KU-357-447

GREAT BOOKS OF THE WESTERN WORLD

GREAT BOOKS
OF THE WESTERN WORLD

ROBERT MAYNARD HUTCHINS, *EDITOR IN CHIEF*

47·

GOETHE

FAUST

PARTS ONE AND TWO

By Johann Wolfgang von Goethe

Translated by George Madison Priest

William Benton, *Publisher*

ENCYCLOPÆDIA BRITANNICA, INC.

CHICAGO · LONDON · TORONTO · GENEVA

THE UNIVERSITY OF CHICAGO

The Great Books
is published with the editorial advice of the faculties
of The University of Chicago

BIOGRAPHICAL NOTE
Johann Wolfgang von Goethe, 1749-1832

GOETHE was born August 28, 1749, at Frankfurt-on-Main. His father was a lawyer of independent means and an imperial councillor; his mother was the daughter of the mayor of Frankfurt. The first sixteen years of his life were spent almost entirely at home, where he gained some acquaintance with the Bible and the classics, Italian, Hebrew, English, music, and drawing.

In 1765 Goethe began his preparation for the law by attending the University of Leipzig. However, it was literature rather than law that occupied him. Moved by his love for a young woman, he began to turn "everything which rejoiced or troubled me into a picture or a poem." A serious breakdown of his health in 1768 cut short his stay at Leipzig. After a long period of convalescence, much of which was devoted to the study of Paracelsus, alchemy, and "natural magic," Goethe went to Strasbourg, where in 1771 he completed his legal training.

While at Strasbourg, Goethe became acquainted with Herder, who, he later remarked, "tore down the curtain which had covered the poverty of German literature." Together they studied Gothic architecture, read Homer, Shakespeare, Ossian, and folksong, and discussed a new German literature. When Goethe returned to Frankfurt in 1771, he had schemes for dramas and various literary works but no strong desire to practise law. That same year he began his first important work, the drama celebrating the sixteenth century robber-knight, Götz von Berlichingen. After a period of several months spent at the imperial courts at Wetzlar, where he knew and loved Lotte Buff, Goethe produced his novel, the Sorrows of Young Werther (1774), written "as by a somnambulist" in four weeks' time. Both the Werther and the Götz, published a year previously, had an enormous success and inaugurated the literary movement known as Sturm und Drang (Storm and Stress). They found many imitators throughout Europe; even the clothes that Werther wore became the fashion; and for a long time thereafter Goethe was known only as the "author of Werther."

Goethe once remarked: "I am like a snake, I slough my skin and start afresh." In 1775, in the midst of his literary triumph, he accepted the invitation of Duke Karl August and moved to the court at Weimar, which was to remain his home for the rest of his life. He was reproached by his friends for abandoning his literary talents, and he soon became so involved with duties of state that for the next ten years he spent little time in writing. He was not long in Weimar before he was entrusted with almost all the offices of the tiny State. As councillor of legation, he attended the privy council and the trial of prisoners. He also had charge of the war and finance commissions as well as the administration of roads, mines, and forests. In 1782 he was raised to the nobility by the emperor and a short time later became president of the chamber.

Partly in connection with his new duties at Weimar, Goethe revived the interest in science that he had first shown at Strasbourg. He took up again the study of anatomy and in 1784 discovered that the intermaxillary bone exists in man in a rudimentary form, thus contributing to the development of the evolutionary doctrine. His experiments with the structure and growth of plants provided him with the material later incorporated in his Metamorphoses of Plants. He also began his work in optics.

Although eminently successful in carrying out his practical duties, Goethe came to regret them as a "terrible disease" which kept him from writing, and "grievously disturbed my creative power." In 1786, determined to escape them for a time, he set out for Italy, disguised as a merchant under the name of Möller. For twenty-two months he remained in Italy and felt that he "found himself again as an artist." Under the influence of what he regarded as the classical spirit, he resolved, "I will occupy myself only with lasting conditions, such as we see in the Greek statues." With that inspiration he re-worked and completed many of the books he had begun previously, including Iphigenie auf Tauris, Torquato Tasso, and Egmont.

After his return to Weimar in 1788, Goethe found it impossible to resume his former life. "My outer man," he wrote, "could not accustom itself to the change." His Italian sojourn had separated him from Charlotte von Stein, whom he had loved for twelve years, and to the scandal of Weimar he took into his house Christine Vulpius, a young factory worker, whom he finally married in 1806. His new classic dramas attracted little attention, and Germany seemed to like only the *Sturm und Drang* literature, which he felt he had left far behind. Schiller had then begun his rise to literary fame, and Goethe at the time felt Schiller was in every way his opposite. He was delighted, however, when Schiller invited him in 1794 to contribute to a new review he was starting. Shortly afterwards, their meeting occurred, inaugurating a friendship which was to last until the younger poet's death in 1805.

Largely under Schiller's influence, Goethe returned to literature with renewed interest. Together they wrote the *Xenian,* attacking the literary foibles of their time. Goethe, to some extent inspired the plays of Schiller, which he produced as the director of the ducal theater. He wrote *Wilhelm Meister's Apprenticeship* (1796), the epic idyll, *Hermann and Dorothea,* and a number of poems. He was also persuaded to resume work upon the Faust legend, which he had begun to dramatize as early as 1774. He had published a fragment of

it in 1790. At the constant urging of Schiller he now completed the first part, which was published in 1808. It immediately won an enthusiastic reception, even from those most opposed to the classicism of the Weimar school.

After Schiller's death Goethe ceased to take any active part in the literary movements of his day, although he continued to direct the Weimar theatre until 1817 and was the recognized dean of German literature. Nor was he much involved with the great political events of his time. He tended to regard Napoleon as the defender of civilization against the Slavs, and in the interview between the two men at Erfurt in 1808 the poet reciprocated the admiration of the French conqueror, who began the meeting by exclaiming: *"Vous êtes un homme."* Goethe still continued to produce a great volume of literary work of all kinds. In 1810 he brought out his *Theory of Color.* The following year he began his autobiography, under the title of *Poetry and Truth. Wilhelm Meister's Travel Years* first appeared in 1821.

In 1824 Goethe returned to work on the second part of *Faust,* and by 1832 the poem was completed. Although often interrupted, the composition of *Faust* had taken Goethe almost sixty years. Shortly after its completion, on March 31, Goethe died. He was buried beside Karl August in the ducal vault at Weimar, to which the remains of Schiller were also removed.

CONTENTS

DEDICATION

Ye wavering forms draw near again as ever
When ye long since moved past my clouded eyes.
To hold you fast, shall I this time endeavour?
Still does my heart that strange illusion prize?
Ye crowd on me! 'Tis well! Your might assever   *5*
While ye from mist and murk around me rise.
As in my youth my heart again is bounding,
Thrilled by the magic breath your train surrounding.

Ye bring with you glad days and happy faces.
Ah, many dear, dear shades arise with you;   *10*
Like some old tale that Time but half erases,
First Love draws near to me and Friendship too.
The pain returns, the sad lament retraces
Life's labyrinthine, erring course anew
And names the good souls who, by Fortune cheated   *15*
Of lovely hours, forth from my world have fleeted.

They do not hear the melodies I'm singing,
The souls to whom my earliest lays I sang;
Dispersed that throng who once to me were clinging,
The echo's died away that one time rang.   *20*
Now midst an unknown crowd my grief is ringing,
Their very praise but gives my heart a pang,
While those who once my song enjoyed and flattered,
If still they live, roam through the wide world scattered.

And I am seized with long-unwonted yearning   *25*
Toward yonder realm of spirits grave and still.
My plaintive song's uncertain tones are turning
To harps aeolian murmuring at will.
Awe binds me fast; tear upon tear falls burning,
My stern heart feels a gentle, tender thrill;   *30*
What I possess, as if far off I'm seeing,
And what has vanished, now comes into being.

I

PRELUDE ON THE STAGE

MANAGER.   DRAMATIC POET.   JESTER.

Manager.   Ye two that have so often stood by me
    In time of need and tribulation,
    Come, say: what hope in any German nation   35
    For what we undertake have ye?
    I much desire to give the crowd a pleasure,
    In chief, because they live and let us live.
    The posts, the boards are up, and here at leisure
    The crowd expects a feast in what we'll give.   40
    They're sitting now with eyebrows raised,
    Quite calmly there, would gladly be amazed.
    I know how one can make all minds akin,
    Yet so embarrassed I have never been.
    In truth, accustomed to the best they're not,   45
    But they have read a really awful lot.
    How shall we plan that all be fresh and new
    And with a meaning, yet attractive too?
    For I do like to see them crowding, urging,
    When toward our booth the stream sets in apace   50
    And with its powerful, repeated surging
    Pours through the strait and narrow gate of grace,[1]
    When still in broad daylight, ere it is four,
    They fight and push their way up to the wicket
    And as the famine-stricken at the baker's door   55
    They nearly break their necks to get a ticket.
    This miracle, upon such varied folk, the poet
    Alone can work; today, my friend, oh, show it!
Poet.   I beg you, of that motley crowd cease telling
    At sight of whom the spirit takes to flight!   60
    Enveil from me the billowing mass compelling
    Us to its vortex with resistless might.
    No, lead me to the tranquil, heavenly dwelling
    Where only blooms for poets pure delight,
    Where Love and Friendship give the heart their blessing,   65
    With godlike hand creating and progressing.
       Ah, all that from the bosom's depths sprang flowing,
    All that from shy and stammering lips has passed,
    Sometimes success and sometimes failure knowing,
    To each wild moment's power a prey is cast.   70
    Oft only after years, in credit growing,
    [1] Cf. Matthew, 7. 14.

2

Doth it appear in perfect form at last.
What gleams is born but for the moment's pages;
The true remains, unlost to after-ages.
Jester.   Could I but hear no more of after-ages!   75
Suppose the thought of them *my* mind engages,
Who'd give the present world its fun?
That will it have and ought to have it too.
The presence of a gallant chap, revealed to you,
I think, is also worth while being shown.   80
Who pleasantly can just himself impart,
Is not embittered by the people's whim;
He likes to have a crowd surrounding him,
More certainly to stir and thrill each heart.
So do be good, show you can set the fashion.   85
Let Fantasy be heard with all her chorus:
Sense, Reason, Sentiment, and Passion;
Yet mark you well! bring Folly too before us!
Manager.   But, more than all, do let enough occur!
Men come to look, to see they most prefer.   90
If, as they gaze, much is reeled off and spun,
So that the startled crowd gapes all it can,
A multitude you will at once have won;
You then will be a much-loved man.
You can compel the mass by mass alone;   95
Each in the end will seek out something as his own.
Bring much and you'll bring this or that to everyone
And each will leave contented when the play is done.
If you will give a piece, give it at once in pieces!
Ragout like this your fame increases.   100
Easy it is to stage, as easy to invent.
What use is it, a whole to fashion and present?
The Public still will pick it all to pieces.
Poet.   You do not feel how bad such handiwork must be,
How little that becomes the artist true!   105
I see, neat gentlemanly botchery
Is now a sovereign rule with you.
Manager.   Reproof like this leaves me quite unoffended!
A man who does his work, effectively intended,
Must stick to tools that are the best for it.   110
Reflect! You have a tender wood to split;
And those for whom you write, just see!
If this one's driven hither by ennui,
Another leaves a banquet sated with its vapours;
And—what the very worst will always be—   115
Many come fresh from reading magazines and papers.
Men haste distraught to us as to the masquerade,
And every step but winged by curiosity;
The ladies give a treat, all in their best arrayed,

And play their part without a fee.
Why do you dream in lofty poet-land?
Why does a full house make you gay?
Observe the patrons near at hand!
They are half cold, half coarse are they.
One, when the play is over, hopes a game of cards;   *125*
A wild night on a wench's breast another chooses.
Why then, with such an aim, poor silly bards,
Will you torment so much the gracious Muses?
Give only more and ever, ever more, I say.
Then from the goal you nevermore can stray.   *130*
Seek to bewilder men—that is my view.
But satisfy them? That is hard to do.—
What is attacking you? Pain or delight?

Poet.   Go hence and seek yourself another slave!
What! Shall the poet take that highest right,   *135*
The Right of Man, that Right which Nature gave,
And wantonly for your sake trifle it away?
How doth he over every heart hold sway?
How doth he every element enslave?
Is it not the harmony that from his breast doth start,   *140*
Then winds the world in turn back in his heart?
When Nature forces lengths of thread unending
In careless whirling on the spindle round,
When all Life's inharmonic throngs unblending
In sullen, harsh confusion sound,   *145*
Who parts the changeless series of creation,
That each, enlivened, moves in rhythmic time?
Who summons each to join the general ordination,
In consecrated, noble harmonies to chime?
Who bids the storm with raging passion lower?   *150*
The sunset with a solemn meaning glow?
Who scatters Springtime's every lovely flower
Along the pathway where his love may go?
Who twines the verdant leaves, unmeaning, slighted,
Into a wreath of honour, meed of every field?   *155*
Who makes Olympus sure, the gods united?
That power of Man the Poet has revealed!

Jester.   Then use these handsome powers as your aid
And carry on this poet trade
As one a love-adventure carries!   *160*
By chance one nears, one feels, one tarries!
And, bit by bit, one gets into a tangle.
Bliss grows, then comes a tiff, a wrangle;
One is enrapt, now one sees pain advance,
And ere one is aware, it is a real romance!   *165*
So let us also such a drama give!
Just seize upon the full life people live!

Each lives it though it's known to few,
And grasp it where you will, there's interest for you.
In motley pictures with a little clarity,   *170*
Much error and a spark of verity,
Thus can the best of drinks be brewed
To cheer and edify the multitude.
Youth's fairest bloom collects in expectation
Before your play and harks the revelation.   *175*
Then from your work each tender soul, intent,
Absorbs a melancholy nourishment.
Then now one thought and now another thought you start;
Each sees what he has carried in his heart.
As yet they are prepared for weeping and for laughter;   *180*
They still revere the flight, illusion they adore.
A mind once formed finds naught made right thereafter;
A growing mind will thank you evermore.

Poet.   Then give me back the time of growing
When I myself was growing too,   *185*
When crowding songs, a fountain flowing,
Gushed forth unceasing, ever new;
When still the mists my world were veiling,
The bud its miracle bespoke;
When I the thousand blossoms broke,   *190*
Profusely through the valleys trailing.
Naught, yet enough had I when but a youth,
Joy in illusion, yearning toward the truth.
Give impulse its unfettered dower,
The bliss so deep 'tis full of pain,   *195*
The strength of hate, Love's mighty power,
Oh, give me back my youth again!

Jester.   Youth, my good friend, you need most in the fight
When enemies come on, hard pressing,
When, clinging to your necks so tight,   *200*
The dearest maidens hang caressing,
When, from afar, a wreath entrances,
Luring to hard-won goal the runner's might,
When, after madly whirling dances,
A man carousing drinks away the night.   *205*
But on the lyre's familiar strings
To play with grace and spirit ever
And sweep with lovely wanderings
Toward goals you choose for your endeavour,
That is your duty, agèd sirs,   *210*
And we revere you for it no less dearly.
Age makes not childish, as one oft avers;
It finds us still true children merely.

Manager.   Words have been interchanged enough,
Let me at last see action too.   *215*

While compliments you're turning—idle stuff!
Some useful thing might come to view.
Why talk of waiting for the mood?
No one who dallies ever will it see.
If you pretend you're poets—good!   220
Command then, poets, poetry!
What we're in need of, that full well you know,
We want to sip strong drink, so go
And start the brew without delay!
Never is done tomorrow what is not done today   225
And one should let no day slip by.
With resolution seize the possible straightway
By forelock and with quick, courageous trust;
Then holding fast you will not let it further fly
And you will labour on because you must.   230
   Upon our German stage, you are aware,
Each tries out what he wishes to display,
So in your work for me today
Scenes, mechanism you are not to spare.
Use both the lights of heaven, great and small;   235
The stars above are yours to squander;
Nor water, fire, nor rocky wall,
Nor beasts nor birds are lacking yonder.
Thus in our narrow house of boards preside
And on through all Creation's circle stride;   240
And wander on, with speed considered well,
From Heaven, through the world, to Hell!

PROLOGUE IN HEAVEN[1]

The LORD.   The HEAVENLY HOSTS.
Afterwards MEPHISTOPHELES.

The THREE ARCHANGELS *come forward.*

Raphael.   The Sun intones, in ancient tourney
  With brother-spheres, a rival song,
  Fulfilling its predestined journey,   245
  With march of thunder moves along.
  Its aspect gives the angels power,
  Though none can ever solve its ways;
  The lofty works beyond us tower,
  Sublime as on the first of days.   250
Gabriel.   And swift beyond where knowledge ranges,
  Earth's splendour whirls in circling flight;
  A paradise of brightness changes
  To awful shuddering depths of night.
  The sea foams up, widespread and surging   255
  Against the rocks' deep-sunken base,
  And rock and sea sweep onward, merging
  In rushing spheres' eternal race.
Michael.   And rival tempests roar and shatter,
  From sea to land, from land to sea,   260
  And, raging, form a circling fetter
  Of deep, effective energy.
  There flames destruction, flashing, searing,
  Before the crashing thunder's way;
  Yet, Lord, Thy angels are revering   265
  The gentle progress of Thy day.
The Three.   Its aspect gives the angels power,
  Since none can solve Thee nor Thy ways;
  And all Thy works beyond us tower,
  Sublime as on the first of days.   270
Mephistopheles.   Since you, O Lord, once more draw near
  And ask how all is getting on, and you
  Were ever well content to see me here,
  You see me also midst your retinue.
  Forgive, fine speeches I can never make,   275
  Though all the circle look on me with scorn;
  Pathos from me would make your sides with laughter shake,
  Had you not laughter long ago forsworn.
  Of suns and worlds I've naught to say worth mention.

[1] Cf. Job, 1. 6-12.

7

How men torment them claims my whole attention.   *280*
Earth's little god retains his same old stamp and ways
And is as singular as on the first of days.
A little better would he live, poor wight,
Had you not given him that gleam of heavenly light.
He calls it Reason, only to pollute   *285*
Its use by being brutaler than any brute.
It seems to me, if you'll allow, Your Grace,
He's like a grasshopper, that long-legged race
That's made to fly and flying spring
And in the grass to sing the same old thing.   *290*
If in the grass he always were reposing!
But in each filthy heap he keeps on nosing.

The Lord.   You've nothing more to say to me?
You come but to complain unendingly?
Is never aught right to your mind?   *295*

Mephistopheles.   No, Lord! All is still downright bad, I find.
Man in his wretched days makes me lament him;
I am myself reluctant to torment him.

The Lord.   Do you know Faust?

Mephistopheles.   The Doctor?

The Lord.   Yes, my servant!

Mephistopheles.   He!
Forsooth, he serves you most peculiarly.   *300*
Unearthly are the fool's drink and his food;
The ferment drives him forth afar.
Though half aware of his insensate mood,
He asks of heaven every fairest star
And of the earth each highest zest,   *305*
And all things near and all things far
Can not appease his deeply troubled breast.

The Lord.   Although he serves me now confusedly,
I soon shall lead him forth where all is clear.
The gardener knows, when verdant grows the tree,   *310*
That bloom and fruit will deck the coming year.

Mephistopheles.   What will you wager? Him you yet shall lose,
If you will give me your permission
To lead him gently on the path I choose.

The Lord.   As long as on the earth he shall survive,   *315*
So long you'll meet no prohibition.
Man errs as long as he doth strive.

Mephistopheles.   My thanks for that, for with the dead I've never got
Myself entangled of my own volition.
I like full, fresh cheeks best of all the lot.   *320*
I'm not at home when corpses seek my house;
I feel about it as a cat does with a mouse.

The Lord.   'Tis well! So be it granted you today!
Divert this spirit from its primal source

And if you can lay hold on him, you may 325
Conduct him downward on your course,
And stand abashed when you are forced to say:
A good man, though his striving be obscure,
Remains aware that there is one right way.
Mephistopheles.   All right! But long it won't endure! 330
I have no fear about my bet, be sure!
When I attain my aim, do not protest,
But let me triumph with a swelling breast.
Dust shall he eat, and that with zest,
As did the famous snake, my near relation.[1] 335
The Lord.   In that too you may play your part quite free;
Your kind I never did detest.
Of all the spirits of negation
The wag weighs least of all on me.
Mankind's activity can languish all too easily, 340
A man soon loves unhampered rest;
Hence, gladly I give him a comrade such as you,
Who stirs and works and must, as devil, do.
But ye, real sons of God, lift up your voice,
In living, profuse beauty to rejoice! 345
May that which grows, that lives and works forever,
Engird you with Love's gracious bonds, and aught
That ever may appear, to float and waver,
Make steadfast in enduring thought!
    Heaven closes, the ARCHANGELS *disperse.*
Mephistopheles [*alone*].   I like to see the Old Man not infrequently, 350
And I forbear to break with Him or be uncivil;
It's very pretty in so great a Lord as He
To talk so like a man even with the Devil.

[1] Cf. Genesis, 3. 14.

The First Part
OF THE TRAGEDY

꘎꘎꘎꘎꘎꘎꘎꘎꘎꘎

NIGHT

In a high-vaulted, narrow Gothic chamber FAUST,
restless in his chair by his desk.

Faust.   I've studied now Philosophy
And Jurisprudence, Medicine,   355
And even, alas! Theology
All through and through with ardour keen!
Here now I stand, poor fool, and see
I'm just as wise as formerly.
Am called a Master, even Doctor too,   360
And now I've nearly ten years through
Pulled my students by their noses to and fro
And up and down, across, about,
And see there's nothing we can know!
That all but burns my heart right out.   365
True, I am more clever than all the vain creatures,
The Doctors and Masters, Writers and Preachers;
No doubts plague me, nor scruples as well.
I'm not afraid of devil or hell.
To offset that, all joy is rent from me.   370
I do not imagine I know aught that's right;
I do not imagine I could teach what might
Convert and improve humanity.
Nor have I gold or things of worth,
Or honours, splendours of the earth.   375
No dog could live thus any more!
So I have turned to magic lore,
To see if through the spirit's power and speech
Perchance full many a secret I may reach,
So that no more with bitter sweat   380
I need to talk of what I don't know yet,
So that I may perceive whatever holds
The world together in its inmost folds,
See all its seeds, its working power,
And cease word-threshing from this hour.   385
   Oh, that, full moon, thou didst but glow
Now for the last time on my woe,
Whom I beside this desk so oft

11

Have watched at midnight climb aloft.
Then over books and paper here   390
To me, sad friend, thou didst appear!
Ah! could I but on mountain height
Go onward in thy lovely light,
With spirits hover round mountain caves,
Weave over meadows thy twilight laves,   395
Discharged of all of Learning's fumes, anew
Bathe me to health in thy healing dew.
　　Woe! am I stuck and forced to dwell
Still in this musty, cursèd cell?
Where even heaven's dear light strains   400
But dimly through the painted panes!
Hemmed in by all this heap of books,
Their gnawing worms, amid their dust,
While to the arches, in all the nooks,
Are smoke-stained papers midst them thrust,   405
Boxes and glasses round me crammed,
And instruments in cases hurled,
Ancestral stuff around me jammed—
That is your world! That's called a world!
　　And still you question why your heart   410
Is cramped and anxious in your breast?
Why each impulse to live has been repressed
In you by some vague, unexplainèd smart?
Instead of Nature's living sphere
In which God made mankind, you have alone,   415
In smoke and mould around you here,
Beasts' skeletons and dead men's bone.
　　Up! Flee! Out into broad and open land!
And this book full of mystery,
From Nostradamus' very hand,   420
Is it not ample company?
The stars' course then you'll understand
And Nature, teaching, will expand
The power of your soul, as when
One spirit to another speaks. 'Tis vain   425
To think that arid brooding will explain
The sacred symbols to your ken.
Ye spirits, ye are hovering near;
Oh, answer me if ye can hear!
　　He opens the book and perceives the sign of the Macrocosm.
What rapture, ah! at once is flowing   430
Through all my senses at the sight of this!
I feel a youthful life, its holy bliss,
Through nerve and vein run on, new-glowing.
Was it a god who wrote these signs that still
My inner tumult and that fill   435

My wretched heart with ecstasy?
Unveiling with mysterious potency
The powers of Nature round about me here?
Am I a god? All grows so clear to me!
In these pure lineaments I see   *440*
Creative Nature's self before my soul appear.
Now first I understand what he, the sage, has said:
"The world of spirits is not shut away;
Thy sense is closed, thy heart is dead!
Up, Student! bathe without dismay   *445*
Thy earthly breast in morning-red!"
   He contemplates the sign.
Into the whole how all things blend,
Each in the other working, living!
How heavenly powers ascend, descend,
Each unto each the golden vessels giving![1]   *450*
On pinions fragrant blessings bringing,
From Heaven through Earth all onward winging,
Through all the All harmonious ringing!
   What pageantry! Yet, ah, mere pageantry!
Where shall I, endless Nature, seize on thee?   *455*
Thy breasts are—where? Ye, of all life the spring,
To whom both Earth and Heaven cling,
Toward whom the withering breast doth strain—
Ye gush, ye suckle, and shall I pine thus in vain?
   He turns the book over impatiently and perceives the sign of the
    EARTH-SPIRIT.
How differently upon me works this sign!   *460*
Thou, Spirit of the Earth, I feel, art nigher.
I feel my powers already higher,
I glow already as from some new wine.
I feel the courage, forth into the world to dare;
The woe of earth, the bliss of earth to bear;   *465*
With storms to battle, brave the lightning's glare;
And in the shipwreck's crash not to despair!
Clouds gather over me—
The moon conceals her light—
The lamp fades out!   *470*
Mists rise—red beams dart forth
Around my head—there floats
A horror downward from the vault
And seizes me!
Spirit invoked! near me, I feel, thou art!   *475*
Unveil thyself!
Ha! how it rends my heart!
To unknown feeling
All my senses burst forth, reeling!

[1] Cf. Genesis, 28. 12.

I feel my heart is thine and to the uttermost!   480
Thou must! Thou must! though my life be the cost!
  He clutches the book and utters the sign of the SPIRIT *in a tone of*
    mystery. A ruddy flame flashes up; the SPIRIT *appears in the*
    flame.
Spirit.   Who calls to me?
Faust [*turning away*].   Appalling apparition!
Spirit.   By potent spell hast drawn me here,
  Hast long been tugging at my sphere,
  And now—
Faust.   Oh woe! I can not bear thy vision!   485
Spirit.   With panting breath thou hast implored this sight,
  Wouldst hear my voice, my face wouldst see;
  Thy mighty spirit-plea inclineth me!
  Here am I!—what a pitiable fright
  Grips thee, thou Superman! Where is the soul elated?   490
  Where is the breast that in its self a world created
  And bore and fostered it? And that with joyous trembling
  Expanded as if spirits, us, resembling?
  Where art thou, Faust, whose voice rang out to me,
  Who toward me pressed with all thy energy?   495
  Is it thou who, by my breath surrounded,
  In all the deeps of being art confounded?
  A frightened, fleeing, writhing worm?
Faust.   Am I, O form of flame, to yield to thee in fear?
  'Tis I, I'm Faust, I am thy peer!   500
Spirit.   In the tides of life, in action's storm,
  Up and down I wave,
  To and fro weave free,
  Birth and the grave,
  An infinite sea,   505
  A varied weaving,
  A radiant living,
  Thus at Time's humming loom it's my hand that prepares
  The robe ever-living the Deity wears.
Faust.   Thou who dost round the wide world wend,   510
  Thou busy spirit, how near I feel to thee!
Spirit.   Thou art like the spirit thou canst comprehend,
  Not me!
      Vanishes.
Faust [*collapsing*].   Not thee!
  Whom then?   515
  I, image of the Godhead!
  And not even like to thee!
      Somebody knocks.
  O death! I know it—'tis my famulus—
  Thus turns to naught my fairest bliss!
  That visions in abundance such as this   520

Must be disturbed by that dry prowler thus!
    WAGNER *in dressing-gown and night-cap, a lamp in his hand.*
    FAUST *turns round impatiently.*

Wagner.   Pardon! I've just heard you declaiming.
   'Twas surely from a Grecian tragic play?
   At profit in this art I'm also aiming;
   For much it can effect today.   525
   I've often heard the boast: a preacher
   Might take an actor as his teacher.

Faust.   Yes, if the preacher is an actor, there's no doubt,
   As it indeed may sometimes come about.

Wagner.   Ah! if thus in his study one must stay,   530
   And hardly sees the world upon a holiday,
   Scarce through a telescope, and far off then,
   How through persuasion shall one lead one's fellow-men?

Faust.   Unless you feel, naught will you ever gain;
   Unless this feeling pours forth from your soul   535
   With native, pleasing vigour to control
   The hearts of all your hearers, it will be in vain.
   Pray keep on sitting! Pray collect and glue,
   From others' feasts brew some ragout;
   With tiny heaps of ashes play your game   540
   And blow the sparks into a wretched flame!
   Children and apes will marvel at you ever,
   If you've a palate that can stand the part;
   But heart to heart you'll not draw men, no, never,
   Unless your message issue from your heart.   545

Wagner.   Yet elocution makes the orator succeed.
   I feel I am still far behind indeed.

Faust.   Seek for the really honest gain!
   Don't be a fool in loudly tinkling dress!
   Intelligence and good sense will express   550
   Themselves with little art and strain.
   And if in earnest you would say a thing,
   Is it needful to chase after words? Ah, yes,
   Your eloquence that is so glittering,
   In which you twist up gewgaws for mankind,   555
   Is unrefreshing as the misty wind,
   Through withered leaves in autumn whispering.

Wagner.   Ah, God! how long is art!
   And soon it is we die.
   Oft when my critical pursuits I ply,   560
   I truly grow uneasy both in head and heart.
   How hard to gain the means whereby
   A man mounts upward to the source!
   And ere man's ended barely half the course,
   Poor devil! I suppose he has to die.   565

Faust.   Parchment! Is that the sacred fountain whence alone

There springs a draught that thirst for ever quells?
Refreshment? It you never will have won
If from that soul of yours it never wells.
Wagner.   Excuse me! But it is a great delight   570
To enter in the spirit of the ages and to see
How once a sage before us thought and then how we
Have brought things on at last to such a splendid height.
Faust.   Oh, yes! Up to the stars afar!
My friend, the ages of aforetime are   575
To us a book of seven seals.[1]
What you call "spirit of the ages"
Is after all the spirit of those sages
In which the mirrored age itself reveals.
Then, truly, that is oft a sorry sight to see!   580
I vow, men do but glance at it, then run away.
A rubbish-bin, a lumber-garret it may be,
At best a stilted, mock-heroic play
With excellent, didactic maxims humming,
Such as in puppets' mouths are most becoming.   585
Wagner.   But, ah, the world! the mind and heart of men!
Of these we each would fain know something just the same.
Faust.   Yes, "know"! Men call it so, but then
Who dares to call the child by its right name?
The few who have some part of it descried,   590
Yet fools enough to guard not their full hearts, revealing
To riffraff both their insight and their feeling,
Men have of old burned at the stake and crucified.
I beg you, friend, it's far into the night,
We must break off our converse now.   595
Wagner.   I'd gladly keep awake for ever if I might
Converse with you in such a learnèd way;
Tomorrow, though, our Easter-Sunday holiday,
This and that question you'll allow.
I've studied zealously, and so   600
I know much now, but all I fain would know.
     Exit.
Faust [*alone*].   How strange a man's not quitted of all hope,
Who on and on to shallow stuff adheres,
Whose greedy hands for hidden treasure grope,
And who is glad when any worm appears!   605
     Dare such a human voice resound
Where spirits near me throng around?
Yet still I thank you, poorest one
Of all the sons of earth, for what you've done.
Torn loose by you, from that despair I'm freed   610
That nearly drove my senses frantic.
That vision, ah! was so gigantic,

[1] Cf. Revelation, 5. 1.

I could but feel myself a dwarf indeed.
   I, image of the Godhead, and already one
Who thought him near the mirror of the Truth Eternal,   *615*
Who revelled in the clearness, light supernal,
And stripped away the earthly son;
I, more than cherub, whose free force
Presumed, prophetic, even now to course,
Creating, on through Nature's every vein,   *620*
To share the life of gods: that!—how must I atone!
A voice of thunder swept me back again.
   I may not dare to call myself thy peer!
What though I had the might to draw thee near,
To hold thee I possessed no might.   *625*
At that ecstatic moment's height
I felt so small, so great;
Thou cruelly didst thrust me back as one
Doomed to uncertain human fate.
Who will instruct me? And what shall I shun?   *630*
Shall I that impulse then obey?
Alas! the deeds that we have done—
Our sufferings too—impede us on life's way.
   To what the mind most gloriously conceives,
An alien, more, more alien substance cleaves.   *635*
When to the good of this world we attain,
We call the better a delusion vain.
Sensations glorious, that gave us life,
Grow torpid in the world's ignoble strife.
   Though Fantasy with daring flight began   *640*
And hopeful toward Infinity expanded,
She's now contented in a little span
When in Time's eddy joy on joy's been stranded.
For Worry straightway nestles deep within the heart,
There she produces many a secret smart.   *645*
Recklessly rocking, she disturbs both joy and rest.
In new disguises she is always dressed;
She may appear as house and land, as child and wife,
As fire, as water, poison, knife.
What never will happen makes you quail,   *650*
And what you'll never lose, always must you bewail.
   I am not like the gods! Feel it I must.
I'm like the worm that burrows through the dust,
That in the dust in which it lived and fed,
Is crushed and buried by a wanderer's tread.   *655*
   Is it not dust that narrows in this lofty wall
Made up of shelves a hundred, is it not all
The lumber, thousandfold light frippery,
That in this world of moths oppresses me?
Here shall I find what is my need?   *660*

Shall I perchance in a thousand volumes read
That men have tortured themselves everywhere,
And that a happy man was here and there?—
Why grinnest thou at me, thou hollow skull?
Save that thy brain, confused like mine, once sought bright day   665
And in the sombre twilight dull,
With lust for truth, went wretchedly astray?
Ye instruments, ye surely jeer at me,
With handle, wheel and cogs and cylinder.
I stood beside the gate, ye were to be the key.   670
True, intricate your ward, but no bolts do ye stir.
Inscrutable upon a sunlit day,
Her veil will Nature never let you steal,
And what she will not to your mind reveal,
You will not wrest from her with levers and with screws.   675
You, ancient lumber, that I do not use,
You're only here because you served my father.
On you, old scroll, the smoke-stains gather,
Since first the lamp on this desk smouldered turbidly.
Far better had I spent my little recklessly   680
Than, burdened with that little, here to sweat!
All that you have, bequeathed you by your father,
Earn it in order to possess it.
Things unused often burden and beset;
But what the hour brings forth, that can it use and bless it.   685
    Why does my gaze grow fixed as if a spell had bound me?
That phial there, is it a magnet to my eyes?
Why does a lovely light so suddenly surround me
As when in woods at night the moonbeam drifts and lies?
    Thou peerless phial rare, I welcome thee   690
And now I take thee down most reverently.
In thee I honour human wit and art.
Thou essence, juice of lovely, slum'brous flowers,
Thou extract of all deadly, subtle powers,
Thy favour to thy Master now impart!   695
I look on thee, and soothed is my distress;
I seize on thee, the struggle groweth less.
The spirit's flood-tide ebbs away, away.
I'm beckoned out, the open seas to meet,
The mirror waters glitter at my feet,   700
To other shores allures another day.
    A fiery chariot floats on airy pinions
Hither to me! I feel prepared to flee
Along a new path, piercing ether's vast dominions
To other spheres of pure activity.   705
This lofty life, this ecstasy divine!
Thou, but a worm, and *that* deservest thou?
Yes! turn thy back with resolution fine

Upon earth's lovely sun, and now
Make bold to fling apart the gate 710
Which every man would fain go slinking by!
Here is the time to demonstrate
That man's own dignity yields not to gods on high;
To tremble not before that murky pit
Where fantasies, self-damned, in tortures dwell; 715
To struggle toward that pass whose narrow mouth is lit
By all the seething, searing flames of Hell;
Serenely to decide this step and onward press,
Though there be risk I'll float off into nothingness.
    So now come down, thou goblet pure and crystalline! 720
From out that ancient case of thine,
On which for many a year I have not thought!
Thou at my fathers' feasts wert wont to shine,
Didst many a solemn guest to mirth incline,
When thee, in pledge, one to another brought. 725
The crowded figures, rich and artful wrought,
The drinker's duty, rhyming to explain them,
The goblet's depths, at but one draught to drain them,
Recall full many a youthful night to me.
Now to no neighbour shall I offer thee, 730
Upon thy art I shall not show my wit.
Here is a juice, one's quickly drunk with it.
With its brown flood it fills thy ample bowl.
This I prepared, I choose this, high upborne;
Be this my last drink now, with all my soul, 735
A festal, lofty greeting pledged to morn!
    He puts the goblet to his lips.
    The sound of bells and choral song.
Chorus of Angels.
                  Christ is arisen!
                  Joy to mortality,
                  Whom earth's carnality,
                  Creeping fatality, 740
                  Held as in prison!

Faust.   What a deep humming, what a clarion tone,
  Draws from my lips the glass with mighty power!
  Ye deep-toned bells, make ye already known
  The Easter-feast's first solemn hour? 745
  Ye choirs, do ye the hymn of consolation sing,
  Which angels sang around the grave's dark night, to bring
  Assurance of new covenant and dower?
Chorus of Women.
                  Rare spices we carried
                  And laid on His breast; 750
                  We tenderly buried

Him whom we loved best;
Cloths and bands round Him,
Spotless we wound Him o'er;[1]
Ah! and we've found Him,   755
Christ, here no more.

Chorus of Angels.

Christ is ascended!
Blessèd the loving one
Who endured, moving one,
Trials improving one,   760
Till they were ended!

Faust.   Ye heavenly tones, so powerful and mild,
Why seek ye me, me cleaving to the dust?
Ring roundabout where tender-hearted men will hear!
I hear the message well but lack Faith's constant trust;   765
The miracle is Faith's most cherished child.
I do not dare to strive toward yonder sphere
From whence the lovely tidings swell;
Yet, wonted to this strain from infancy,
Back now to life again it calleth me.   770
In days that are no more, Heaven's loving kiss
In solemn Sabbath stillness on me fell;
Then rang prophetical, full-toned, the bell;
And every prayer was fervent bliss.
A sweet, uncomprehending yearning   775
Drove me to wander on through wood and lea,
And while a thousand tears were burning,
I felt a world arise for me.
Of youth's glad sports this song foretold me,
The festival of spring in happy freedom passed;   780
Now memories, with childlike feeling, hold me
Back from that solemn step, the last.
Sound on and on, thou sweet, celestial strain!
The tear wells forth, the earth has me again!

Chorus of Disciples.

Though He, victorious,   785
From the grave's prison,
Living and glorious,
Nobly has risen,
Though He, in bliss of birth,
Creative Joy is near,   790
Ah! on the breast of earth
We are to suffer here.
He left His very Own
Pining for Him we miss;
Ah! we bemoan,   795
Master, Thy bliss!

[1] Cf. John, 19. 40; Mark, 16. 1; Luke, 23. 56.

Chorus of Angels.

Christ is arisen
Out of Corruption's womb!
Burst bonds that prison,
Joy over the tomb!   *800*
Actively pleading Him,
Showing love, heeding Him,
Brotherly feeding Him,
Preaching, far speeding Him,
Rapture succeeding Him,   *805*
To you the Master's near,
To you is here!

OUTSIDE THE GATE OF THE TOWN

All sorts of people are walking out

Some Young Workmen.   Why are you going off that way?
Others.   We're going to the Hunters' Lodge today.
The Former.   But toward the Mill we'd like to wander.   *810*
Workman.   Go to the River Inn, that's my advice.
A Second.   The road that way is far from nice.
The Others.   What will you do?
A Third.   Go with them yonder.
A Fourth.   Come up to Burgdorf! There you'll surely find
   The prettiest girls and beer, the finest kind,   *815*
   Besides a first-rate sort of scrap.
A Fifth.   How you do swagger! What a chap!
   Does your skin itch a third time for a row?
   I will not go, I fear that place somehow.
Servant-Girl.   No, no, I'll go back toward the town.   *820*
Another.   We'll find him by those poplars certainly.
The First.   But that is no great luck for me!
   At your side he'll go walking up and down;
   He never dances but with you.
   With your fun what have I to do?   *825*
The Second.   Today he's surely not alone; he said
   His friend would be with him, the curly-head.
Student.   By thunder! how the whacking wenches stride!
   We must go with them, brother, come along.
   Strong beer, tobacco with a bite, and, on the side,   *830*
   A servant-maid decked out, for these I long.
Citizen's Daughter.   I say, just see those fine young blades!
   It really is an insult. See!
   They could have had the best of company
   And run here after serving-maids!   *835*
Second Student [*to the first*].
   Not quite so fast! There come two others, there behind,

Quite neatly dressed and rather striking.
One of them is my neighbour too, I find,
And she is greatly to my liking.
They go their way now quite demurely,   *840*
Yet in the end, they'll take us with them surely.
The First.   No, friend! To feel constrained is too depressing.
Quick then! lest we should lose the wilder prey.
The hand that wields the broom on Saturday
Will Sunday treat you with the best caressing.   *845*
Citizen.   No, that new burgomaster I don't like a bit.
Now since he's in, he's daily bolder every way,
And for the town, what does he do for it?
Are things not growing worse each day?
Now more than ever we must all submit,   *850*
And more than ever must we pay.
Beggar [*sings*].

Good gentlemen and ladies pretty,
So flushed of cheek and fine of dress,
May it please you, look on me with pity,
And see and soften my distress!   *855*
Let me not vainly grind here waiting!
Who likes to give, alone is gay.
A day all men are celebrating,
Be it for me a harvest day.

Another Citizen.   I know naught better on a Sunday or a holiday   *860*
Than chat of wars and warlike pother,
When off in Turkey, far away,
The people clash and fight with one another.
We stand beside the window, drain our glasses,
And see how each gay vessel down the river passes,   *865*
Then in the evening homeward wend our ways,
Blessing with joy sweet peace and peaceful days.
Third Citizen.   Yes, neighbour! I would leave things so;
Each other's skulls they well may crack,
And everything may topsyturvy go,   *870*
If only things at home stay in the old, old track.
Old Woman [*to two* CITIZENS' DAUGHTERS].
My! How dressed up! You beautiful young dears!
Who would not gape now if he met you?
But not so haughty! Have no fears!
What you desire I know well how to get you.   *875*
Citizen's Daughter.   Come, Agatha, away! I take great heed
That with such witches no one sees me go;
Yet to me on St. Andrew's night, indeed,
My future lover she did really show.
The Other.   She showed me mine too in the crystal ball,   *880*
So soldier-like, with others swift to dare;

I look about, I seek him everywhere,
But I can't find him, not at all.
Soldiers.

> Castles with lofty
> Ramparts retaining,   *885*
> Maids who are haughty,
> Scornful, disdaining,
> Fain I'd be gaining!
> Bold is the venture,
> Grand is the pay!   *890*
>   We let the trumpet
> Summon us, wooing,
> Calling to pleasure,
> Oft to undoing.
> That is a storming!   *895*
> Life in its splendour!
>   Maidens and castles
> Both must surrender.
> Bold is the venture,
> Grand is the pay!   *900*
> Then are the soldiers
> Off and away.

FAUST *and* WAGNER.

Faust.   From the ice they are freed, the stream and brook,
By the Spring's enlivening, lovely look;
The valley's green with joys of hope;   *905*
The Winter old and weak ascends
Back to the rugged mountain slope.
From there, as he flees, he downward sends
An impotent shower of icy hail
Streaking over the verdant vale.   *910*
Ah! but the Sun will suffer no white,
Growth and formation stir everywhere,
'Twould fain with colours make all things bright,
Though in the landscape are no blossoms fair.
Instead it takes gay-decked humanity.   *915*
Now turn around and from this height,
Looking backward, townward see.
Forth from the cave-like, gloomy gate
Crowds a motley and swarming array.
Everyone suns himself gladly today.   *920*
The Risen Lord they celebrate,
For they themselves have now arisen
From lowly houses' mustiness,
From handicraft's and factory's prison,
From the roof and gables that oppress,   *925*
From the bystreets' crushing narrowness,

From the churches' venerable night,
They are all brought out into light.
See, only see, how quickly the masses
Scatter through gardens and fields remote;   930
How down and across the river passes
So many a merry pleasure-boat.
And over-laden, almost sinking,
The last full wherry moves away.
From yonder hill's far pathways blinking,   935
Flash to us colours of garments gay.
Hark! Sounds of village joy arise;
Here is the people's paradise,
Contented, great and small shout joyfully:
"Here I am Man, here dare it to be!"   940
Wagner.   Doctor, to walk with you is ever
An honour and a profit, though
I'd here not care to stray alone—no, never—
Because to all that's vulgar I'm a foe.
This fiddling, shrieking, bowling—all this revel   945
To me's a sound detested long;
They riot as if driven by the Devil,
And call it a pleasure, call it a song.
Peasants under the linden tree. [Dance and song.]
     The shepherd decked him for the dance,
In ribbons, vest, and wreath to prance,   950
Adorned with fine arraying.
Now round the linden lass and lad
Were thronging, dancing there like mad.
Hurrah! Hurrah!
Hurrah-a-rah-a-rah!   955
Thus fiddle-bow was playing.
     He crowded and he pushed in haste,
Then bumped into a maiden's waist,
Elbow against her laying.
The lively damsel turned her head: 960
"I find that stupid, now!" she said.
Hurrah! Hurrah!
Hurrah-a-rah-a-rah!
"Don't be so rude and swaying!"
     Then round and round they winged their flight,   965
They danced to left, they danced to right,
All petticoats displaying.
They grew so red, they grew so warm,
Then rested panting, arm in arm,
Hurrah! Hurrah!   970
Hurrah-a-rah-a-rah!
On hip the elbow staying.
     "I say, don't make so free with me!

How many fooled his bride-to-be,
Deceiving and betraying!"   975
And yet he coaxed her to one side,
And from the linden far and wide:
Hurrah! Hurrah!
Hurrah-a-rah-a-rah!
Rang shouts and fiddle-playing.   980
Old Peasant.   Good Doctor, this is fine of you,
That you don't scorn us here today,
And now amid this crowding throng,
A highly-learnèd man, you stray.
Hence take in turn the finest mug   985
That with a fresh, cool drink we've filled.
I pledge you, sir, and wish aloud
Not only that your thirst be stilled:
For every drop the mug conveys,
A day be added to your days!   990
Faust.   I take the refreshing drink and thus I too
Return the health with thanks to all of you.
The people gather round in a circle.
Old Peasant.   Forsooth, it is indeed well done
That you on happy days appear.
You have aforetime with us too   995
Been kind when days were evil here!
Full many a one stands here alive,
Whom your good father still did wrest
From burning fever's deadly rage
When he set limits to the pest.   1000
And you as well, a young man then,
To every sick man's house you went around.
Many a corpse did men bring forth,
But from within you came out sound,
Withstanding many a test severe;   1005
The Helper over us helped our helper here.
All.   Health to the man whom we have tried,
Long may he be our help and guide!
Faust.   To Him on High with reverence bend,
Who teaches help and help doth send!   1010
He goes on with WAGNER.
Wagner.   Oh, what a feeling you must have, great man,
Thus venerated by this multitude!
Oh, happy he who, through his own gifts, can
Draw such a gain, such gratitude!
The father shows you to his brood,   1015
Each asks and hastes and nearer draws;
The fiddle stops, the dancers pause.
You go, they stand in rows to see.
The caps are quickly lifted high;

A little more and they would bend the knee 1020
As if the Holy Sacrament came by.
Faust.   Only a few steps farther, up to yonder stone!
Here let us rest a little from our straying.
Here often, wrapped in thought, I sat alone
And tortured me with fasting and with praying. 1025
In hope full rich, firm in the faith possessed,
With tears, sighs, wringing hands, I meant
To force the Lord in Heaven to relent
And end for us the fearful pest.
The crowd's applause now sounds like scorn to me. 1030
Oh, could you but within me read
How little, son and father, we
Were worthy such a fame and meed!
My father was a simple, worthy man,
Who over Nature and her every sacred zone, 1035
Quite honestly, in his odd plan
Mused with a wayward zeal that was his own,
Who, with adepts their presence lending,
Shut him in that black kitchen where he used,
According to receipts unending, 1040
To get the contraries together fused.
There was a lover bold, a lion red,
Who to the lily in a tepid bath was wed.
Both, tortured then with flames, a fiery tide,
From one bride-chamber to another pass. 1045
Thereon appeared, with motley colours pied,
The youthful queen within the glass.
Here was the medicine; the patients died,
And no one questioned: who got well?
Thus we with hellish nostrums, here 1050
Within these mountains, in this dell,
Raged far more fiercely than the pest.
I gave the poison unto thousands, ere
They pined away; and I must live to hear
The shameless murderers praised and blessed. 1055
Wagner.   How can you give yourself to such lament?
Does not a good man do his part
In practising transmitted art
Exactly and with good intent?
If you revere your father as a youth, 1060
Gladly from him you will receive;
If as a man you further knowledge and the truth,
Then can your son a higher goal achieve.
Faust.   Oh, happy he who still hopes that he can
Emerge from Error's boundless sea! 1065
What man knows not, is needed most by man,
And what man knows, for that no use has he.

But what fair blessing that this hour can show
Let's not with mournful thoughts like these embitter!
Behold how in the evening sunset-glow 1070
The green-encircled hamlets glitter.
The sun retreats—the day, outlived, is o'er—
It hastens hence and lo! a new world is alive!
Oh, that from earth no wing can lift me up to soar
And after, ever after it to strive! 1075
I'd see in that eternal evening beam,
Beneath my feet, the world in stillness glowing
Each valley hushed and every height agleam,
The silver brook to golden rivers flowing.
The mountain wild with all its gorges 1080
Would hinder not the godlike course for me;
Before astounded eyes already surges,
With bays yet warm, the open sea.
And yet at last the god seems to be sinking;
But new impulse awakes, to light 1085
I hasten on, eternal brightness drinking,
Before me day, behind me night,
Above me heaven, and under me the billow.
A lovely dream, the while the glory fades from sight.
Alas! To wings that lift the spirit light 1090
No earthly wing will ever be a fellow.
Yet 'tis inborn in everyone, each fancies
His feeling presses upward and along,
When over us lost amid the blue expanses
The lark sings down his showering song, 1095
When over rough heights of firs and larches
The outspread eagles soaring roam,
And over lakes and over marshes
The crane strives onward toward his home.
Wagner. I've often had capricious, odd hours of my own, 1100
Yet such an impulse I have never known.
One's sated soon if on the woods and fields he look;
I'll never envy any bird his wing.
How differently the joys of spirit bring
Us on from page to page, from book to book! 1105
Then winter nights become so sweet and fair,
A blessèd life warms up our every limb;
And ah! if one unrolls a parchment really rare,
The whole of Heaven descends on him.
Faust. By one impulse alone are you impressed. 1110
Oh, never learn to know the other!
Two souls alas! are dwelling in my breast;
And each is fain to leave its brother.
The one, fast clinging, to the world adheres
With clutching organs, in love's sturdy lust; 1115

The other strongly lifts itself from dust
To yonder high, ancestral spheres.
Oh, are there spirits hovering near,
That ruling weave, twixt earth and heaven are rife,
Descend! come from the golden atmosphere   *1120*
And lead me hence to new and varied life!
Yea! were a magic mantle only mine,
To bear me to strange lands at pleasure,
I would not barter it for costliest treasure,
Not for the mantle of a king resign.   *1125*

Wagner.   Oh, call them not, the well-known swarms
That streaming spread throughout the murky air;
In every quarter they prepare
A danger for mankind in a thousand forms,
Sharp spirit-fangs press from the north   *1130*
Upon you here with arrow-pointed tongues;
And from the east, now parching, they come forth
And feast themselves upon your lungs;
And when the south wind from the desert drives
Those that heap glow on glow upon your brain,   *1135*
The west wind brings the swarm that first revives,
Then drowns you and the field and plain.
They like to hear, on mischief gaily bent,
They like to hearken, for they like to try
To fool us, pose as if from Heaven sent,   *1140*
And lisp like angels when they lie.
But let us go! The world's already grey,
The air grows chill, the mists of evening fall!
'Tis now we treasure home the most of all—
Why do you stand and stare? What is the trouble?   *1145*
What in the gloaming seizes you in such a way?

Faust.   You see that black dog streaking through the grain and stubble?
Wagner.   I saw him long since; not important did he seem to me.
Faust.   Observe him well! What do you take the beast to be?
Wagner.   Why, just a poodle; in his way he's worrying   *1150*
In his attempt to find his master's traces.
Faust.   But do you note how in wide spiral rings he's hurrying
Around us here and ever nearer chases?
And if I err not, there's a trail behind him!
Along his path a fiery eddy flies.   *1155*
Wagner.   Only a plain black poodle do I see. Don't mind him!
I think it's an illusion of your eyes.
Faust.   He seems in magic nooses to be sweeping
Around our feet, a future snare to bind.
Wagner.   I see he doubts, he's timidly around us leaping,   *1160*
Two strangers—not his master—does he find.
Faust.   The circle narrows; he's already near!
Wagner.   You see a dog! It is no spectre here.

He snarls and doubts, now on his belly see him crawl,
He wags his tail, dog-habits all.   *1165*
Faust.   Come here! And be a friend with us!
Wagner.   It is a beast and, poodle-like, ridiculous.
Stand quiet and he'll sit up too;
Speak to him and he'll scramble up on you;
Lose something and he'll bring it back again,   *1170*
Leap into water for your cane.
Faust.   You're likely right. I find no trace remaining
Of any spirit; it is all mere training.
Wagner.   By any dog, if he but be well trained,
Even a wise man's liking may be gained,   *1175*
Yes, he deserves your favour thoroughly,
A clever pupil of students, he.

They go into the gateway of the town.

STUDY

Faust [entering with the poodle].

Meadow and field have I forsaken,
That deeps of night from sight enroll;
A solemn awe the deeps awaken,   *1180*
Rousing in us the better soul.
No wild desires can longer win me,
No stormy lust to dare and do;
The love of all mankind stirs in **me,**
The love of God is stirred anew.[1]   *1185*

Be quiet, poodle! Don't make such a riot!
Why at the threshold do you sniff the air?
Lie down behind the stove in quiet!
My best of cushions I will give you there.
As on the hillside pathway, leaping   *1190*
And running about, you amused us best,
So take now too from me your keeping,
But as a welcome, silent guest.

Ah, when the friendly lamp is glowing
Again within our narrow cell,   *1195*
Through heart and bosom light comes flowing
If but the heart knows itself well.
Then Reason once again discourses
And Hope begins to bloom again;
Man yearns to reach life's flowing sources,   *1200*
Ah! to the Fount of Life attain.

[1] Cf. Spinoza, *Ethics*, v. 20.

Snarl not, you poodle! To the sacred strain
That now doth all my soul surround,
Is suited not that bestial sound.
We know full well that men deride whate'er 1205
They do not understand
And that before the Good and Fair,
Which oft is hard for them, they grumble;
And will the dog, like them too, snarl and bumble?
But ah! I feel already, with a will the best, 1210
Contentment wells no longer from my breast.
But wherefore must the stream so soon run dry
And we again thus thirsting lie?
I have experienced this in ample measure.
And yet this feeling has its compensation; 1215
We learn the supernatural to treasure.
Our spirits yearn toward revelation
That nowhere glows more fair, more excellent,
Than here in the New Testament.
To open the fundamental text I'm moved, 1220
With honest feeling, once for all,
To turn the sacred, blest original
Into my German well-beloved.
     He opens a volume and applies himself to it.
'Tis written: "In the beginning was the Word!"
Here now I'm balked! Who'll put me in accord? 1225
It is impossible, the *Word* so high to prize,
I must translate it otherwise
If I am rightly by the Spirit taught.
'Tis written: In the beginning was the *Thought!*
Consider well that line, the first you see, 1230
That your pen may not write too hastily!
Is it then *Thought* that works, creative, hour by hour?
Thus should it stand: In the beginning was the *Power!*
Yet even while I write this word, I falter,
For something warns me, this too I shall alter. 1235
The Spirit's helping me! I see now what I need
And write assured: In the beginning was the *Deed!*
   If I'm to share this room with you,
Poodle, then leave off howling,
Then leave off growling! 1240
Such a distracting fellow I can't view
Or suffer to have near me.
One of us two, or I or you,
Must quit this cell, I fear me.
I'm loath your right as guest thus to undo. 1245
The door is open, you've a passage free.
But what is this I now must see!
Can that happen naturally?

Is it phantom? Is it reality?
How long and broad the poodle grows! 1250
He rises up in mighty pose,
'Tis not a dog's form that he shows!
What spectre have I sheltered thus?
He's like a hippopotamus
With fiery eyes, jaws terrible to see. 1255
Oh, mine you are most certainly.
For such as your half-hellish crew
The Key of Solomon will do.[1]

Spirits [*in the corridor*].
            Captured is someone within!
            Stay without, none follow in! 1260
            Like a fox in a snare
            Quakes an ancient hell-lynx there.
            But now give heed!
            Hover hence, hither hover,
            Under, over, 1265
            And he soon himself has freed.
            Can ye avail him,
            Oh, do not fail him!
            For he has already done
            Much to profit us, each one. 1270

Faust.   First, to deal with this beast's core,
   I will use the Spell of Four:

            Salamander must be glowing,
            Undine self-coiling,
            Sylph vanish in going, 1275
            Kobold keep toiling.

            Who would ignore
            The elements four,
            Their powers
            And dowers, 1280
            No master he
            Over spirits can be.

            Vanish in fiery glow,
            Salamander!
            Gurgling, together flow, 1285
            Undine!
            In meteoric beauty shine,
            Sylph!
            Bring homely help,

[1] A book containing directions for exorcizing the four elements.

Incubus! Incubus!   *1290*
Step forth and end the charm for us.

None of the Four
Hides in the beast.
He lies quite calmly, grins evermore;
I've not yet hurt him in the least.   *1295*
Thou'lt hear me longer
Conjure thee stronger!

Art thou, fellow, one
That out of Hell has run?
Then see this Sign!   *1300*
Before which incline
Black cohorts e'er!
It swells up now with bristling hair.

Thou reprobated,
Canst rede His token?   *1305*
The Ne'er-originated,
The Never-spoken,
Who every Heaven has permeated,
He! wantonly immolated![1]

Behind the stove, held by my spells,   *1310*
Like an elephant it swells,
And all the space it fills complete.
In vapour it will melt away.
Mount not up to the ceiling! Lay
Thyself down at thy Master's feet!   *1315*
I threaten not in vain as thou canst see.
With holy fire I'll shrivel thee!
Do not await
The light thrice radiate!
Do not await   *1320*
The strongest art at my command!

MEPHISTOPHELES *steps forth from behind the stove while the*
    vapour is vanishing. He is dressed as a travelling scholar.
Mephistopheles.   Wherefore this noise? What does my lord
    command?
Faust.   So this, then, was the kernel of the brute!
    A travelling scholar it is? The *casus* makes me smile.
Mephistopheles.   To you, O learnèd sir, I proffer my salute!   *1325*
    You made me sweat in vigorous style.
Faust.   What is your name?
Mephistopheles.   The question seems but cheap
    From one who for the Word has such contempt,

[1] Cf. Ephesians, 4. 10; John, 19. 34; Revelation, 1. 7.

Who from all outward show is quite exempt
And only into beings would delve deep.   *1330*
Faust.   The being of such gentlemen as you, indeed,
In general, from your titles one can read.
It shows itself but all too plainly when men dub
You Liar or Destroyer or Beëlzebub.[1]
Well now, who are you then?
Mephistopheles.   Part of that Power which would   *1335*
The Evil ever do, and ever does the Good.
Faust.   A riddle! Say what it implies!
Mephistopheles.   I am the Spirit that denies!
And rightly too; for all that doth begin
Should rightly to destruction run;   *1340*
'Twere better then that nothing were begun.
Thus everything that you call Sin,
Destruction—in a word, as Evil represent—
That is my own, real element.
Faust.   You call yourself a part, yet whole you're standing there.   *1345*
Mephistopheles.   A modest truth do I declare.
A man, the microcosmic fool, down in his soul
Is wont to think himself a whole,
But I'm part of the Part which at the first was all,
Part of the Darkness that gave birth to Light,   *1350*
The haughty Light that now with Mother Night
Disputes her ancient rank and space withal,
And yet 'twill not succeed, since, strive as strive it may,
Fettered to bodies will Light stay.
It streams from bodies, it makes bodies fair,   *1355*
A body hinders it upon its way,
And so, I hope, it has not long to stay
And will with bodies their destruction share.
Faust.   Now I perceive your worthy occupation!
You can't achieve wholesale annihilation   *1360*
And now a retail business you've begun.
Mephistopheles.   And truly thereby nothing much is done.
What stands out as the opposite of Naught—
This Something, this your clumsy world—for aught
I have already undertaken,   *1365*
It have I done no harm nor shaken
With waves and storms, with earthquakes, fiery brand.
Calm, after all, remain both sea and land.
And that accursèd trash, the brood of beasts and men,
A way to get at them I've never found.   *1370*
How many now I've buried in the ground!
Yet fresh, new blood forever circulates again.
Thus on and on—one could go mad in sheer despair!
From earth, from water, and from air

[1] Cf. John, 8. 44; Revelation, 9. 11; Matthew, 12. 24; Mark, 3. 22.

A thousand germs evolving start,   *1375*
  In dryness, moisture, warmth, and cold!
  Weren't it for fire which I withhold,
  I'd have as mine not one thing set apart.
Faust.   So to that Power never reposing,
  Creative, healing, you're opposing   *1380*
  Your frigid devil's fist with might and main.
  It's clenched in spite and clenched in vain!
  Seek something else to undertake,
  You, Chaos' odd, fantastic son!
Mephistopheles.   We'll really ponder on what can be done   *1385*
  When my next visits here I make.
  But may I for the present go away?
Faust.   Why you should ask, I do not see.
  Though we have only met today,
  Come as you like and visit me.   *1390*
  Here is a window, here a door, for you,
  Besides a certain chimney-flue.
Mephistopheles. Let me own up! I cannot go **away;**
  A little hindrance bids me stay.
  The witch's foot upon your sill I see.   *1395*
Faust.   The pentagram? That's in your way?
  You son of Hell explain to me,
  If that stays you, how came you in today?
  And how was such a spirit so betrayed?
Mephistopheles.   Observe it closely! It is not well **made;**   *1400*
  One angle, on the outer side of it,
  Is just a little open, as you see.
Faust.   That was by accident a lucky hit!
  And are you then my captive? Can that be?
  By happy chance the thing's succeeded!   *1405*
Mephistopheles.   As he came leaping in, the poodle did not heed it.
  The matter now seems turned about;
  The Devil's in the house and can't get out.
Faust.   Well, through the window—why not there withdraw?
Mephistopheles.   For devils and for ghosts it is a law: *1410*
  Where they slipped in, there too must they go out.
  The first is free, the second's slaves are we.
Faust.   Does Hell itself have its laws then?
  That's fine! A compact in that case might be
  Concluded safely with you gentlemen?   *1415*
Mephistopheles.   What's promised, you'll enjoy with naught
    subtracted,
  With naught unduly snipped off or exacted.
  But that needs more than such a brief consideration
  And we'll discuss it soon in further conversation.
  But now, most earnestly I pray,   *1420*
  For this time let me go away.

Faust. One moment longer do remain;
   Tell me at last some pleasant news.
Mephistopheles. Let me go now, I'll soon be back again;
   Then you may question as you choose.   1425
Faust. I've never set a snare for you;
   You walked, yourself, into this net tonight.
   Let him who holds the Devil hold him tight!
   He'll not so soon catch him anew.
Mephistopheles. If it so please you, I'm prepared, indeed,   1430
   To lend you company, but take good heed:
   It's on condition that my arts beguile
   The time for you in worthy style.
Faust. I'll gladly see your arts, in that you're free,
   Though only if you please with artistry!   1435
Mephistopheles. More for your senses, friend, you'll gain
   In this one hour than you'd obtain
   In a whole year's monotony.
   All that the tender spirits sing you,
   The lovely images they bring you,   1440
   Are not an empty sorcery.
   They will delight your sense of smell,
   They will refresh your palate well,
   And blissful will your feeling swell.
   Of preparation there's no need,   1445
   We're here together, so proceed!
Spirits.
              Vanish, ye darkling
              Vaultings above him!
              More lovely gleaming,
              Blue ether beaming,   1450
              Gaze down, benign!
              Now are the darkling
              Clouds disappearing!
              Faint stars are sparkling,
              Gentler suns nearing   1455
              Hitherward shine.
              Graces, adorning
              Sons of the morning,
              Spirit-like, bending,
              Wavering, hover.   1460
              Yearning unending
              Follows them over;
              Ribbons a-trailing,
              Fluttering, veiling,
              Wide spaces cover,   1465
              Cover the bower,
              Where, with deep feeling,
              Lovers are dreaming,

Life-pledges sealing.
Bower by bower!   *1470*
Tendrils out-streaming!
Heavy grape's gushing,
In the vats plunging;
Out from the cushing
Winepresses lunging,   *1475*
Wine-streams are whirling;
Foaming and purling
Onward o'er precious
Pure stones they wind them,
Leave heights behind them,   *1480*
Broad'ning to spacious
Fair lakes, abounding
Green hills surrounding.
Wingèd creation,
Sipping elation,   *1485*
Sunward is fleeting,
Bright islands meeting,
Flying to meet them
On the waves dancing,
Rhythmic, entrancing,   *1490*
Where we, to greet them,
Hear a glad chorus,
See o'er the meadows
Dancers like shadows,
Flitting before us,   *1495*
Playing, regaling,
Hills some are scaling;
Others are swimming,
Lakes swiftly skimming;
Playfully trailing,   *1500*
Other ones flitter,
All for existent,
All for the distant
Stars as they glitter
Rapturous Love.   *1505*

Mephistopheles. He sleeps! Well done, ye tender, airy throng!
Ye truly lulled him with your song,
And for this concert I am in your debt.
You're not the man to keep the Devil captive yet!
Enchant him with a dream's sweet imagery,   *1510*
Plunge him into an ocean of untruth!
But now, to break this threshold's sorcery,
I have to get a rat's sharp tooth.
To conjure long I do not need;
Already one is rustling and it soon will heed.   *1515*
    The lord of all the rats and mice,

Of flies and frogs and bugs and lice,
Bids you now venture to appear
And gnaw upon this threshold here
Where he is dabbing it with oil.   1520
Already you come hopping forth. Now to your toil!
Quick to the work! The point that held me bound
There on the outer edge is found.
Just one bite more—'tis done! Begone!
Now, Faustus, till we meet again, dream on!   1525
Faust awakening. Am I again a victim of delusion?
That streaming throng of spirits—gone are they?
Dreamt I the Devil through some mere illusion?
Or did a poodle only leap away?

STUDY
FAUST. MEPHISTOPHELES.

Faust. A knock? Come in! Who now will bother me?   1530
Mephistopheles. 'Tis I.
Faust.   Come in!
Mephistopheles.   Full three times must it be.
Faust. Come in, then!
Mephistopheles.   Fine! I like that! All is well!
I hope we'll bear with one another and agree!
For I, your every crotchet to dispel,
Am here all dressed up like a noble squire,   1535
In scarlet, gold-betrimmed attire:
A little cloak of heavy silk brocade,
Here on my hat a tall cock's-feather too,
Here at my side a long and pointed blade;
And now, to make it brief, I counsel you   1540
That you too likewise be arrayed,
That you, emancipated, free,
Experience what life may be.
Faust. I'll feel, whatever my attire,
The pain of life, earth's narrow way.   1545
I am too old to be content with play,
Too young to be without desire.
What can the world afford me now?
Thou shalt renounce! Renounce shalt thou!
That is the never-ending song   1550
Which in the ears of all is ringing,
Which always, through our whole life long,
Hour after hour is hoarsely singing.
I but with horror waken with the sun,
I'd fain weep bitter tears, because I see   1555
Another day that, in its course, for me
Will not fulfil one wish—not one,

Yea, that the foretaste of each joy possessed
With carping criticism half erases,
That checks creation in my stirring breast   *1560*
With thousands of life's grinning faces.
I too, when darkness sinks down o'er me,
Must anxious stretch me on my bed;
There, too, no rest comes nigh my weary head,
For savage dreams will rise before me.   *1565*
The god that dwells within my soul
Can stir to life my inmost deeps.
Full sway over all my powers he keeps,
But naught external can he ever control.
So Being like a load on me is pressed,   *1570*
I long for death, existence I detest.
Mephistopheles.   And yet Death never is a wholly welcome guest.
Faust.   Ah, happy he around whose brow Death binds
The blood-stained wreath mid victory's blaze,
Whom in a maiden's arms Death finds   *1575*
After a dance's maddening maze.
Oh, would that I, beneath the lofty Spirit's sway,
Enrapt, had rendered up my soul and sunk away!
Mephistopheles.   And yet that night, those juices brown
A certain man did not drink down.   *1580*
Faust.   Spying is your delight, is that not so?
Mephistopheles.   Omniscient am I not, yet many things I know.
Faust.   Though, from the frightful frenzy reeling,
A sweet, familiar tone drew me away,
Though what remained of childlike feeling   *1585*
Was duped by echoes of a happier day,
I now curse all that, round the soul, enfolds it
With dazzling lures and jugglery,
And, banned within this cave of sorrows, holds it
With blinding spells and flattery.   *1590*
Cursed, before all, the high adherence
To some opinion that ensnares the mind!
Cursed be the blinding of appearance
That holds our senses thus confined!
Cursed be dissembling dream-obsessions,   *1595*
The fraud of fame, a name's enduring life!
Cursed all that flatters as possessions,
As slave and plough, as child and wife!
Cursed too be Mammon, when with treasures
He stirs us on to deeds of might,   *1600*
When he, for lazy, idle pleasures,
Lays down for us the cushions right!
Cursed be the grape's sweet juice deceiving!
Cursed Love's supreme, delicious thrall!
A curse on Hoping! on Believing!   *1605*

And cursed be Patience most of all!
Chorus of Spirits [*invisible*].
                    Woe! Woe!
                    Thou hast destroyed
                    The beautiful world,
                    With powerful fist;   *1610*
                    'Tis smashed, downward hurled!
                    A demigod dashed it to bits!
                    We're trailing
                    The ruins on to the Void,
                    And wailing   *1615*
                    Over the beauty lost and gone!
                    Mighty one
                    Midst the sons of earth,
                    Splendider
                    Build it again,   *1620*
                    Build it aloft in thy breast!
                    And life's new quest
                    Commence
                    With clearer sense,
                    And songs of cheer   *1625*
                    Anew shalt hear!

Mephistopheles.

                    These are the little folk
                    Of those whom I evoke.
                    Hark how they to joy and deed
                    Sagely bid you to give heed!   *1630*
                    Into life they would,
                    Far from solitude
                    There stagnate sap and sense,
                    Persuade and lure you hence.

Cease with your brooding grief to play   *1635*
That, like a vulture, eats your life away.
The worst of company will let you find
That you're a man among mankind.
But yet I don't mean that I'll thrust
You midst the rabble men don't trust.   *1640*
I'm not one of the Great;
Still, if through life you'll go with me,
In that case I'll agree
With pleasure to accommodate
You, on the spot belong to you.   *1645*
I'll be your comrade true
And if to your liking I behave,
I'll be your servant, be your slave!
Faust.   And what in turn am I to do for you?
Mephistopheles.   That is a long way off! Pray don't insist.   *1650*

Faust.   No, no! The Devil is an egoist
  And not "for God's sake!" only will he do
  What will another's needs assist.
  Tell me your terms both plain and clear!
  Such servants in the house bring danger near.   *1655*
Mephistopheles.   *Here* to your service I will bind **me;**
  Beck when you will, I will not pause or rest;
  But in return when *yonder* you will find me,
  Then likewise shall you be at my behest.
Faust.   The *yonder* is to me a trifling matter.   *1660*
  Should you this world to ruins shatter,
  The other then may rise, its place to fill.
  'Tis from this earth my pleasure springs,
  And this sun shines upon my sufferings;
  When once I separate me from these things,   *1665*
  Let happen then what can and will.
  And furthermore I've no desire to hear
  Whether in future too men hate and love,
  And whether too in yonder sphere
  There is an *under* or *above*.   *1670*
Mephistopheles.   In this mood you can dare to go **my ways.**
  Commit yourself; you shall in these next days
  Behold my arts and with great pleasure too.
  What no man yet has seen, I'll give to you.
Faust.   Poor devil! What have you to give?   *1675*
  Was any human spirit, struggling to ascend,
  Such as your sort could ever comprehend?
  Still, have you food on which no man can live?
  Have you red gold that runs through, without rest,
  Quicksilver-like, the hand it's in?   *1680*
  A game at which men never win?
  A maiden who while on my breast
  Will with my neighbour ogle and conspire?
  The joys divine of honour, once possessed,
  Which vanish like a meteor's fire?   *1685*
  Show me the fruit which, ere it's plucked, will rot,
  And trees that every day grow green anew!
Mephistopheles.   Such a commission frights me not;
  Such treasures I can serve to you.
  But, my good friend, the time approaches when we could   *1690*
  In peace and quiet feast on something good.
Faust.   If ever I lay me on a bed of sloth in peace,
  That instant let for me existence cease!
  If ever with lying flattery you can rule me
  So that contented with myself I stay,   *1695*
  If with enjoyment you can fool me,
  Be that for me the final day!
  That bet I offer!

Mephistopheles. Done!
Faust.   Another hand-clasp! There!
  If to the moment I shall ever say:
  "Ah, linger on, thou art so fair!"   *1700*
  Then may you fetters on me lay,
  Then will I perish, then and there!
  Then may the death-bell toll, recalling
  Then from your service you are free;
  The clock may stop, the pointer falling,   *1705*
  And time itself be past for me!
Mephistopheles. Consider well, we'll not forget it.
Faust. Your perfect right to that I'll not deny.
  My action was not rash, I'll not regret it.
  As soon as I stagnate, a slave am I,   *1710*
  And whether yours or whose, why should I ask?
Mephistopheles. Then at a Doctor's-feast this very day
  I'll act as servant and fulfil my task.
  But one thing still: in case of life or death, I pray,
  Give me a written line or two.   *1715*
Faust. What, pedant! Something written do you ask of me?
  Was neither man nor word of man yet known to you?
  Is it not enough that this my spoken word
  Disposes of my days for all eternity?
  Does not the world rush on, in all its currents stirred,   *1720*
  And should a promise have a hold on me?
  Yet to our hearts we've taken this conceit.
  Who gladly would its hold undo?
  Blest he whose bosom is with breachless faith replete,
  No sacrifice will that man ever rue.   *1725*
  But any stamped and written parchment sheet
  Is like a ghost that all men shrink to view.
  The spoken word dies forthwith in the quill;
  Leather and wax remain our masters still.
  What, Evil Spirit, do you want of me?   *1730*
  Brass, marble, parchment, paper? Name it then!
  Am I to write with graver, chisel, pen?
  I offer you your choice quite free.
Mephistopheles. How can you talk so heatedly,
  Exaggerate in such a way?   *1735*
  Just any little sheet will do, it's all the same.
  With one wee drop of blood you sign your name.
Faust. If this will satisfy you, then I say:
  Let us agree and put the farce to this odd use.
Mephistopheles. Blood is a quite peculiar juice.   *1740*
Faust. Fear not! This league with you I shall not break!
  The aim and goal of all my energy
  Is to fulfil the promise I now make.
  I've puffed myself too high, I see;

Only within your ranks do I deserve to be.   *1745*
The Mighty Spirit spurned me with a scoff,
And Nature turns herself away from me.
The thread of thought is broken off,
To me all learning's long been nauseous.
In depths of sensuality   *1750*
Let us our glowing passions still!
In magic's veils impervious
Prepared at once be every marvel's thrill!
Come, let us plunge into Time's rushing dance,
Into the roll of Circumstance!   *1755*
There may then pain and joyance,
Successes and annoyance,
Alternately follow as they can.
Only restlessly active is a man!
Mephistopheles.   To you no goal is set, nor measure.   *1760*
If you should like to nibble everything,
To snatch up something on the wing,
May all agree with you that gives you pleasure!
Fall to, I say, and don't be coy.
Faust.   You hear indeed, I do not speak of joy.   *1765*
Life's wildering whirl be mine, its painfulest enjoyment,
Enamoured hate, and quickening annoyment.
My bosom, of all thirst for knowledge cured,
Shall close itself henceforth against no woe;
Whatever to all mankind is assured,   *1770*
I, in my inmost being, will enjoy and know,
Seize with my soul the highest and most deep;
Men's weal and woe upon my bosom heap;
And thus this self of mine to all their selves expanded,
Like them I too at last be stranded.   *1775*
Mephistopheles.   Oh, trust me who for many a thousand year
Have chewed this crust, it is so hard at best
That twixt the cradle and the bier
That ancient leaven no man can digest.
Trust one like me: this Whole is wrought   *1780*
And fashioned only for a God's delight!
He dwells in an eternal light;
Us into darkness He has brought;
To you are suited only day and night.
Faust.   Ah, but I will!
Mephistopheles.   Well said and right!   *1785*
And yet I fear there is but one thing wrong;
For life is short and art is long.
I'd think you'd let yourself be taught.
Associate you with a poet; then, in thought,
You leave the gentleman full sweep,   *1790*
Upon your honoured head to heap

Each good and noble quality:
The lion's mood,
The stag's rapidity,
The fiery blood of Italy,   *1795*
The Northman's hardihood.
The secret for it? Let him find
How magnanimity and cunning are combined,
How with a youth's hot impulse you may fall
In love according to a plan.   *1800*
Might I myself know such a gentleman,
Him Mr. Microcosm I would call.

Faust.   What am I if I strive in vain
To win the crown of all mankind which, though afar,
All senses struggle to obtain?   *1805*

Mephistopheles.   You at the end are—what you are.
Put on your head perukes with a million locks,
Put on your feet a pair of ell-high socks,
You after all will still be—what you are.

Faust.   I feel that I have made each treasure   *1810*
Of human mind my own in vain,
And when at last I sit me down at leisure,
No new-born power wells up within my brain.
I'm not a hair's-breadth more in height
Nor nearer to the Infinite.   *1815*

Mephistopheles.   My good sir, you observe this matter
As men these matters always see;
But we must manage that much better
Before life's pleasures from us flee.
Your hands and feet too—what the devil!—   *1820*
Your head and seed are yours alone!
Yet all with which I gaily revel,
Is it on that account the less my own?
If for six stallions I can pay,
Aren't all their powers added to my store?   *1825*
I am a proper man and dash away
As if the legs I had were twenty-four!
Quick, then! Let all reflection be,
And straight into the world with me!
A chap who speculates—let this be said—   *1830*
Is very like a beast on moorland dry,
That by some evil spirit round and round is led,
While fair, green pastures round about him lie.

Faust.   But how shall we begin?

Mephistopheles.   We'll just get out, so come!
Bah! what a place of martyrdom!   *1835*
What kind of life is this you lead?
Boring the youngsters and yourself indeed!
Leave that to Master Paunch, your neighbour!

    Why plague yourself by threshing straws?

    The best that you can know with all your labour,   *1840*

    You dare not tell the striplings raw.

    Right now I hear one in the passageway.

Faust.   I cannot possibly see him today.

Mephistopheles.   He's waited long, the poor young chap;

    Uncomforted, he must not go away.   *1845*

    Come, let me have your gown and cap;

    I in that costume? What a precious fit!

       He dresses himself up.

    Now you can leave things to my wit!

    I only need a quarter of an hour.

    And then our lovely tour, meanwhile prepare for it!   *1850*

       Exit FAUST

Mephistopheles [*in* FAUST's *long robe*].

    Humanity's most lofty power,

    Reason and knowledge, pray despise!

    Let but the Spirit of all Lies

    With works of dazzling magic blind you;

    Then, absolutely mine, I'll have and bind you!   *1855*

    To him has Fate a spirit given

    That, uncurbed, ever onward sweeps,

    Whose striving, by too hasty impulse driven,

    The joys of this earth overleaps.

    Him will I drag through wild life whirling past,   *1860*

    Through all that is unmeaning, shallow stuff;

    I'll see him struggle, weaken, and stick fast!

    Before his greedy lips that can not feast enough

    Shall hover food and drink as if for some grand revel;

    Refreshment will he all in vain implore;   *1865*

    And had he not surrendered to the Devil,

    Still were he lost forevermore.

       A STUDENT *enters*

Student.   I've been here just a little while or so

    And come to pay an humble call,

    To talk with you, a man to know,   *1870*

    One who is named with reverence by all.

Mephistopheles.   You please me greatly by your courtesy!

    A man like many another one you see.

    Have you already looked about elsewhere?

Student.   I beg you, take me in your kindly care!   *1875*

    I come with every good intention,

    Fresh blood, and money, though not much to mention.

    My mother scarcely would permit my going.

    I'd fain learn here abroad something worth knowing.

Mephistopheles.   Well, now you're at the proper place.   *1880*

Student.   Yet, frankly, would I could my steps retrace!

    Within these walls the lecture hall,

I do not like it here at all.
It is a space that's so confined;
One sees no green nor any tree,   *1885*
And in the halls with benches lined,
Sight, hearing, thought, all go from me.
Mephistopheles.   That only comes with habit, so
A child takes not its mother's breast
Quite willingly in the beginning, though   *1890*
Soon nourishes itself with zest.
So at the breasts of Wisdom nursed,
Each day you'll lust for them the more athirst.
Student.   I'll cling about her neck with joy,
But say what means thereto I shall employ.   *1895*
Mephistopheles.   Ere you go on, explain your views.
Which is the faculty you choose?
Student.   I'd like right learnèd to become; what is
On earth I'd gladly comprehend,
To heaven itself my range extend,   *1900*
Know all of nature and the sciences.
Mephistopheles.   Then you are on the proper way
But must not let yourself be lured astray.
Student.   Body and soul I'm for it bent;
Yet there would please me, I must say,   *1905*
A little freedom and divertisement
Upon a pleasant summer holiday.
Mephistopheles.   Make use of time, its course so soon is run,
Yet system teaches you how time is won.
I counsel you, dear friend, in sum,   *1910*
That first you take *collegium logicum.*
Your spirit's then well broken in for you,
In Spanish boots[1] laced tightly to,
That you henceforth may more deliberately keep
The path of thought and straight along it creep,   *1915*
And not perchance criss-cross may go,
A-will-o'-wisping to and fro.
Then you'll be taught full many a day
What at one stroke you've done alway,
Like eating and like drinking free,   *1920*
It now must go like: One! Two! Three!
In fact, when men are fabricating thought,
It goes as when a weaver's masterpiece is wrought.
One treadle sets a thousand threads a-going,
And to and fro the shuttle flies;   *1925*
Quite unperceived the threads are flowing,
One stroke effects a thousand ties.
Then some philosopher steps in, and he

[1]Instruments of torture favoured by the Spanish Inquisition, consisting of long iron gaiters screwed tighter and tighter around the legs.

Will demonstrate to you it so must be:
The first was so, the second so, *1930*
And thus the third and fourth are so;
And if no first nor second had been there,
The third and fourth one would be never.
All students prize that everywhere,
But are they weavers? No, they're not that clever. *1935*
Who'll know aught living and describe it well,
Seeks first the spirit to expel.
He then has the component parts in hand
But lacks, alas! the spirit's band.
Encheirisis naturae,[1] Chemistry names it so, *1940*
Mocking herself but all unwitting though.
Student.   I can't quite understand you, I confess.
Mephistopheles.   Next time, be sure, you will have more success,
When you have learned how to reduce
And classify all by its use. *1945*
Student.   I feel as stupid after all you've said
As if a miller's wheel were whirling in my head.
Mephistopheles.   And next—the first of all worth mention—
To Metaphysics you must give attention,
And see that you profoundly strive to gain *1950*
What is not suited for the human brain.
For what goes in or won't go in the head,
A brilliant phrase will serve you in good stead.
Yet, first of all for this half-year,
Observe the best of systems here *1955*
You take five lectures daily—understand?
And when the clock strikes, be on hand!
Be well prepared before the start,
With paragraphs well got by heart,
So later you can better look *1960*
And see he says naught save what's in the book;
But write away as unabated
As if the Holy Ghost dictated!
Student.   You will not need to say that to me twice!
I can foresee how much I'll gain from this advice; *1965*
Because what one has down in black and white
It is a comfort to take home at night.
Mephistopheles.   But come now, choose a faculty!
Student.   I can't adjust myself to Law—not possibly.
Mephistopheles.   I can't blame that in you, it's no demerit. *1970*
This science as it really is I see.
Statutes and laws that we inherit
Like an eternal malady
Go trailing on from race to race
And furtive shift from place to place. *1975*

[1]Manipulation of nature.

To nonsense reason turns, and benefit to worry.
Woe unto you that you're a grandchild, woe!
For of the law that was born with us, no!
Of that, alas! there never is a query.

Student. You have increased my own disgust. The youth   *1980*
Whom you instruct is blessed in sooth!
I'm now almost inclined to try Theology.

Mephistopheles. I would not wish to lead you so astray.
In what this science teaches, it would be
So hard to shun the false, misleading way;   *1985*
So much of hidden poison lies therein,
You scarce can tell it from its medicine.
'Tis best here too that only one be heard
And that you swear then by the master's word.
Upon the whole—to words stick fast!   *1990*
Then through a sure gate you'll at last
Enter the templed hall of Certainty.

Student. Yet in each word some concept there must be.

Mephistopheles. Quite true! But don't torment yourself too
    anxiously;
For at the point where concepts fail,   *1995*
At the right time a word is thrust in there.
With words we fitly can our foes assail,
With words a system we prepare,
Words we quite fitly can believe,
Nor from a word a mere iota thieve.   *2000*

Student. Pardon, I keep you here with many a question,
But I must cause more trouble still.
Concerning Medicine as well you will
Not make some pithy, keen suggestion?
Three years! how quickly they are past!   *2005*
And, God! the field is far too vast.
If but some sign is indicated,
A man can sooner feel his way.

Mephistopheles [*aside*]. With this dry tone I am now satiated;
The downright devil I must once more play.   *2010*
    Aloud.
Medicine's spirit one can grasp with ease.
The great and little world you study through,
To let things finally their course pursue
As God may please.
It's vain that you in search of knowledge roam and drift,   *2015*
Each only learns what learn he can;
Yet he who grasps the moment's gift,
He is your proper man.
You are moreover quite well-built, beside,
Will never lack for boldness too;   *2020*
And if you only in yourself confide,

All other souls confide in you.
Learn chiefly how to lead the women; be assured
That all their "Ohs" and "Ahs," eternal, old,
So thousandfold, 2025
Can at a single point be cured;
And if you half-way decorously come,
You have them all beneath your thumb.
A title first must make them comprehend
That your art many arts doth far transcend. 2030
By way of welcome then you touch all matters
For sake of which, long years, another flatters.
Learn how the little pulse to squeeze
And then with sly and fiery glances seize
Her freely round the slender hips to see 2035
How firmly laced up she may be.
Student. Now that looks better! Now one sees the where and how!
Mephistopheles. Dear friend, all theory is grey,
And green the golden tree of life.
Student. I vow,
It's all just like a dream to me. 2040
Another time I'll bore you, if I may,
To hear your wisdom through and through.
Mephistopheles. All that I can I'll gladly do.
Student. It is impossible for me to go away
Before I hand my album here to you. 2045
Will your grace grant this favour to me too?
Mephistopheles. Oh, very well!
He writes and gives it back.
Student [*reads*]. Eritis sicut Deus, scientes bonum et malum.[1]
He closes the book reverently and takes his leave.
Mephistopheles. Follow the ancient text and heed my coz the snake;
With all your likeness to God you'll sometimes tremble and quake. 2050
Faust *enters.*
Faust. Now whither shall we go?
Mephistopheles. Whither it pleases you.
We'll see the little world and then we'll see the great.
With how much joy and how much profit too
You'll sponge the whole course through until you graduate.
Faust. But with my beard so long I may 2055
Quite lack life's free and easy way.
In this attempt no luck will come to me;
I never fitted in society at all.
With other men I feel myself so small;
I'll feel embarrassed constantly. 2060
Mephistopheles. For that, good friend, this is the remedy I give:
Just trust yourself, then you'll know how to live.

---

[1]"Ye shall be as God, know good and evil." Cf. Genesis, 3. 5.

Faust. We'll leave the house but how shall we set out?
 Have you a horse, a servant, carriage, anywhere?
Mephistopheles. We'll only spread this mantle out   *2065*
 And have it bear us through the air.
 You'll take upon this daring flight
 No heavy luggage, only light.
 A bit of fiery air—I'll have it ready here—
 Will lift us from this earth without ado,   *2070*
 And if we're light, we'll go up swiftly too.
 I must congratulate you on your new career.

AUERBACH'S CELLAR IN LEIPSIC
DRINKING-BOUT OF JOLLY COMPANIONS

Frosch. Will no one drink? and no one laugh?
 I'll teach you how to look so wry!
 You're everyone like sodden chaff   *2075*
 And always used to blaze sky-high!
Brander. That's your fault; you don't add a single stroke,
 No beastliness and not one silly joke.
Frosch [*pours a glass of wine over* BRANDER'S HEAD].
 There you have both!
Brander.   You twofold beast!
Frosch. That's what you asked me for, at least!   *2080*
Siebel. If any quarrel, throw 'em out!
 Come, sing with all your lungs, boys, swill and shout!
 Up! Holla! Ho!
Altmayer.   My God! I'm done for! Here!
 Some cotton wool! The fellow bursts my ear.
Siebel. When vaulted ceilings echo back our song,   *2085*
 Then first we feel the bass is deep and strong.
Frosch. Quite right! Then out with him who takes a thing amiss!
 Ah! tara lara da!
Altmayer.   Ah! tara lara da!
Frosch. The throats are tuned for this!
 He sings.
                 Dear Holy Roman Empire! Say,   *2090*
                 How does it stick together?

Brander. A nasty song! Shame! a political song!
 A wretched song! Thank God each morning, brother,
 That for the Roman Empire you don't need to bother!
 There is at least one gain I am most thankful for,   *2095*
 That I'm not Kaiser and not Chancellor.
 And yet we must not fail to have a ruler. Stay!
 Let us elect a Pope! What do you say?
 You know the kind of quality that can
 Bear down the scale and elevate the man.   *2100*

Frosch [*sings*].

> Soar aloft, Dame Nightingale,
> Ten thousand times my sweetheart hail!

Siebel.   No greeting to a sweetheart! I'll not hear of this!
Frosch.   You will not hinder me! My sweetheart, hail! A kiss!
　　He sings.

> Lift the latch! In silent night.   2105
> Lift the latch! The lover wakes.
> Drop the latch! The morning breaks.

Siebel.   Yes, sing on, praise and brag of her with all your might!
　I will in my own time be sure to laugh at you.
　She once led me astray, she'll do it to you too.   2110
　Give her a kobold for her lovesick yearning!
　At some cross-road let him go woo her.
　Let some old buck, from Blocksberg[1] homeward turning,
　Still on the gallop, bleat "Good Evening!" to her.
　A gallant fellow of real flesh and blood   2115
　Is for that wench a deal too good.
　I'll hear no greetings to that lass
　But such as smash her window-glass.
Brander [*pounding on the table*].
　Give heed! Give heed! Lend me your ear!
　You, sirs, confess that I know what is what.   2120
　Some lovesick folk are sitting here,
　And so in honour due their present lot
　I must contribute to their night's good cheer.
　Give heed! A brand-new song 'twill be!
　And sing the chorus lustily!   2125
　　He sings.

> There once in a cellar lived a rat,
> Had a paunch could scarce be smoother,
> For it lived on butter and on fat,
> A mate for Doctor Luther.
> But soon the cook did poison strew   2130
> And then the rat, so cramped it grew
> As if it had love in its body.

Chorus [*shouting*].

> As if it had love in its body.

Brander.

> It flew around, and out it flew,
> From every puddle swilling,   2135
> It gnawed and scratched the whole house
>   through,
> But its rage was past all stilling.
> It jumped full oft in anguish mad,

[1]Usually called the Brocken, the legendary meeting-place of witches.

But soon, poor beast, enough it had,
As if it had love in its body.   *2140*

Chorus.

As if it had love in its body.

Brander.

By anguish driven in open day
It rushed into the kitchen,
Fell on the hearth and panting lay,
Most pitiably twitchin'.   *2145*
Then laughed the poisoner: "Hee! hee! hee!
It's at its last gasp now," said she,
"As if it had love in its body."

Chorus.

"As if it had love in its body."

Siebel.   How these dull chaps enjoy themselves! Now that's   *2150*
A fine old art, so it would seem,
To scatter poison for poor rats!
Brander.   They stand so high in your esteem?
Altmayer.   See the old tub, so bald and fat!
Misfortune makes him mild and tame;   *2155*
He sees in any bloated rat
His very own image, quite the same.
         FAUST *and* MEPHISTOPHELES *enter.*
Mephistopheles.   Before all else I now must let you view
The doings of a jovial crew,
That you may see how smoothly life can flow along.   *2160*
To this crowd every day's a feast and song.
With little wit and much content,
Each, on his own small round intent,
Is like a kitten with its tail.
While no sick headache they bewail   *2165*
And while their host will still more credit give,
Joyous and free from care they live.
Brander.   Those people come directly from a tour,
You see it in their strange, odd ways;
They've not been here an hour, I'm sure.   *2170*
Frosch.   In truth, you're right! My Leipsic will I praise!
A little Paris, one that cultivates its people.
Siebel.   Who are these strangers, do you think?
Frosch.   Leave it to me! Give me a brimming drink
And from these chaps I'll worm the truth   *2175*
As one draws out a young child's tooth.
To me they seem of noble family,
So proud and discontented they appear to be.
Brander.   They're mountebanks, I'll lay a bet with you!
Altmayer.   Perhaps!
Frosch.   Pay heed, I'll make them feel the screw!   *2180*

Mephistopheles [*to* FAUST].   These chaps don't scent the Devil out
   And would not if he had them by the snout!
Faust.   We greet you, sirs!
Siebel.   Thanks and to you the same!
      In a low tone, looking at MEPHISTOPHELES *askance.*
      Why is that fellow's one foot lame?
Mephistopheles.   We'll sit with you if you'll permit the liberty.   2185
   Instead of some good drink which is not here,
   We shall enjoy your company's good cheer.
Altmayer.   A very pampered man you seem to be.
Frosch.   I guess you started late from Rippach on your way.
   Can you have supped with Master Hans[1] tonight?   2190
Mephistopheles.   We passed him by without a stop today!
   We spoke with him last time. He'd quite
   A lot about his cousins to convey,
   Charged us with greetings to each one.
      He bows toward FROSCH.
Altmayer [*in a low tone*].   You got it then! He knows!
Siebel.   A cunning
   fellow, he!   2195
Frosch.   Just wait a bit, I'll get him on the run.
Mephistopheles.   If I mistake not, didn't we
   Hear practised voices sing in chorus?
   In truth, a song must perfectly
   Reëcho from this vaulted ceiling o'er us!   2200
Frosch.   Are you perchance a virtuoso?
Mephistopheles.   Oh no! The zest is great, ability but so-so.
Altmayer.   Give us a song!
Mephistopheles.   A lot, if that way you incline.
Siebel.   But let it be a brand-new strain!
Mephistopheles.   We have returned quite recently from Spain,   2205
   The lovely land of melody and wine.
      He sings.

                  A king there once was reigning,
                  Who cherished a great big flea—

Frosch.   Hear that! A flea! Did you quite grasp the jest?
   I say, a flea's a tidy guest.   2210
Mephistopheles [*sings*].

                  A king there once was reigning,
                  Who cherished a great big flea;
                  No little love attaining,
                  As his own son loved he.
                  He called his tailor hireling,   2215

----

[1]Hans Arsch of Rippach, a stock name for a simple-minded, boorish person. Rippach
is a village a few miles southwest of Leipsic.

The tailor to him flew:
"Ho, measure now the squireling
For coat and breeches too."

Brander.   Be sure to tell that man of stitches
That he must measure to a hair,   2220
And if his head is dear to him, I swear,
No wrinkles must be in those breeches!
Mephistopheles.

In silk and velvet splendid
He now was always dressed,
By ribbons gay attended,   2225
A cross upon his breast.
Was minister created,
A mighty star did sport;
Then all his kin, elated,
Became great lords at court.   2230

Lord, lady, and dependent
Were plagued and sore distressed;
The queen and her attendant
Were bitten by the pest.
And yet they dared not whack them   2235
Nor scratch by day or night.
We smother and we crack them
Whenever we feel them bite.
Chorus [*shouting*].
We smother and we crack them
Whenever we feel them bite.   2240

Frosch.   Bravo! Bravo! That was splendid!
Siebel.   And so should every flea be ended!
Brander.   Point your fingers and squeeze them fine!
Altmayer.   Long live freedom! Long live wine!
Mephistopheles.   A glass to honour freedom I would gladly clink   2245
If but your wines were better fit to drink.
Siebel.   We do not want to hear such talk again!
Mephistopheles.   I only fear the landlord might complain;
Else I would treat each worthy guest
With what our cellar offers of the best.   2250
Siebel.   Do bring it on! The risk be mine.
Frosch.   Produce a good glass and we'll praise your wine.
But don't give us a sample all too small;
If I'm to play the solemn judge at all,
A right good mouthful I require.   2255
Altmayer [*in a low tone*].   They're from the Rhine, I scented that
before.
Mephistopheles.   Fetch me a gimlet!

Brander.   Say, why that desire?
  You haven't got the casks outside the door?
Altmayer.   Back there the landlord keeps his tool-kit placed.
Mephistopheles [*taking the gimlet, to* FROSCH].
  Now say, what do you want to taste?   2260
Frosch.   What do you mean? Have you so many kinds?
Mephistopheles.   I leave the choice to each. Make up your minds!
Altmayer [*to* FROSCH].
  You're licking your chops now! Be careful, steady!
Frosch.   'Tis well! If I'm to choose, it's Rhine wine I propose.
  The best of gifts is what the fatherland bestows.   2265
Mephistopheles [*boring a hole in the edge of the table at the place
    where* FROSCH *is sitting*].   Get us some wax at once, to have the
    stoppers ready!
Altmayer.   Ah! These are tricks! It's jugglery!
Mephistopheles [*to* BRANDER].   And you?
Brander.   Champagne's the stuff for
  me,
  And bubbling, sparkling, must it be.
    MEPHISTOPHELES *is boring holes; one of the others has meanwhile
    made the stoppers and plugged the holes.*
Brander.   What's foreign we can't always shun,   2270
  So far from us must good things often be.
  A genuine German can't abide the French, not one,
  But of their wines he drinks most cheerfully.
Siebel [*as* MEPHISTOPHELES *comes near his place*].
  I do not like the sour, I'd have you know;
  Give me a glass that's really sweet!   2275
Mephistopheles [*boring*].   You'll see, at once Tokay will flow.
Altmayer.   No, gentlemen, just look me in the face! I see't,
  You're only fooling us, it is a jest.
Mephistopheles.   Oh! Oh! With such a noble guest
  That were a bit too much to dare!   2280
  Be quick about it and declare!
  What kind of wine then shall I serve?
Altmayer.   Oh, any! Don't keep asking! I don't care!
    After all the holes are bored and plugged.
Mephistopheles [*with strange gestures*].
      Clustered grapes the vine bears!
      And horns the he-goat wears!   2285
      The wine is juicy, wood the vine;
      The wooden table too can give forth **wine.**
      A view of nature, deep and clear!
      Only believe! A miracle's here!

  Now draw the stoppers and enjoy your fill!   2290
All [*while they pull out the stoppers and the wine desired runs into
  each one's glass*].   O beauteous fountain flowing at our will!

Mephistopheles.   But watch, I say, that not a drop you spill!
  They drink repeatedly.
All [*sing*].
<blockquote>
We're just as happy as cannibals,
As if we were five hundred swine!
</blockquote>

Mephistopheles.   Behold how happy is this folk—it's free!   2295
Faust.   I think now I would like to go away.
Mephistopheles.   But first give heed to a display
  Of glorious bestiality.
Siebel [*drinks carelessly; the wine is spilt upon the ground and turns
  into flame*].   Help! Hell's on fire! It's burning me!
Mephistopheles [*conjuring the flame*].   Be quiet, friendly element! 2300
  To the young men.
  This time 'twas but a flame that Purgatory sent.
Siebel.   What's that? Just wait! For that you will pay dear.
  You don't know who we are, that's clear.
Frosch.   Don't try that game a second time, I say!
Altmayer.   I think we'd better bid him gently go away.   2305
Siebel.   What, sir! You venture to provoke us
  And carry on your hocus-pocus?
Mephistopheles.   Silence, old wine-butt!
Siebel.   Broomstick, you!
  Will you insult me to my nose?
Brander.   Just wait a bit, 'twill soon be raining blows!   2310
Altmayer [*draws a stopper out of the table; fire leaps out at him*].
  I burn! I burn!
Siebel.   It's sorcery!
  The rogue's an outlaw! Come, thrust home with me!
  They draw their knives and rush at MEPHISTOPHELES.
Mephistopheles [*with solemn gestures*].
<blockquote>
False form and word appear,
Change place and sense's sphere!
Be there and here!   2315
</blockquote>
  They stand amazed and look at each other.
Altmayer.   Where am I? What a lovely land!
Frosch.   Vineyards! Do I see right?
Siebel.   Grape clusters close at hand!
Brander.   Here underneath this foliage green,
  See, what a bunch! What grapes are to be seen!
  He seizes SIEBEL *by the nose. The others do the same, one to the
  other, and raise their knives.*
Mephistopheles [*as before*].   Error, loose from their eyes the band! 2320
  And mark you how the Devil's jesting goes.
  He vanishes with FAUST. *The fellows start back from one another.*
Siebel.   What's up?
Altmayer.   How's this?
Frosch.   Was that your nose?

Brander [*to* SIEBEL].   And yours I'm holding in my hand!
Altmayer.   That was a blow, it staggered me down to my toes!
　　I can't stand up, get me a chair!   2325
Frosch.   Out with it, say, what's happened?
Siebel.   Where,
　　Oh, where's that rascal? If I find him now,
　　He shan't escape alive, I vow.
Altmayer.   With my own eyes I saw him riding through
　　The cellar-door—upon a wine-cask too!   2330
　　I feel a weight like lead about my feet!
　　　Turning toward the table.
　　My God! I wonder if the wines still flow?
Siebel.   It was a swindle, lies, 'twas all a cheat.
Frosch.   Yet I drank wine or thought it so.
Brander.   But how about the grapes? What was that anyway?   2335
Altmayer.   One should believe no miracles? Oh, say!

WITCH'S KITCHEN

A great cauldron stands over the fire on a low hearth. In the steam
which rises from it, various figures become visible. A Female
Ape sits by the cauldron and skims the foam off it, taking care
that it does not run over. The Male Ape, with the Young Apes,
sits beside it and warms himself. Walls and ceiling are decked
out with the strangest articles of witches' furniture.

FAUST.   MEPHISTOPHELES.

Faust.   I am repelled by this mad sorcery.
　　I shall get well, you promise me,
　　In this chaotic craziness?
　　Shall I demand an old crone's remedy?   2340
　　And will the dirty, boiling mess
　　Divest my body of some thirty years?
　　Woe's me, if there's naught better you can find!
　　For now my hope already disappears.
　　Has nature not, has not a noble mind,   2345
　　Discovered somewhere any balm?
Mephistopheles.   My friend, you talk once more as if you're calm.
　　By natural means you can acquire a youthful look,
　　But it is in another book
　　And is a chapter strange to see.   2350
Faust.   Still I will know it.
Mephistopheles.   Good! To have a remedy
　　Without physician, money, sorcery:
　　Betake yourself into the fields without delay,
　　Begin to dig and hack away,
　　Maintain yourself, your thought and feeling,   2355
　　Within a circle quite confined and fixed;

Take nourishment of food that is not mixed;
Live with the beasts as beast, nor deem it base
To spread the field you reap with your own dung.
Be sure, this method's best in any case,   2360
Though eighty years of age, still to be young.
Faust.   I am not used to that; I can't submit
To take the spade in hand and dig and ditch.
For me a narrow life is quite unfit.
Mephistopheles.   So then there is no help save from the witch.   2365
Faust.   But why the old beldame? What is your notion?
Can you yourself not brew the potion?
Mephistopheles.   That were a lovely pastime on my part!
Meanwhile a thousand bridges I could rear.
We can't depend alone on science or on art,   2370
The work demands a deal of patience too.
A quiet spirit's busy many a year,
For time alone produces potent brew.
And all that is a part of it
Is wondrous as one must admit!   2375
It's true, the Devil taught her how to do it,
And yet the Devil can not brew it.
        Catching sight of THE BEASTS.
How delicate the breed! Just see!
That is the maid! The man is he!
        To THE BEASTS.
It seems the dame is not at home with you.   2380
The Beasts.

                    To a rollicking crew
                    Out she flew
                    By the chimney-flue!

Mephistopheles.   How long is it her wont to roam from here?
The Beasts.   As long as it takes to warm a paw.   2385
Mephistopheles [*to* FAUST].   How do you think the dainty beasts
    appear?
Faust.   Absurd as anyone I ever saw.
Mephistopheles.   I say, this kind of conversation
I carry on with greatest delectation.
        To THE BEASTS.
Accursèd puppets! Come and tell,   2390
What are you querling in that stuff?
The Beasts.   A beggars' soup that's watered well.
Mephistopheles.   Then you've a public large enough.
The Male Ape [*sidles up to* MEPHISTOPHELES *and fawns on him*].
                    Oh, do throw the dice,
                    Make me rich in a trice,   2395
                    And do let it win me!
                    It all is so bad,

If money I had,
Good sense would be in me.

Mephistopheles.   How fortunate the ape would think himself, could 2400
   he
  But also risk some money in a lottery!
    Meanwhile THE YOUNG APES *have been playing with a great globe*
    which they now roll forward.
The Male Ape.

     That is the world!
     It mounts, now whirled,
    Its fall will follow,
     Like glass it rings. 2405
     Soon break such things!
     Within it's hollow.
     Here bright it gleams,
     Here brighter beams.
     I am alive! 2410
     My dear son, strive
     To keep away!
     For you must die!
     'Tis made of clay,
     In bits 'twill fly. 2415

Mephistopheles.

     What means the sieve?

The Male Ape [*takes it down*].

     Came you to thieve,
     I would know you directly.
  He runs to THE FEMALE APE *and makes her look through it.*
     Look through the sieve!
     Know you the thief? 2420
     Dare not name him exactly?

Mephistopheles [*going nearer to the fire*].
     And then this pot?

Male Ape and Female Ape.
     The half-witted sot!
     He knows not the pot,
     He knows not the kettle! 2425
Mephistopheles.

     Unmannerly beast!
The Male Ape.

     Take the brush at least
     And sit on the settle!

He makes MEPHISTOPHELES *sit down.*

Faust [who all this time has been standing before a mirror, now going near it, now going away from it].

What do I see? What form divinely fair
Within this magic mirror is revealed?   2430
Oh lend me, Love, thy swiftest wing and bear
Me hence into her wondrous field!
Alas! If from this spot I dare
But stir, or if I venture to go near,
Then dim as through a mist doth she appear!   2435
The fairest image of a woman! Can it be,
Is it possible? Can woman be so fair?
Must I in that recumbent body there
Behold of all the heavens the epitome?
Can one so fair be found on earth?   2440

Mephistopheles.   Well, if a God for six whole days, my friend,
Toils hard and says "Ah, bravo!" at the end,[1]
Then something rather neat must come to birth.
For this time gaze till you are satiate.
I know how I can find you such a treasure   2445
And he who as a bridegroom has the happy fate
To lead her home, is blessed beyond all measure!

> FAUST *continues to look in the mirror.* MEPHISTOPHELES, *stretching himself on the settle and playing with the brush, continues to speak.*

I sit here like a king upon his throne;
I hold the sceptre here, I lack the crown alone.

The Beasts [who meanwhile have been playing all sorts of odd confused antics, bring a crown to MEPHISTOPHELES *with a loud outcry].*

> Oh, please be so good   2450
> With sweat and with blood
> The crown to belime!

> *They handle the crown awkwardly and shatter it into two pieces with which they jump about.*

> It's done for! and we,
> We speak and we see,
> We hear and we rhyme.   2455

Faust [facing the mirror].   Woe's me! How nearly crazy do I feel!
Mephistopheles [pointing to THE BEASTS*].*
Now my head too almost begins to reel.
The Beasts.

> And if we succeed
> And all fits indeed,
> Will thoughts in it be!   2460

Faust [as above].   My breast begins to burn in me!
Let's go away immediately!

[1]Cf. Genesis 1. 31.

Mephistopheles [*in the same attitude as above*].
   Well, now at least one has to say,
   There are some honest poets anyway.
     The cauldron which THE FEMALE APE *has neglected, begins to*
      boil over; a great flame arises which streams up the chimney.
      THE WITCH *comes careering down through the flame with hor-*
      rible cries.
The Witch.
          Ow! Ow! Ow! Ow!   2465
          You damnèd beast! Accursèd sow!
          Neglecting kettle, scorching me now!
          Accursèd beast!
   Espying FAUST *and* MEPHISTOPHELES.
          What is that here?
          Who are you here?   2470
          What will you wreak?
          Who is the sneak?
          May pangs of hell
          Burn your bones well!

    She plunges the skimming-ladle into the cauldron and sprinkles
    flames toward FAUST, MEPHISTOPHELES, *and* THE BEASTS. THE
      BEASTS *whimper.*
Mephistopheles [*who reverses the brush which he has been holding*
  and strikes among the glasses and pots].
          In two! In two!
          There lies the brew!   2475
          There lies the glass!
          Let the joke pass
          As beat, you ass,
          To melodies from you!   2480

    As THE WITCH *steps back full of rage and horror.*
   Do you know me? You skeleton! You fright!
   Do you know me, your lord and master?
   What holds me back that I don't smite
   And crush you and your ape-sprites with disaster?
   Have you no more respect before the doublet red?   2485
   Can you not recognize the tall cock's-feather?
   Was this my face hid altogether?
   My name forsooth I should have said?
The Witch.   My rough salute, sir, pardon me!
   But yet no horse's-foot I see.   2490
   Your pair of ravens, where are they?
Mephistopheles.   This time I'll pardon you that you were rough,
   For it's a long time, sure enough,
   Since we have crossed each other's way.
   Culture that licks and prinks the world anew,   2495

Has reached out to the Devil too.
The northern phantom now is seen nowhere;
Where do you see the horns, the claws, and tail?
And as concerns the foot which I can't spare,
My credit socially it would impair;   2500
So I, as many young men do, avail
Myself of false calves now for many a year.

The Witch [*dancing*]. I almost lose my senses and my brain—oh,
    dear!
To see Squire Satan once more here!
Mephistopheles. That title, woman, I forbid it me!   2505
The Witch. Why? Has it done you any injury?
Mephistopheles. That's been known as a fable many a season;
But men have things no better for that reason.
Free are they from the Evil One; the evil are still here.
Just call me Baron, that will satisfy me.   2510
Like other cavaliers I am a cavalier.
My noble blood you don't deny me;
This is the coat of arms I bear, see here!
    He makes an indecent gesture.
The Witch [*laughs immoderately*].
Ha! Ha! That is your very way!
Just as you ever were, you are a rogue today!   2515
Mephistopheles [*to* FAUST]. My friend, learn well and understand,
This is the way to take a witch in hand.
The Witch. Now, gentlemen, what say you I shall do?
Mephistopheles. A good glass of the well-known juice,
Yet I must beg the oldest sort of you.   2520
A double strength do years produce.
The Witch. With pleasure! Here I have a bottle
From which I sometimes wet my throttle,
Which has no more the slightest stink;
I'll gladly give a little glass to you.   2525
    In a low tone.
And yet this man, if unprepared he drink,
He can not live an hour, as you know too.
Mephistopheles. He is a friend of mine whom it will profit well;
I would bestow your kitchen's best on him.
So draw your circle, speak your spell,   2530
Give him a cup full to the brim!

    THE WITCH *with curious gestures draws a circle and places marvel-
    lous things in it; meanwhile the glasses begin to ring, the caul-
    dron to sound and make music. Lastly, she brings a large book
    and places the* APES *in a circle so as to make them serve as a
    reading-desk and hold the torch. She beckons* FAUST *to come
    near her.*
Faust [*to* MEPHISTOPHELES]. What is to come of all this? Say!
These frantic gestures and this crazy stuff?

This most insipid, fooling play,
I've known and hated it enough. 2535
Mephistopheles. Nonsense! She only wants to joke us;
I beg you, do not be so stern a man!
Physician-like, she has to play some hocus-pocus
So that the juice will do you all the good it can.
He obliges FAUST *to step into the circle.*
The Witch [*begins to declaim, with great emphasis, from the book*].
This you must ken! 2540
From one make ten,
And two let be,
Make even three,
Then rich you'll be.
Skip o'er the four! 2545
From five and six,
The Witch's tricks,
Make seven and eight,
'Tis finished straight;
And nine is one, 2550
And ten is none,
That is the witch's one-time-one!

Faust. I think the old hag's talking in delirium.
Mephistopheles. Much more of it is still to come.
I know it well, thus doth the whole book chime; 2555
I've squandered over it much time,
For perfect contradictions, in the end,
Remain mysterious alike for fools and sages.
The art is old and new, my friend.
It was the way in all the ages, 2560
Through Three and One, and One and Three,
Error instead of truth to scatter.
Thus do men prate and teach untroubledly.
With fools who'll bandy wordy chatter?
Men oft believe, if only they hear wordy pother, 2565
That there must surely be in it some thought or other.
The Witch [*goes on*].
The lofty power
Of Wisdom's dower
From all the world is hidden!
Who takes no thought, 2570
To him it's brought,
Without a care, unbidden.

Faust. What nonsense is she chanting here before us?
My head's near splitting from her shrieking.
I seem to hear a whole, great chorus, 2575
A hundred thousand idiots speaking.

Mephistopheles.   Enough, O Sibyl excellent, enough!
  Give us your drink, the precious stuff,
  And fill the goblet quickly to the brim.
  Since he's my friend, the drink will not hurt him.   2580
  A man of numerous degrees, he's quaffed
  Already many a goodly draught.
      THE WITCH *with many ceremonies pours the drink into a goblet.*
      As FAUST *lifts it to his mouth, a light flame rises.*
Mephistopheles.   Quick, down with it! And make an end!
  Your heart will be delighted by the drink.
  You are the Devil's bosom friend,   2585
  And yet, afraid of fire, you shrink?
      THE WITCH *breaks up the circle.* FAUST *steps out.*
Mephistopheles.   Quick, now, away! You must not rest.
The Witch.   May you enjoy the small gulp's savour!
Mephistopheles [*to* THE WITCH]. If I can do you any favour,
  Then on Walpurgis Night make your request.   2590
The Witch.   Here is a song! If sometimes sung, you'll see
  In what a special way it will affect you.
Mephistopheles [*to* FAUST].   Come quickly and let me direct you;
  You must perspire—that needs must be—
  So that the potent juice all through you flow.   2595
  I'll teach you afterward to value noble leisure,
  And soon you'll feel with thrilling pleasure
  How Cupid stirs and leaps and trips it to and fro.
Faust.   Let me but briefly gaze once more into the glass,
  Ah, too fair seemed that woman's form!   2600
Mephistopheles.   No, no! A model that no woman can surpass,
  You'll see anon alive and warm.
      In a low tone.
  With this drink in your body, soon you'll greet
  A Helena in every girl you meet.

A STREET
FAUST.   MARGARET [*passing by*].

Faust.   My fair young lady, may I make so free   2605
  As to lend you my arm and company?
Margaret.   I'm not a lady, am not fair;
  I can go home without your care.
      She frees herself and exits.
Faust.   By heaven, but this child is fair!
  I've never seen her equal anywhere!   2610
  So virtuous, modest, through and through,
  Yet with a bit of curtness too.
  Her ruby lips, her cheek's clear bloom,
  I'll not forget till the day of doom!

And then how she casts down her eyes,   *2615*
Stamped deeply in my heart it lies!
How curt and short were her replies,
That fills me with sheer ecstasy!
    MEPHISTOPHELES *appears.*

Faust.   Hear, you must get that girl for me!
Mephistopheles.   Well, which one, then?
Faust.   She just went by.   *2620*
Mephistopheles.   That one? She was just coming from her priest,
Absolved from every sin, down to the least.
Hard by the chair I stole quite nigh.
She's innocent in deed and thought
And went to confession all for naught.   *2625*
Over her I have no power.
Faust.   She's over fourteen years old even so.
Mephistopheles.   My word! You talk like gay Lothario
Who covets for himself each lovely flower
And fancies, puffed up, there's no honour, no,   *2630*
Nor favour that he may not cull;
But yet that is not always possible.
Faust.   Sir Master Worshipful, I beg you, pause
And leave me in peace with all your laws!
And this I say—few words are best—   *2635*
Unless that sweet young maiden lays
Her head this night upon my breast,
At midnight we've gone different ways.
Mephistopheles.   Consider well what can and can not be.
I'll need at least some fourteen days   *2640*
But to scent out an opportunity.
Faust.   Had I but seven hours' rest, no need
Of devil would I have, to lead
A little creature such as this astray.
Mephistopheles.   You're talking almost like a Frenchman. Pray   *2645*
Don't let yourself be vexed beyond due measure.
What good is it to reap immediate pleasure?
The joy's not near so great, I say,
As if you first prepare the ground
With every sort of idle folly,   *2650*
Knead and make ready your pretty dolly,
As many Romance tales expound.
Faust.   I've appetite without that too.
Mephistopheles.   Now jests aside, no more ado.
With that good, lovely child, indeed,   *2655*
I tell you once for all, we can't use speed.
There's nothing here to take by storm;
To strategy we must conform.
Faust.   Get something that the angel owns for me!
Oh, lead me to her place of rest!   *2660*

Get me a kerchief from her breast,
A garter to my ecstasy!
Mephistopheles.   Now just to prove that I will be
Of helpful service in your agony,
We'll lose no moment in delay.   2665
I'll lead you to her room this very day.
Faust.   And shall I see her? have her?
Mephistopheles.   No!
For she'll be at a neighbour's for a chat or so.
While she is gone, all by yourself you may
Enjoy her atmosphere till you are sated   2670
And feast on all the hope of joys anticipated.
Faust.   Can we go there?
Mephistopheles.   It is too early yet.
Faust.   Provide a gift for her and don't forget.
        Exit.
Mephistopheles.   Ah, gifts at once? That's good! He'll make a hit!
Full many a lovely place I know   2675
And many a treasure buried long ago.
I must survey the ground a bit.
        Exit.

EVENING

A NEAT LITTLE ROOM

Margaret [plaiting and binding up her braids of hair].
I would give something, could I say
Who was that gentleman today!
Right gallant did he seem to be   2680
And of some noble family.
That from his brow I could have told—
Else he would not have been so bold.
        Exit.

MEPHISTOPHELES *and* FAUST.

Mephistopheles.   Come! come in! and on tiptoe!
Faust [after a silence].   Leave me alone here, I entreat!   2685
Mephistopheles [peering about].
Not every girl keeps things so neat.
        Exit.
Faust [looking up and around].   Welcome, O thou sweet twilight
        glow
That through this shrine art stirring to and fro.
Sweet agony of love, possess this heart of mine,
Thou who on dews of hope dost live and yet dost pine.   2690
What sense of quiet breathes around,
Of order, of contentedness!
What riches in this poverty abound!

Within this prison, ah! what blessedness!
> *He throws himself on the leather arm-chair by the bed.*
Oh, welcome me, thou who the world now gone   2695
Didst once receive in joy and sorrow, open-armed!
How often, ah! around this fathers'-throne
A flock of children clinging swarmed!
And, thankful for the Christmas gift, maybe
My darling here, her childish cheeks filled out,   2700
Kissed grandsire's withered hand devotedly.
I feel, O maid, thy spirit radiate
Abundance, order, round about,
That, motherly, instructs thee day by day,
Bids thee the cloth upon the table neatly lay,   2705
Even make the sand at thy feet decorate.
O darling hand! So godlike in thy ministry!
The hut becomes a realm of Heaven through thee.
And here!
> *He lifts one of the bed curtains.*
> > What bliss and awe lay hold on me!
Here for whole hours I fain would tarry.   2710
O Nature! Here didst thou in visions airy
Mould her, an angel in nativity.
Here lay the child; with warm life heaving
The tender bosom filled and grew;
And here, with pure and holy weaving,   2715
The image of the gods was wrought anew!
> And thou, O Faust, what led thee here? I feel
My very inmost being reel!
What wouldst thou here? What weights thy heart so sore?
O wretched Faust! I know thee now no more.   2720
> Does magic play about me, sweet and rare?
Some force impelled me to enjoy without delay,
And now in dreams of love I seem to float away!
Are we the sport of every puff of air?
> And if this very moment she might enter here,   2725
For thy rash conduct how wouldst thou atone!
Thou, great big lout, how small wouldst thou appear!
How, melted at her feet, thou wouldst lie prone!

Mephistopheles [*enters*].   Be quick! I see her coming down the
> lane.
Faust.   Away! I'll never come back here again!   2730
Mephistopheles.   Here is a casket, of some weight,
Which I got elsewhere as a bait.
Here, put it in the press, this minute;
She'll lose her senses, I swear it to you.
In fact, I put some trinkets in it,   2735
Enough another nobler maid to woo;
But still a child's a child, and play is play.

Faust. I don't know if I should?
Mephistopheles. Why ask you, pray?
 Do you perhaps intend to hoard the treasure?
 Then I'd advise you in your lustfulness   *2740*
 To waste no more sweet hours of leisure
 And spare me further strain and stress.
 I hope that you're not greedy!
 I rub my hands, I scratch my head—
  He puts the casket in the press and turns the lock again.
 Away and speedy!—   *2745*
 To turn the sweet young child that she be led
 To satisfy your heart's desire and will;
 And you look around
 As if to a lecture you were bound,
 As if before you, living still,   *2750*
 Stood Physics and Metaphysics grey!
 But off! away!
  Exeunt.
Margaret [*with a lamp*].   Here is such close, such sultry air!
  She opens the window.
 And yet it's really not so warm out there.
 I feel so strange—I don't know how—   *2755*
 I wish that Mother came home now.
 From head to foot I'm shuddering—
 I'm but a foolish, fearsome thing!
  She begins to sing while she undresses.
     There was in Thule olden
     A king true till the grave,   *2760*
     To whom a beaker golden
     His dying mistress gave.
      Naught prized he more, this lover,
     He drained it at each bout;
     His eyes with tears brimmed over,   *2765*
     As oft he drank it out.
      And when he came to dying,
     His towns and his lands he told,
     Naught else his heir denying
     Except the beaker of gold.   *2770*
      Around him knight and vassal,
     At a royal feast sat he
     In his fathers' lofty castle,
     The castle by the sea.
      There the old pleasure-seeker   *2775*
     Drank, standing, life's last glow,
     Then hurled the sacred beaker
     Into the waves below.
      He saw it plunging, drinking,
     And sinking in the sea,   *2780*

And so his eyes were sinking,
Never one drop more drank he.

*She opens the press to put away her clothes and catches sight of
the little jewel-casket.*

How came this lovely casket in my press?
Indeed I turned the lock most certainly.
It's very strange! What's in it I can't guess.   2785
Someone has brought it as a pledge maybe,
And on it Mother loaned a bit.
Here on the ribbon hangs a little key,
I really think I'll open it.
What is that? God in Heaven! See!   2790
I've never seen such things as here!
Jewels! A noble lady might appear
With these on any holiday.
This chain—how would it look on me?
Ah, whose can all this splendour be?   2795
She adorns herself with it and steps before the mirror.
Were but the earrings mine! I say
One looks at once quite differently.
What good is beauty? blood of youth?
All that is nice and fine, in truth;
However, people pass and let it be.   2800
They praise you—half with pity, though, be sure.
Toward gold throng all,
To gold cling all,
Yes, all! Alas, we poor!

A PROMENADE

FAUST *walking thoughtfully up and down.* MEPHISTOPHELES
joins him.

Mephistopheles.   By every despisèd love! By the red-hot fires of   2805
    Hell!
Would I knew something worse, to curse by it as well!
Faust.   What is the matter? What's so badly vexing you?
I've never seen before a face that looked that way.
Mephistopheles.   Off to the Devil I'd betake myself this day
If I myself were not a devil too!   2810
Faust.   What has gone wrong? Why thus behave?
It suits you well to rant and rave!
Mephistopheles.   Just think, the gems for Gretchen that I got,
    A wretched priest has bagged the lot!
The mother gets to see the stuff   2815
And starts at once to feel a secret shuddering.
The woman has a scent that's fine enough,

Forever in her prayer-book she delights to snuff,
And smells it out in every single thing
If it be sacred or profane;   2820
So in those gems she noses till it's plain
That they held little blessing, little good.
"My child," she cried, "to keep unrighteous **gain**
Perturbs the soul, consumes the blood.
We'll dedicate it to the Mother of our Lord,   2825
With heavenly manna She'll reward!"[1]
Then Gretchen drew her mouth askew;
She thought: "It is a gift-horse, it is true,
And surely godless is not he
Who brought it here so handsomely."   2830
The mother summoned in a priest who **came**
And when he'd scarce perceived the game,
Got much contentment from the sight.
He said: "So one is minded right!
Who overcometh, winneth a crown.[2]   2835
The Church hath a good stomach ever,
Whole countries hath she gobbled down,
And yet hath over-eaten never;
The Church alone, dear ladies, best
Can all unrighteous goods digest."   2840

Faust.   That is a custom that men oft pursue;
    A Jew and king can do it too.

Mephistopheles.   With that he bagged brooch, **chain, and rings,**
    As if mere toadstools were the things,
    And thanked them neither less nor more   2845
    Than were it a basketful of nuts he bore.
    He promised them all heavenly pay
    And greatly edified thereby were they.

Faust.   And Gretchen?

Mephistopheles.   Now sits restless. What **she would**
    She knows not, neither what she should,   2850
    Thinks of the jewels night and day,
    Still more on him who brought them to her.

Faust.   The darling's grief distresses me.
    Quick! get new ornaments to woo her.
    The first ones were not much to see.   2855

Mephistopheles.   Oh yes, Milord thinks all is mere child's-play!

Faust.   Make haste and do things as I like them done.
    Into her neighbour's graces win your way!
    Devil, don't be like mush and move so slow.
    Fetch some new ornaments—up, now, and run!   2860

Mephistopheles.   Yes, gracious sir, with all my heart I'll go.
      Exit FAUST.

[1]Cf. Revelation, 2. 17.
[2]*ibid.*

Such an enamoured fool would puff and blow
Sun, moon, and stars into thin air
Just as a pastime for his lady fair.
  Exit.

THE NEIGHBOUR'S HOUSE

Martha [*alone*]. God pardon my dear husband! He   *2865*
 Has truly not done well by me!
 Off in the world to go and roam
 And leave me on the straw at home!
 Sure, I did naught to vex him, truly,
 And, God knows, always loved him duly.   *2870*
  She weeps.
 Perhaps he's even dead!—Oh, cruel fate!
 If I but had a death-certificate!
  MARGARET *enters.*
Margaret. Dame Martha!
Martha.   Gretchen dear, what can it be?
Margaret. My knees almost sink under me!
 There in my press I've found again   *2875*
 Just such a casket—and of ebony,
 And things! magnificent they are,
 Much richer than the first, by far!
Martha. You must not tell that to your mother;
 She would confess it like the other.   *2880*
Margaret. Ah, only look! ah, see now, do!
Martha [*decking her out*]. You lucky, lucky creature, you!
Margaret. Alas, these jewels I can never wear
 At church or on the street, I'd never dare!
Martha. Come often over here to me   *2885*
 And here put on the jewels secretly.
 Stroll up and down before the mirror for a season;
 We'll have our own sweet joy of it.
 And then there'll be a feast-day or some other reason
 When one lets people see them, bit by bit.   *2890*
 A chain at first, a pearl then in your ear; your mother
 Scarce will see it, we'll coin some fib or other.
Margaret. But both the caskets! Who could bring
 Them both? Some wrong is in this thing!
  Someone knocks.
 Good Heaven! My mother—can that have been?   *2895*
Martha [*peeping through the curtain*].
 It's some strange gentleman! Come in!
  MEPHISTOPHELES *enters.*
Mephistopheles. I'm very bold to walk in right away;
 The pardon of the ladies I must pray.
  He steps back respectfully in the presence of MARGARET.

Dame Martha Schwerdtlein I would like to find!

Martha.   I'm she! What has the gentleman upon his mind?   2900

Mephistopheles [*aside to her*].   I know you now, that is enough for me.
    You have a most distinguished guest, I see.
    Excuse the liberty I took! If it is not too soon,
    I'll come again this afternoon.

Martha [*aloud*].   Imagine, child, of all things on this earth!   2905
    The gentleman thinks you of noble birth.

Margaret.   I am a poor, young thing, as you can see.
    The gentleman is far too kind to me.
    The ornaments and jewels aren't my own.

Mephistopheles.   Ah, it is not the ornaments alone;   2910
    You've such a manner, so refined a way!
    How glad I am that I may stay!

Martha.   What is your errand? I would like to hear—

Mephistopheles.   I wish my tidings brought more cheer!
    I hope you'll not make me repent this meeting: 2915
    Your husband's dead and sends a greeting.

Martha.   Is dead? That faithful heart! Oh, woe!
    My husband's dead! I'm dying! Oh!

Margaret.   Ah! don't despair, Dame Martha dear!

Mephistopheles.   Prepare the mournful tale to hear!   2920

Margaret.   That's why I would not love while I draw breath;
    Such loss as this would make me grieve to death.

Mephistopheles.   Joy must sorrow, sorrow joy must know.

Martha.   Relate the ending of his life to me!

Mephistopheles.   In Padua he's buried, midst a row   2925
    Of graves close to St. Anthony,
    In holy ground that was well blessed,
    Forever cool his bed of rest.

Martha.   Did you bring nothing else beside?

Mephistopheles.   Oh yes, a weighty, great petition: 2930
    Three hundred masses are you to provide!
    My pockets? They have naught. Thus endeth my commission!

Martha.   What? Not a medal? Not a trinket? Such
    As every journeyman deep in his pouch doth hide,
    As a remembrance puts aside,   2935
    And rather hungers, rather begs, than touch?

Mephistopheles.   Madame, that grieves me much, but let me say,
    He truly did not throw his cash away;
    And deeply did he all his faults deplore,
    Yes, and bewailed his ill luck still much more.   2940

Margaret.   Alas, the bad luck men do meet!
    Full many a requiem for him will I pray.

Mephistopheles.   You're fit, I think, to wed this very day;
    You are so lovable and sweet.

Margaret.   That would not do as yet. Ah, no!   2945

Mephistopheles.   If not a husband, be it for the while a beau.

For, of the greatest gifts of Heaven, it is one
  To have within our arms a lover dear.
Margaret.   That's not the custom of the country here.
Mephistopheles.   Custom or not! At any rate it's done.   *2950*
Martha.   Tell on, oh, please!
Mephistopheles.   I stood where dying he was laid.
  'Twas not a dung-heap; somewhat better it was made
  Of rotting straw; but as a Christian did he die,
  Thinking he owed far greater penance for his life.
  "How deeply must I hate myself," I heard him cry,   *2955*
  "To leave my business so, my wife!
  Alas, the recollection's killing me.
  If she could but forgive me in this life!"
Martha [*weeping*].   The good man! I forgave him long since—
    truthfully!
Mephistopheles.   "But she, God knows, was more to blame than I!"   *2960*
Martha.   He lies! What! at the grave's brink—so to lie!
Mephistopheles.   He fabled as he breathed his last, be sure,
  If I am only half a connoisseur.
  "I could not gape for pastime," so he said;
  "First children, then to get them bread,   *2965*
  And bread in all the broadest sense, I swear;
  Yet never could I eat in peace my share."
Martha.   To all my love, fidelity, he gave no thought,
  Nor to my drudgery by night and day?
Mephistopheles.   Not so; he thought of it most warmly as he ought.   *2970*
  He said: "From Malta once I sailed away
  And ardently for wife and children did I pray.
  Then Heaven favoured us in gracious measure
  Because our ship a Turkish vessel caught
  Which to the mighty Sultan bore a treasure.   *2975*
  Then valour was rewarded as was fit,
  And I received moreover, as one ought,
  My own well-measured share of it."
Martha.   Oh what? Oh where? Perhaps he buried it?
Mephistopheles.   Who knows where the four winds have carried   *2980*
    it?
  A pretty miss adopted him as her dear friend
  When he, in Naples strange, was circulating;
  She gave him love and troth so unabating
  That he felt the results until his blessèd end.
Martha.   The scamp! The robber of his children, he!   *2985*
  And all that want and all that misery
  Could not prevent the shameful life he led!
Mephistopheles.   Well, he has paid for it and now he's dead.
  If I were now in your place here,
  I'd mourn for him a well-bred year,   *2990*
  Meanwhile be on the lookout for a sweetheart new.

Martha.   Ah, God! Another like the first I knew,
  I'll hardly find on earth again!
  There scarce could be a dearer little fool than mine.
  Only to roam he was too much inclined, and then   *2995*
  He loved those foreign women, also foreign wine,
  And that accursed dice-throwing.
Mephistopheles.   Now, now, things could have gone and still be
  going,
  If he perchance as much in you
  Had overlooked on his part too.   *3000*
  I swear, on terms like these, if you'd agree,
  I'd ask you to exchange a ring with me.
Martha.   The gentleman is pleased to jest.
Mephistopheles [*aside*].   Now to make off betimes were best!
  She'd hold the very Devil to his word.   *3005*
      To GRETCHEN.
  How is your heart? Has it been stirred?
Margaret.   What means the gentleman?
Mephistopheles [*aside*].   You innocent, sweet dear!
    Aloud.
  Ladies, good-by!
Margaret.   Good-by!
Martha.   Oh, quickly let me hear
  The evidence I'd like to have and save:
  Where, how, and when my darling died and where his grave.   *3010*
  Of order I have always been a friend,
  And in our *Weekly* I would like to read his end.
Mephistopheles.   Yes, my good woman, what two witnesses attest
  Is always known as truth made manifest,
  And with me I've a splendid mate.   *3015*
  I tell you, I'll take him before a magistrate.
  I'll bring him here.
Martha.   Oh, do that, do!
Mephistopheles.   And this young lady, will she be here too?
  A gallant chap! and travelled far has he
  And shows young ladies every courtesy.   *3020*
Margaret.   Before the gentleman I'd flush with shame.
Mephistopheles.   Before no king this earth could name.
Martha.   Behind my house and in my garden then,
  This evening we'll await the gentlemen.

A STREET
FAUST.   MEPHISTOPHELES.

Faust.   How goes it? Will it work? soon win the game?   *3025*
Mephistopheles.   Ah, bravo! Do I find you all aflame?
  Gretchen will in a brief time be your own.
  This evening you will see her all alone

At Neighbour Martha's; that's a woman made
For go-between and gypsy trade.   3030
Faust. 'Tis well!
Mephistopheles. Yet something's wanted from us too.
Faust. One service may demand another as its due.
Mephistopheles. We have in due form only to attest
That her good spouse's outstretched limbs repose
In Padua, in consecrated soil at rest.   3035
Faust. Most wise! We first must make the journey, I suppose!
Mephistopheles. Sancta Simplicitas! Of that there is no need;
You don't know much, but still depose.
Faust. If that's your best, I tear your plan asunder.
Mephistopheles. O saintly man! Then you would be a saint   3040
indeed!
Is it the first time in your life
You've borne false witness? Well, I wonder!
Of God, the world, and what therein is rife,
Of man, what stirs within his heart and brain,
Have you no definition given with might and main?   3045
With brazen brow and dauntless breast?
And if you'll only probe things truly,
You knew of them—you must confess it duly—
No more than of this Schwerdtlein's death and place of rest!
Faust. You are and you remain a liar, sophist too.   3050
Mephistopheles. Yes, if one did not have a little deeper view.
Will you not presently cajole
Poor Gretchen—in all honour too—and swear
To her the love of all your soul?
Faust. Aye, swear it from my heart.
Mephistopheles.   Fine, I declare!   3055
Then there'll be talk of love, fidelity eternal,
Of one almighty force supernal—
Will that too issue from your heart alone?
Faust. Have done! It will!—And when I'm feeling,
When for the feeling, for my senses' reeling,   3060
I seek for names and yet find none,
Then through the world with every sense sweep on,
Toward all the loftiest phrases, grasping, turn,
And this the glow from which I burn,
Endless, eternal, aye, eternal name,   3065
Is that a devilish, lying game?
Mephistopheles. And yet I'm right!
Faust.   Take heed! Mark this from me,
I beg of you, and spare my lungs:
He who maintains he's right—if his the gift of tongues—
Will have the last word certainly.   3070
So come, this prating rouses my disgust;
I'll say you're right, especially since I must.

A GARDEN

MARGARET *on* FAUST'S *arm*, MARTHA *and* MEPHISTOPHELES, *walking up and down.*

Margaret.   I feel the gentleman is only sparing me,
   So condescends that I am all confused.
   A traveller is so much used   3075
   To bear with things good-naturedly.
   I know too well, my poor talk hardly can
   Amuse you, an experienced man.
Faust.   One glance from you, one word, more entertains
   Than all the wisdom that this world contains.   3080
      He kisses her hand.
Margaret.
   Don't incommode yourself! How can my hand be kissed by you?
   It is so ugly and so rough!
   What work is there that I've not had to do?
   My mother's more than strict enough.
      They pass on.
Martha.   And you, sir, are you always on the go?   3085
Mephistopheles.   Alas, that business, duty, drive us so!
   With how much pain one goes from many a place,
   And even so, one simply must not stay.
Martha.   In active years perhaps 'tis well this way,
   Thus freely round and round the world to race;   3090
   But then the evil times come on apace,
   And as a bachelor to drag on to the grave alone,
   That has been good for no one, you must own.
Mephistopheles.   With dread I see it far away.
Martha.   Then, worthy sir, consider while you may!   3095
      They pass on.
Margaret.   Yes, out of sight is out of mind!
   To you so easy is this courtesy;
   But many friends you always find,
   More sensible than I can be.
Faust.   O dear one! Trust me, that which men call sense   3100
   Is oft but vanity and narrowness.
Margaret.   But why? Tell me.
Faust.   Ah, that simplicity, that innocence,
   That neither its own sacred value knows!
   That lowliness, humility, those gifts supreme
   That loving Nature's bounteous hand bestows—   3105
Margaret.   Though you may think of me a moment only,
   I'll have, ah, time enough to think of you and dream.
Faust.   You are then often lonely?
Margaret.   Yes, for our household is but small,
   And yet one has to look to all.   3110

We have no maid—must cook, sweep, sew, and knit,
And early run about and late;
And Mother is in all of it
So accurate!
Not that in spending she must feel confined;   3115
We could branch out far more than many do.
My father left a pretty property behind,
A house outside the town, a little garden too.
Yet now I've pretty quiet days. My brother,
He is a soldier lad.   3120
My little sister's dead.
A deal of trouble with the child did I go through;
Yet once more would I gladly undertake the bother,
I loved the child so much.
Faust.   An angel, if like you.
Margaret.   I brought it up and it was fond of me.   3125
Father had died when it was born;
We gave our mother up for lost, so worn
And wretched, lying there, was she.
And she grew well so slowly, bit by bit,
She could not think of suckling it   3130
Herself, the poor babe pitifully wee,
And so I brought it up, and quite alone,
With milk and water; so it became my own.
Upon my arm and in my lap it threw
Itself about, was friendly too, and grew.   3135
Faust.   You've surely felt the purest happiness.
Margaret.   But also many weary hours, I must confess.
The wee thing's cradle stood at night
Beside my bed; it scarcely might
Just stir; I was awake;   3140
Sometimes I had to give it drink, sometimes to take
It in with me, sometimes from bed arise
And dandle up and down the room to hush its cries;
And at the wash-tub stand at daylight's break,
Then to the marketing and to the hearth attend.   3145
Tomorrow too just like today, so without end.
Thus, sir, one's spirits are not always of the best,
But in return one relishes both food and rest.
      They pass on.
Martha.   Poor women have things hard, it's true;
A bachelor's not easy to convert.   3150
Mephistopheles.   It but depends upon the like of you,
For then my present ways I might desert.
Martha.   Speak out, sir, is there none you've ever met?
Has your heart never bound itself as yet?
Mephistopheles.   One's own good wife and hearth, we're told,   3155
Are worth as much as pearls and gold.

Martha. I mean, if you have never felt a passion?

Mephistopheles. I've always been received in very courteous
>   fashion.

Martha. I mean: has love in earnest never stirred your breast?

Mephistopheles. With ladies one should never dare to jest. 3160

Martha. Ah, you don't understand me!

Mephistopheles. That distresses me!
>   And yet I understand—most kindly would you be.
>   *They pass on.*

Faust. Did you, O little angel, straightway recognize
>   Me when I came into the garden?

Margaret. Did you not see that I cast down my eyes? 3165

Faust. That liberty I took, you'll pardon?
>   The daring impudence that day
>   When coming from the church you went your way?

Margaret. I was confused; to me it never had
>   Occurred; no one could say of me what's bad. 3170
>   Ah, thought I, in your manner, then, has he
>   Seen something bold, unmaidenly?
>   It seemed to strike him right away
>   To have some dealings with this girl without delay.
>   Yet I confess I know not why my heart 3175
>   Began at once to stir to take your part.
>   But with myself I was right vexed, it's true,
>   That I could not become more vexed toward you.

Faust. Sweet darling!

Margaret. Wait a bit!
>   *She plucks a star-flower and picks off the petals, one after the other.*

Faust. What's that? A nosegay?

Margaret. No,
>   It's just a game.

Faust. What?

Margaret. You will laugh at me, do go! 3180
>   *She pulls off the petals and murmurs.*

Faust. What are you murmuring?

Margaret [*half aloud*]. He loves me—loves me not!

Faust. Sweet, heavenly vision!

Margaret [*goes on*]. Loves me—not—loves me—not—
>   *Plucking off the last petal with lovely joy.*
>   He loves me!

Faust. Yes, my child! and let this blossom's word
>   Be oracle of gods to you! He loves you! 3185
>   You understand that word and what it means? He loves you!
>   *He seizes both her hands.*

Margaret. I'm all a-tremble!

Faust. Oh, shudder not! But let this look,
>   Let this hand-pressure say to you
>   What is unspeakable: 3190

To give one's self up wholly and to feel
A rapture that must be eternal!
Eternal!—for its end would be despair.
No! no end! no end!

> MARGARET *presses his hands, frees herself, and runs away. He*
> *stands a moment in thought and then follows her.*

Martha [*coming*].   The night comes on.
Mephistopheles.   Yes, and we must away.   *3195*
Martha.   I'd ask you make a longer stay;
  But it's a wicked place, here roundabout,
  As if no one had naught to carry through
  And naught to do
  But gape at all the neighbours going in and out.   *3200*
  One's talked about, do all one may.
  And our dear couple?
Mephistopheles.   Up that walk I saw them whirr,
  The wanton butterflies!
Martha.   He seems to take to her.
Mephistopheles.   And she to him. So runs the world away.

A GARDEN HOUSE

> MARGARET *runs in, hides behind the door, holds the tip of her*
> *fingers to her lips, and peers through the crevice.*

Margaret.   He's coming!
Faust [*enters*].   Rogue, it's thus you tease!   *3205*
  I've caught you!
> *He kisses her.*
Margaret [*embracing him and returning the kiss*].
          Best of men, I love you from my heart!
> MEPHISTOPHELES *knocks.*
Faust [*stamping*].   Who's there?
Mephistopheles.   A friend!
Faust.   A beast!
Mephistopheles.   I think it's time to part.
Martha [*enters*].   Yes, sir, it's late.
Faust.   Mayn't I escort you, please?
Margaret.   My mother would—Good-by!
Faust.   Must I go then?
  Good-by!
Martha.   Adieu!
Margaret.   But soon to meet again!   *3210*
> FAUST *and* MEPHISTOPHELES *exeunt.*
Margaret.   Dear God! The things that such a man
  Can think of! Everything! I only can
  Stand there before him shamed and quivering
  And answer "Yes" to everything.

I am a poor unknowing child, and he—   3215
I do not see what he can find in me.
   Exit.

FOREST AND CAVERN

Faust [alone].   Spirit sublime, thou gav'st me, gav'st me all
For which I prayed. Thou hast not turned in vain
Thy countenance to me in fire and flame.
Thou gav'st me glorious nature as a royal realm,   3220
The power to feel and to enjoy her. Not
Amazed, cold visits only thou allow'st;
Thou grantest me to look in her deep breast
Even as in the bosom of a friend.
Thou leadest past a series of the living   3225
Before me, teaching me to know my brothers
In silent covert and in air and water.
And when the storm roars screeching through the forest,
When giant fir tree plunges, sweeping down
And crushing neighbouring branches, neighbouring trunks,   3230
And at its fall the hills, dull, hollow, thunder:
Then leadest thou me to the cavern safe,
Show'st me myself, and my own heart becomes
Aware of deep mysterious miracles.
And when before my gaze the stainless moon   3235
Soothing ascends on high: from rocky walls
And from damp covert float and soar about me
The silvery forms of a departed world
And temper contemplation's austere joy.
   Oh, that for man naught perfect ever is,   3240
I now do feel. Together with this rapture
That brings me near and nearer to the gods,
Thou gav'st the comrade whom I now no more
Can do without, though, cold and insolent,
He lowers me in my own sight, transforms   3245
With but a word, a breath, thy gifts to nothing.
Within my breast he fans with busy zeal
A savage fire for that fair, lovely form.
Thus from desire I reel on to enjoyment
And in enjoyment languish for desire.   3250
Mephistopheles [appears].   Have you now led this life quite long
   enough?
How can it long have any charm for you?
'Tis well, indeed, for once to try the stuff,
But then, in turn, away to something new!
Faust.   I wish that you had something else to do   3255
Than on a happy day to plague me like a pest.
Mephistopheles.   Now, now! I'll gladly let you rest!
You do not dare to say this seriously.

A comrade mad, ungracious, cross,
Would truly be a trifling loss.   3260
The livelong day one's hands are full as they can be.
What he would like for one to do or leave alone,
His lordship's face will never let one see.
Faust.   So! That is just the proper tone:
You now want thanks for boring me.   3265
Mephistopheles.   Without me how would you, Earth's wretched son,
Have kept on living? What would you have done?
Your hodge-podge of imagination—balderdash!
At least I've cured you now and then of all that trash.
In fact, if I had not been here at all,   3270
You'd long since sauntered off this earthly ball.
Why here within the cavern's rocky rent
Thus sit your life away so owl-like and alone?
Why from the sodden moss and dripping stone
Sip, like a toad, your nourishment?   3275
A fine sweet way to pass the time. I'll bet
The Doctor's in your body yet.
Faust.   Can you conceive what new vitality
This walking in the desert works in me?
Yes, could you sense a force like this,   3280
You would be devil enough to grudge my bliss.
Mephistopheles.   It's more than earthly, such delight!
To lie in night and dew on mountain height,
Embracing earth and heaven blissfully,
Puffing one's self and deeming one a deity;   3285
To burrow through earth's marrow, onward pressed
By prescient impulse, feel within one's breast
All six days' work, in haughty power enjoy and know
I can't tell what, soon all creation overflow
In rapturous love, lost to all sight the child of clay,   3290
And then the lofty intuition
   With a gesture.
Ending—I dare not say in what fruition!
Faust   Shame on you!
Mephistopheles.   That's not to your liking, eh?
You have the moral right to cry out "Shame!"
Before chaste ears one must not name   3295
What chaste hearts can't dispense with, just the same!
In short, I grudge you not the pleasure of evasion,
Of lying to yourself upon occasion;
But you will not stick long to that, it's clear.
Again you are already spent,   3300
And if this goes on longer, you'll be rent
To shreds by madness or by agony and fear.
Enough of this! Your darling sits at home apart
And more and more she's feeling caged and sad.

Your image never leaves her mind and heart,   3305
The all-consuming love she bears you is half mad.
First came your passion like the furious current
Of brooklets swollen high from melted snow.
Into her heart you poured the torrent,
And now again your brooklet's running low.   3310
I think, instead of sitting throned in forests wild
It would become so great a lord
To seek the poor, young, silly child
And give her for her love some due reward.
To her the time grows pitiably long.   3315
She stands beside the window, sees the clouds that stray
Over the old town wall and far away.
"Were I a little bird!" so goes her song,
All day long and half the night long.
She's mostly sad, at times is gay,   3320
At times is quite wept out, and then,
It seems, is calm again,
And is in love alway.

Faust.   Serpent! Serpent!

Mephistopheles [*aside*].   Good! I'll bet
That I will get you yet!   3325

Faust.   Infamous fiend! Off, get you hence!
And do not name that lovely woman!
Nor yet desire for her sweet body summon
Again before my half-distracted sense!

Mephistopheles.   What would you then? She thinks that you have
flown,   3330
And half and half you are, as you must own.

Faust.   I'm near to her, however far I were,
I never can forget nor yet lose her;
I envy even the Body of the Lord
Whenever her sweet lips touch the Adored.   3335

Mephistopheles.   Well said, my friend! Oft have I envied you indeed
The twin-pair that among the roses feed.[1]

Faust.   Off, pander!

Mephistopheles.   Fine! You rail and it's a joke to me.
The God who fashioned youth and maid
At once perceived the noblest trade   3340
Was that He make them opportunity.
Be off! That is a cause of woe!
It's to your darling's chamber you're to go,
Not to your death, indeed!

Faust.   How am I, in her arms, by Heaven blessed?   3345
Though I grow warm upon her breast,
Do I not always feel her need?
Am I not still the fugitive? unhoused and roaming?

[1]Cf. The Song of Solomon, 4. 5.

The monster without goal or rest
That like a cataract from rock to rock roared foaming   3350
To the abyss, by greed and frenzy headlong pressed?
She at one side, still with her childlike senses furled,
Upon the alpine meadow in the cottage small,
With all her homely joys and cares, her all,
Within that little world;   3355
And I, the God-detested,
Not enough had I
That all the rocks I wrested
And into pieces made them fly!
Her did I have to undermine, her peace!   3360
Thou, Hell, didst have to have this sacrifice!
Help, Devil, make it brief, this time of agony!
What must be done, let it at once be so!
Then may her fate plunge crushing down on me,
And she with me to ruin go!   3365
Mephistopheles.   How it seethes again and how again it glows!
You fool, go and console your pretty dear!
When such a brain as yours no outlet knows,
It straightway fancies that the end is near.
Long life to him who bravely dares!   3370
At other times you've been of quite a devilish mind.
Naught more absurd in this world can I find
Than is a devil who despairs.

GRETCHEN'S ROOM

Gretchen [*at her spinning-wheel, alone*].
                    My peace is gone,
                    —My heart is sore—   3375
                    I'll find it, ah, never,
                    No, nevermore!
                       When he is not near,
                    My grave is here;
                    My world is all   3380
                    Turned into gall.
                       My poor, poor head
                    Is all a-craze,
                    And my poor wits
                    All in a maze.   3385
                       My peace is gone,
                    —My heart is sore—
                    I'll find it, ah, never,
                    No, nevermore!
                       To see him only   3390
                    At the window I stay,
                    To meet him only

From home I stray.
　His noble form,
His bearing so high,   *3395*
And his lips so smiling,
And the power of his eye,
　His flowing speech's
Magic bliss,
His hands' fond clasp,   *3400*
And, ah, his kiss!
　My peace is gone,
—My heart is sore—
I'll find it, ah, never,
No, nevermore!   *3405*
　My bosom yearns
Toward him to go.
Ah! might I clasp him
And hold him so,
　And kiss his lips   *3410*
As fain would I,
Upon his kisses
To swoon and die!

MARTHA'S GARDEN

MARGARET.　FAUST.

Margaret.　Promise me, Henry!
Faust.　　　　　　　　　What I can!
Margaret.　How do you feel about religion? Tell me, **pray.**   *3415*
　You are a dear, good-hearted man,
　But I believe you've little good of it to say.
Faust.　Hush, hush, my child! You feel my love for you.
　For those I love, I'd give my blood and body too,
　Would no one of his feelings or of church bereave.   *3420*
Margaret.　That's not enough. We must believe!
Faust.　Must we?
Margaret.　　　　Ah, could I but impress you, Henry dear!
　The Holy Sacraments you also don't revere.
Faust.　I do revere them.
Margaret.　　　　　　　But without desire, alas!
　It's long since you confessed or went to mass.   *3425*
　Do you believe in God?
Faust.　　　　　　　My darling, who dare say:
　"I believe in God"? You may
　Ask priest or sage, and you'll receive
　What only seems to mock and stay
　The asker.
Margaret.　So you don't believe?   *3430*

Faust. Sweet vision, don't misunderstand me now!
  Who dare name Him?
  And who avow:
  "I believe in Him"?
  Who feels and would   3435
  Have hardihood
  To say: "I don't believe in Him"?
  The All-Enfolder,
  The All-Upholder,
  Enfolds, upholds He not   3440
  You, me, Himself?
  Do not the heavens over-arch us yonder?
  Does not the earth lie firm beneath?
  Do not eternal stars rise friendly
  Looking down upon us?   3445
  Look I not, eye in eye, on you,
  And do not all things throng
  Toward your head and heart,
  Weaving in mystery eternal,
  Invisible, visible, near to you?   3450
  Fill up your heart with it, great though it is,
  And when you're wholly in the feeling, in its bliss,
  Name it then as you will,
  Name it Happiness! Heart! Love! God!
  I have no name for that!   3455
  Feeling is all in all;
  Name is but sound and smoke,
  Beclouding Heaven's glow.
Margaret. That's all quite nice and good to know;
  Much the same way the preacher talks of it,   3460
  Only in words that differ just a bit.
Faust. Wherever the light of Heaven doth shine,
  All hearts repeat it, everywhere, and each
  In its own speech;
  Then why not I in mine?   3465
Margaret. To hear it thus, it's passable, and still I doubt it;
  In spite of it all there is some hitch about it,
  For you have no Christianity.
Faust. Dear child!
Margaret.   It long has been a grief to me
  That I see you in such company.   3470
Faust. How so?
Margaret.   The man who is with you as your mate,
  Deep in my inmost soul I hate.
  In all my whole life there's not a thing
  That's given my heart so sharp a sting
  As that man's hostile face has done.   3475
Faust. Don't fear him, my precious one!

Margaret.   His presence makes my blood run so chill,
And toward all others I bear good-will;
But although to see you I yearn and long,
With uncanny horror that man makes me shrink.   *3480*
He is a knave, I really do think!
God forgive me if I'm doing him wrong!
Faust.   Such queer birds there must also be.
Margaret.   I'd not like to live with one like him!
If he but comes inside the door, you see   *3485*
Him look always so scoffingly
And so half grim.
For nothing has he any real sympathy;
It's written on his forehead, one can see
That in his sight no soul can be dear.   *3490*
I feel so happy in your arm,
So free, so yielding, and so warm,
And yet my heart grows stifled whenever he is near.
Faust.   O you foreboding angel, you!
Margaret.   It overcomes me so much too,   *3495*
That when he but only comes our way,
I even think I've no more love for you,
And when he's there, I nevermore could pray;
That eats into my heart; and so you too
Must feel, dear Henry, as I do.   *3500*
Faust.   You simply have antipathy!
Margaret.   I must go now.
Faust.   Ah, can there never be
Upon your bosom one calm, little hour of rest,
To mingle soul with soul, press breast to breast?
Margaret.   Ah, if I only slept apart!   *3505*
For you I'd gladly leave the bolt undrawn tonight,
But then my mother's sleep is light;
And were we found by her, dear heart,
I would fall dead upon the spot!
Faust.   No need of that! You angel, fear it not!   *3510*
Here is a little phial! Only three
Drops in her drink, and pleasantly
Deep slumber will enfold her like a charm!
Margaret.   For your sake what would I not do?
I hope it will not do her harm!   *3515*
Faust.   If so, my love, would I thus counsel you?
Margaret.   If I but look at you, O best of men,
I know not what compels me to your will.
I've done so much, your wishes to fulfil,
There's almost nothing left for me to do.   *3520*
      Exit.
      MEPHISTOPHELES appears.
Mephistopheles.   The little monkey! Is she gone?

Faust.   You've spied again!
Mephistopheles.   I've heard it all and understood,
  The Doctor was put through the catechisms.
  I hope that it will do you good.
  Girls have a great desire to know, it's true,   3525
  If one is sleek and pious, true to ancient isms.
  They think: if there he knuckles, us he'll follow too.
Faust.   You monster, you've not seen
  How this soul true and dear,
  Full of the faith she hath,   3530
  That quite alone must mean
  Eternal bliss to her, torments herself with awful fear
  To think the man she loves is doomed by endless wrath.
Mephistopheles.   You lover super-sensual, sensual too,
  A damsel leads you by the nose.   3535
Faust.   O monstrous progeny of fire and filthy spew!
Mephistopheles.   And physiognomy quite masterly she knows.
  She feels she knows not how when I'm about,
  And in my mask a hidden meaning sees.
  She feels that I'm a dæmon, without doubt,   3540
  Perhaps the very Devil, if you please!
  Well now—tonight?
Faust.   What's that to you?
Mephistopheles.   I have my pleasure in it too!

AT THE WELL

GRETCHEN *and* LISBETH *with jugs.*

Lisbeth.   Of our friend Babbie you've not heard?
Gretchen.   I seldom go where people are—no, not a word.   3545
Lisbeth.   It's true, Sibylla told me so today!
  So after all she's played the fool, I say.
  That comes of all her airs!
Gretchen.   How so?
Lisbeth.   It stinks.
  She's feeding two now when she eats and drinks.
Gretchen.   Ah!   3550
Lisbeth.   So now it's served her right, in truth.
  How long she's hung upon that youth!
  That was a promenading,
  To village and to dance parading!
  Had ever as the first to shine,   3555
  He always courted her with tarts and wine;
  She fancied her beauty was something fine,
  Was yet so lost to honour she had no shame
  To take his presents as they came.
  'Twas cuddling and kissing, on and on;   3560
  And now, you see, the floweret's gone!

Gretchen.　　The poor thing!

Lisbeth.　　　　　　　　What! You pity her? I don't!

When girls like us were spinning, mother's wont

At night was never to let us out,

But she! With her sweet love she'd stand about.　　　*3565*

On the door-bench, in the hallway dim,

No hour became too long for her or for him.

Now she can knuckle under in full view

And in a sinner's shift do penance too.

Gretchen.　　He'll take her of course to be his wife.　　*3570*

Lisbeth.　　He'd be a fool! A lively lad

Has plenty elbow-room elsewhere.

Besides, he' gone.

Gretchen.　　　　　　That is not fair!

Lisbeth.　　If she gets him, she'll find her luck is bad.

The boys will dash her wreath on the floor,　　　*3575*

And we will strew chaff before her door.

　　Exit.

Gretchen [*going home*].　　How I could once so stoutly flay

When some poor maiden went astray!

How I could find no words enough

At others' sins to rail and scoff!　　　*3580*

Black as it seemed, I made it blacker still,

But never black enough to suit my will;

I blessed myself! So proud I've been!

Now I'm myself laid bare to sin!

Yet—all that drove me, all I would,　　　*3585*

God! was so dear! ah, was so good!

THE RAMPARTS

In a niche of the wall a devotional image of the Mater Dolorosa
with jugs for flowers in front of it.

Gretchen [*is putting fresh flowers in the jugs*].

　　　　　　Oh, bend Thou,

　　　　　　Mother of Sorrows; send Thou

　　　　　　A look of pity on my pain.

　　　　　　Thine heart's blood welling　　　*3590*

　　　　　　With pangs past telling,

　　　　　　Thou gazest where Thy Son hangs slain.

　　　　　　Thou, heavenward gazing,

　　　　　　Art deep sighs raising

　　　　　　On high for His and for Thy pain.　　　*3595*

　　　　　　Who feeleth

　　　　　　How reeleth

This pain in every bone?
All that makes my poor heart shiver,
Why it yearneth and doth quiver,   3600
Thou dost know and Thou alone!

Wherever I am going,
How woe, woe, woe is growing,
Ah, how my bosom aches!
When lonely watch I'm keeping,   3605
I'm weeping, weeping, weeping,
My heart within me breaks.

The plants before my window
I wet with tears—ah, me!—
As in the early morning   3610
I plucked these flowers for Thee.

Ah, let my room but borrow
The early sunlight red,
I sit in all my sorrow
Already on my bed.   3615

Help! rescue me from death and stain!
Oh, bend Thou,
Mother of Sorrows; send Thou
A look of pity on my pain!

NIGHT
The street before GRETCHEN'S *door.*

Valentine [*a soldier, Gretchen's brother*].
When I've sat with a jovial crowd   3620
Where many a man has boasted loud
And fellows then have praised to me
The beauty of maidens noisily
And drowned the praises with full cup,
Upon my elbow well propped up   3625
Secure in my repose I've sat and so
Heard all the braggadocio.
I've stroked my whiskers, smiling, bland,
And grasped the full cup in my hand
And said: "Let each man have his way!   3630
But is there one in all the land
Like my dear Gretchen, who can hold
A candle to my sister? Say!"
Hear! hear! clink-clink! about it went;
Some cried: "He's right! She is of all   3635

Her sex the pride and ornament!"
Then dumb sat all the boasters bold.
And now!—I could tear out my hair
And try to run straight up a wall!
With stinging speeches, nose in air,   3640
Each scurvy knave may taunt and sneer!
I'll sit like one accursed by debt
And at each casual word I'll sweat!
Though I would like to smash and maul them,
Still, liars I could never call them.   3645
　　What's coming here? What sneaks in view?
If I mistake not, there are two.
If he is one, swift at his hide I'll drive!
He shall not leave this spot alive!
FAUST.　MEPHISTOPHELES.
Faust.　How from the window of yon sacristy   3650
Upward the glow of that eternal taper shimmers,
And weak and weaker sideward glimmers,
And darkness round it presses nigh!
So in my bosom do night shadows gather.
Mephistopheles.　I'm like a sentimental tom-cat, rather,   3655
That stealthy sneaks by fire-escapes,
Along the walls quite softly scrapes.
I feel quite like myself in this, I must confess:
A bit of thievish greed, a bit of rammishness.
So even now, I feel, through every vein   3660
Is spooking glorious Walpurgis Night.
Just two days hence it comes again.
Then why one keeps awake, one knows aright!
Faust.　Meanwhile does not a treasure rise in air
That I see glimmering back there?   3665
Mephistopheles.　Ere long you can proceed with pleasure
To raise the kettle and its treasure.
Not long ago I took a squint,
Saw splendid lion-dollars[1] in 't.
Faust.　But not a trinket, not a ring,   3670
To ornament my darling girl?
Mephistopheles.　I saw among them some such thing,
A kind of necklace made of pearl.
Faust.　So it is well! I do not find it pleasant
To go to her without a present.   3675
Mephistopheles.　It should not really trouble you
To have some pleasure gratis too.
Now since the sky glows with a starry throng,
A very masterpiece you'll hear.
I'll sing to her a moral song,   3680

---

[1]Coins minted first perhaps in Bohemia with the royal Bohemian lion stamped on them, perhaps first in Louvain, which the Germans called Löwen (Lions).

More surely to beguile her ear.
   He sings to his guitar.

What dost before
Thy lover's door,
Katrin, before
The world with light is laden?   *3685*
Let, let it be!
He lets in thee
As maid, but he
Will let thee out no maiden.

Maids, heed aright!   *3690*
Is it done quite?
Ah, then good-night!
Poor things, he will not linger!
For your own sake,
No robber take,   *3695*
When love he'd make,
Save with the ring on finger![1]

Valentine [*steps forth*].   Whom lure you here? God's-element!
  O you rat-catcher, cursèd slinger!
  To the Devil first the instrument!   *3700*
  To the Devil afterwards the singer!
Mephistopheles. He's broken my guitar! There's no more use in it.
Valentine. A skull's now going to be split!
Mephistopheles [*to* FAUST]. Don't give way, Doctor! Quick! Don't
    tarry!
  Keep close by as I lead the way.   *3705*
  Out with your duster, out, I say!
  Thrust hard at him and I will parry.
Valentine. Then parry that!
Mephistopheles.   And why not, pray?
Valentine. That too!
Mephistopheles.   Sure!
Valentine.   I believe the Devil's in the fray!
  What's this? My hand's already going lame.   *3710*
Mephistopheles [*to* FAUST]. Thrust home!
Valentine [*falls*].   O woe!
Mephistopheles.   Now is the lubber
    tame!
  But quick away! We must at once be gone,
  For even now a murd'rous cry arises.
  With the police quite nicely I get on
  But fare but ill with the assizes.   *3715*
Martha [*at a window*]. Out, neighbours, out!
Gretchen [*at a window*].   Here, bring a light!
Martha [*as above*]. They rail and scuffle, yell and fight.

    [1]Cf. Ophelia's song, *Hamlet*, iv, 5.

People.   Already one is lying there! He's dead!
Martha [*coming out*].   The murderers! Where have they run?
Gretchen [*coming out*].   Who's lying here?
People.   Your mother's son!   3720
Gretchen.   Almighty One! What misery!
Valentine.   I'm dying! That is quickly said
    And quicker still can be.
    Why, women, stand and howl and wail?
    Come here and listen to my tale!   3725
        They all come around him.
    My Gretchen, see! Young are you still
    And shrewd enough by no means quite.
    You manage your affairs but ill.
    In confidence I tell you, what is more,
    Since once for all now you're a whore,   3730
    So be one then outright!
Gretchen.   My brother! God! What words to me!
Valentine.   In this game let our Lord God be!
    Now what is done is done, alas!
    And as things can, so will they come to pass.   3735
    With one you started secretly,
    And more of them there soon will be.
    When a dozen men have had you down,
    You're common then to all the town.
        When Shame at first is given birth,   3740
    She is smuggled in upon this earth,
    And then the veil of night is thrown
    Around her ears and head;
    Yes, one would gladly murder her instead.
    But when both proud and great she's grown,   3745
    By daylight then she goes forth openly,
    And yet has not become more fair to see.
    The loathsomer her face, straightway
    The more she seeks the light of day.
        I see the time already nearing   3750
    When townsfolk, honest and God-fearing,
    As from an infectious body shrinking,
    Past you, you whore, will hurry slinking.
    In heart and body you'll despair
    If they but look you in the face!   3755
    No more a golden chain you'll wear,
    No more beside the altar take your place!
    In fine lace collar to your pleasure
    You'll dance no more a happy measure.
    In some dark corner you will hide   3760
    Among beggars and cripples, side by side.
    Even if God His pardon give,
    On earth you shall accursèd live!

Martha.　Commend your soul to God! Can it then be
　You'll cap your other sins with blasphemy?　　　　　　　*3765*
Valentine.　Could I but to your withered body limp,
　You shameless woman, coupling pimp!
　Then I indeed might hope to win
　Forgiveness plenty for each sin.
Gretchen.　My brother! Oh, what agony!　　　　　　　*3770*
Valentine.　I tell you, let the weeping be!
　When you from honour went apart,
　You stabbed me to the very heart.
　Now through the slumber of the grave
　I go to God, a soldier brave.　　　　　　　　　　　*3775*
　　Dies.

CATHEDRAL

Mass, Organ, and Singing.

GRETCHEN *among many people,* EVIL SPIRIT *behind* GRETCHEN.
Evil Spirit.　How different, Gretchen, it was with thee,
　When thou, still full of innocence,
　Here to the altar cam'st,
　Out of the well-worn, little book
　Didst prattle prayers,　　　　　　　　　　　　　*3780*
　Half childhood's play,
　Half God in thy heart!
　Gretchen!
　Where are thy thoughts?
　Within thy heart　　　　　　　　　　　　　　　*3785*
　What foul misdeed?
　Is it for thy mother's soul thou prayest, who
　　Through thee to long, long torment fell asleep?
　Upon thy door-sill, whose the blood?
　—Beneath thy heart already　　　　　　　　　　*3790*
　Is there not stirring swelling life
　That tortureth itself and thee
　With its foreboding presence?
Gretchen.　Woe! Woe!
　Would I were free of thoughts　　　　　　　　　*3795*
　That go within me hither and thither
　Against my will!
Choir.　Dies irae, dies illa
　Solvet saeclum in favilla.[1]
　　Sound of the organ.
Evil Spirit.　Wrath grips thee!　　　　　　　　　*3800*
　The last trumpet sounds!
　The graves are trembling!

---

[1]"Day of wrath, that day shall dissolve the world in ashes": the first lines of the dirge on Judgment Day, composed in the thirteenth century, probably by Thomas of Celano.

And thy heart,
From rest in ashes
To flaming torments   3805
Raised up, re-created,
Trembling ascends!

Gretchen.   Would I were away from here!
It seems to me as if the organ
Would stifle my breathing,   3810
As if my inmost heart
Were melted by the singing.

Choir.   *Judex ergo cum sedebit,*
      Quidquid latet adparebit,
      Nil inultum remanebit.   3815

Gretchen.   I'm stifling here!
The walls and pillars
Imprison me!
The vaulted arches
Crush me!—Air!   3820

Evil Spirit.   Hide thyself! Sin and shame
Remain not hidden.
Air? Light?
Woe's thee!

Choir.   *Quid sum miser tunc dicturus?*   3825
      Quem patronum rogaturus,
      Cum vix justus sit securus?

Evil Spirit.   The faces of the Glorified
Will turn away from thee;
To thee their hands to offer   3830
Will the Pure shudder.
Woe!

Choir.   *Quid sum miser tunc dicturus?*

Gretchen.   Neighbour! Your smelling-salts!
      She falls in a swoon.

WALPURGIS NIGHT[1]

The hartz mountains
Region of Schierke and Elend.
FAUST. MEPHISTOPHELES.

Mephistopheles.   If you'd a broomstick, wouldn't that be fine?   3835
I wish the sturdiest he-goat were mine.
Our goal's still far off and this way is rough.

Faust.   As long as I feel fresh afoot, I say

[1]The night between April 30 and May 1, when witches are reputed to hold carnival on
the Brocken, or Brocksberg, a peak about 3600 feet high and the most lofty in the Hartz
Mountains. Walpurgis was an English Benedictine nun long resident in Germany
(eighth century).

For me this knotted staff's enough.

What good is it when one cuts short the way? 3840

To loiter through the labyrinth of valleys

And then to mount these cliffs, whence sallies

The ever bubbling, leaping spring,

That is the spice that makes such paths worth wandering!

Already springtime in the birches stirs, 3845

It's even felt already by the firs;

Should not our members also feel effect?

Mephistopheles.   Forsooth, no trace of that can I detect!

I'm feeling wintry in my every limb;

Upon my path I should like frost and snow. 3850

How sadly rises, red and incomplete, the dim

Moon's disc with its belated glow

Lighting so ill that at each step or so

One runs against a rock, against a tree!

Let's ask a will-o'-the-wisp to lend his flicker! 3855

I see one there just flaming merrily.

Hey, friend! May I bid you to help us get on quicker?

Why will you blaze away so uselessly?

Do be so good and light us up the hill!

Will-o'-the-Wisp.   Out of respect for you I hope I'll find 3860

A way to curb my nature's flighty will;

Our course, as heretofore, is zigzag still.

Mephistopheles.   Ho! Ho! You think you'll imitate mankind.

Go on and in the Devil's name, but straight! Now mind!

Or else I'll blow your flickering light clean out. 3865

Will-o'-the-Wisp.   You are the master of the house, I have no doubt,

And I'll accommodate myself to you with glee.

But do reflect! The mountain's magic-mad today,

And if a will-o'-the-wisp must show the way,

You must not take things all too seriously. 3870

Faust, Mephistopheles, Will-o'-the-Wisp [*in alternating song*].

Spheres of dream and necromancy,

We have entered them, we fancy.

Lead us well, for credit striving,

That we soon may be arriving

In the wide and desert spaces. 3875

I see trees there running races.

How each, quickly moving, passes,

And the cliffs that low are bowing,

And the rocks, long nose-like masses,

How they're snoring, how they're blowing! 3880

Over stones and grass are flowing

Brook and brooklet downward fleeting.

Hear I murmuring? Hear I singing?

Hear sweet plaints of love entreating,

Voices of those blest days ringing? 3885

What we're loving, hopeful yearning!
And the echo, like returning
Tales of olden times, resoundeth!
   Hoo-hoo! Shoo-hoo! Nearer soundeth
Cry of owlet, jay, and plover!   *3890*
Are they all awake remaining?
Salamanders, through the cover,
Long-limbed, fat-paunched, are they straining?
And the roots, like serpents, winding
Out of rock and sand, unbinding,   *3895*
Stretch out fetters strange to scare us,
To affright us and ensnare us.
Living, sturdy gnarls uncanny
Stretch out polypus-antennæ
Toward the wanderer. Mice are teeming   *3900*
In a thousand colours, streaming
Through the moss and through the heather!
And the glow-worms fly, in swarming
Columns, ever forming
A bewildering escort hither.   *3905*
   Tell me, do we stay or whether
We are going onward thither?
All, all seems to be gyrating,
Rocks and trees that make grimaces,
Lights that wander, changing places,   *3910*
Multiplying, self-inflating.

Mephistopheles.   Grab my mantle's hem, hold tightly!
  Here's a midway peak where nightly
  Man, astounded, sees and knows
  How in the mountain Mammon glows.[1]   *3915*
Faust.   How strangely glimmers through the gorges,
  Like morning's red, a turbid glow!
  Down the abyss itself it forges,
  Cleaving its way through gulfs far, far below.
  Vapour floats yonder, there is steam up-leaping,   *3920*
  Here shines a glow through mist and haze,
  Then like a slender thread it's creeping,
  Then forth it breaks like fountain-sprays.
  Here for a long way it goes winding
  Along the vale in a hundred veins   *3925*
  And here—a corner crowding, binding—
  In sudden isolation wanes.
  There sparks are sprinkling like a shower
  Of widely scattered golden sand.
  And see the rocky walls! They tower,   *3930*
  They kindle and like ramparts stand.

[1]Cf. Matthew, 6. 24.

Mephistopheles. Does not Sir Mammon splendidly
　　Light up the palace for his revelry?
　　You see all this! What luck you've had!
　　But hark! Now come the guests in tumult mad. 3935
Faust. How through the air the tempest raves!
　　It smites my neck, shock after shock!
Mephistopheles. You must lay hold on these old ribs of rock;
　　Else it will hurl you down to these abysses' graves.
　　A mist is making night more dark. 3940
　　How through the woods it crashes! Hark!
　　Scared away, the owls are flying.
　　Hearken! Columns split and quiver
　　In palaces of green undying.
　　The branches sigh and breaking shiver! 3945
　　The tree-trunks' mighty groaning!
　　The roots are creaking and moaning!
　　In frightfully entangled fall
　　They crash together, one and all,
　　And through the wreck-over-strewn abysses 3950
　　The tempest howls and hisses.
　　Voices over us! Do you hear?
　　Now far off and now more near?
　　All the mountain-side along
　　Streams a furious magic song! 3955

Witches [*in Chorus*].
　　　　　　The witches to the Brocken go;
　　　　　　The grain is green, the stubble aglow.
　　　　　　There gathers all the mighty host;
　　　　　　Sir Urian[1] sits uppermost.
　　　　　　So goes it over stone and stock; 3960
　　　　　　The witch breaks wind, and stinks the buck.

A Voice. Alone old Baubo's[2] coming now;
　　She's riding upon a farrow sow.
Chorus.
　　　　　　So honour to whom honour is due!
　　　　　　In front, Dame Baubo! Lead the crew! 3965
　　　　　　A sturdy sow with mother astride,
　　　　　　All witches follow in a tide.

A Voice. Which way did you come here?
A Voice. 　　　　　　　　　　　The Ilsenstein[3] way.
　　I peeped in the owl's nest there today.
　　She made great eyes at me!

[1]The Devil.
[2]Baubo, a figure from classical mythology, symbolizes gross sensuality.
[3]A tall, clifflike rock a few miles from the Brocken.

A Voice.   Oh, fare on to Hell!   3970
  Why ride so pell-mell?
A Voice.   Just see how she's flayed me!
  The wounds she has made me!

Witches [*Chorus*].
          The way is broad, the way is long;
          What is that mad and crazy throng?   3975
          The broomstick pokes, the pitchfork thrusts,
          The infant chokes, the mother busts.

Wizards [*Half Chorus*].
          We steal along, like snails' our pace;
          All women beat us in the race.
          If toward Hell we set our pace,   3980
          By a thousand steps they win the race.

Other Half.
          Not so precisely do we take it,
          In a thousand steps may woman make it;
          Yet though she hastes as ever she can,
          In a single leap it's done by man.   3985

A Voice [*from above*].   Come with us from the cliff-bound mere!
A Voice [*from below*].   We'd like to go with you up there.
  We wash and we're scoured all bright and clean,
  But sterile still as we've always been.

Both Choruses.
          The wind is stilled, the stars take flight,   3990
          The dismal moon fain hides its light;
          In whiz and whirr the magic choir
          By thousands sputters out sparks of fire.

A Voice [*from below*].   Halt there! Ho, there! Ho!
A Voice [*from above*].   Who calls out from the cleft below?   3995
A Voice [*below*].   Take me too! Take me too!
  I'm climbing now three hundred years
  And I can never reach the summit.
  I want to be among my peers.

Both Choruses.
          The broomstick bears, and bears the stock,   4000
          The pitchfork bears, and bears the buck.
          Who cannot lift himself today,
          Is a lost man for aye and aye.

Half-Witch [*below*].   I've tripped behind so many a day,
  And now the others are far away!   4005

I've no repose at home, and yet
Here too there's none for me to get.

Chorus of Witches.
    Salve puts a heart in every hag,
    Good as a sail is any rag;
    A good ship every trough is too.   *4010*
    You'll fly not 'less today you flew.

Both Choruses.
    And when we glide the peak around,
    Then sweep along upon the ground;
    Bedeck both far and wide the heather
    With all your witchdom's swarm together. *4015*
  They settle down.
Mephistopheles. They crowd and shove, they rush and clatter,
 They hiss and whirl, they pull and chatter,
 They sputter, stink and burn and flare!
 A real witch-element, I swear!
 Keep close or soon we'll be a parted pair.   *4020*
 Where are you?
Faust [at a distance]. Here!
Mephistopheles.   Already snatched up there?
 Then I must exercise my rightful sway.
 Make way! Squire Voland[1] comes! Make way, sweet folk, make way!
 Here, Doctor, hold to me! and now in one quick rush
 Let us get out of all this crush;   *4025*
 It is too crazy even for the likes of me.
 Hard by there something gleams with a quite peculiar glare;
 A something draws me to that shrubbery.
 Come, come! We'll go and slip in there.
Faust. Spirit of Contradiction! On! and lead the way! *4030*
 It was a very clever notion, I must say;
 We seek the Brocken on Walpurgis Night,
 Yet choose to isolate ourselves when near the height!
Mephistopheles. What motley flames! Just look along the heather!
 There is a jolly club together.   *4035*
 In little circles one is not alone.
Faust. I'd rather be up yonder, I must own.
 Already whirling smoke and glow come into view.
 A host is streaming to the Devil! See them ride!
 Full many a riddle there must be untied.   *4040*
Mephistopheles. Yet many a riddle will be tied anew.
 Just let the great world whiz and riot;
 We'll house us meanwhile here in quiet.
 We've known it as a fact of ancient date
 That men make little worlds within the great. *4045*
 [1]The Devil.

I see young witches stripped and naked over there
And old ones wisely veiled, they don't go bare.
For my sake be a friend to all;
The fun is great, the trouble small.
I hear the sound of instruments arise!   4050
Accursèd din! One must get used to that ado.
Come! Come with me! It can't be otherwise.
I'll step up here; I'll introduce you too,
And thus in debt to me bind you anew.
That is no little space. What say you, friend?   4055
Just look out there! You scarce can see the end.
A hundred fires are burning, tier on tier.
They dance, they cook, they drink, make love, and chat.
Now say, where's something better than all that?

Faust. In introducing us, will you appear   4060
As devil or magician here?

Mephistopheles. True, I'm much used to go incognito,
But on a gala day one lets one's orders show.
No garter[1] have I to distinguish me,
But here the horse's foot is honoured and in place.   4065
You see that snail there? See her groping face!
Already, creeping hither steadily,
She's scented something out in me.
Though I should wish it, I cannot belie me here.
But come! From fire to fire we'll make a tour,   4070
I'll be the go-between and you the wooer.
   To some who are sitting around dying embers.
You agèd sirs, what are you doing in the rear?
I'd praise you if right nicely in the midst I found you,
With riot, youthful revelry around you.
At home there's solitude enough for everyone.   4075

General. What trust in nations can one place?
However much for them one may have done.
In peoples' as in women's grace
Youth stands supreme over everyone.

Minister. Now all too far away from right are men,   4080
I praise the good and old, and duly;
When we were all-in-all, ah, truly,
The real, real golden age was then.

Parvenu. We too weren't stupid, I'll be bound.
Oft what we did, we shouldn't rightly;   4085
But now the world turns round and round,
And just when we would hold things tightly.

Author. Who now in any case will read
A book with contents middling clever?
And as for dear young folks, indeed,   4090
They're pert and saucy now as never.

[1]An allusion to the English Order of the Garter.

Mephistopheles [*who all at once appears very old*].
    I feel that men are ripe for Judgment Day,
    Since no more up the witches' mount I'll climb;
    And since my cask drains turbidly away,
    So too the world declines in dregs and slime.   *4095*

Huckster-Witch.   You gentlemen, don't pass by so!
    Let such an opportunity not go!
    Look at my wares attentively;
    Here are all sorts of things to see.
    Yet in my shop, sirs, there is naught—   *4100*
    Its like on earth you will not find—
    That at some time or other has not wrought
    Dire harm both to the world and to mankind.
    No dagger's here which has not streamed with blood,
    No cup which has not poured a hot, consuming flood   *4105*
    Of poison into some quite healthy frame,
    No gem that has not brought some lovely maid to shame,
    Nor sword that has not made a truce miscarry
    Or, from behind maybe, has stabbed no adversary.

Mephistopheles.   Dear Coz, you understand but badly times like
    these: *4110*
    What's done is past! What's past is done!
    Provide yourself with novelties!
    By novelties alone can we be won.

Faust.   If I'm not to forget myself, I must watch out!
    That's what I call a fair beyond all doubt.   *4115*

Mephistopheles.   Upward strives the whirling throng;
    You think you shove, and you are shoved along.

Faust.   Who can that be?

Mephistopheles.   Observe her with great care!
    That's Lilith.

Faust.   Who?

Mephistopheles.   Adam's first wife.[1] Beware
    That lovely hair of hers, those tresses   *4120*
    Which she incomparably delights to wear!
    The young man whom she lures into their snare
    She will not soon release from her caresses.

Faust.   Yonder sit two, one old and one young thing.
    They have already done some right good capering.   *4125*

[1]Jewish tradition ascribes to Adam a first wife named Lilith. After the creation of Eve, Lilith is said to have become the mistress of a devil, seducing men and pursuing children. She has been identified with the "female" of Gen. 1. 27, and with the "screech owl" (or "night monster") of Isaiah, 34. 14. (Gen. 1. 27: So God created man in his own image, in the image of God created he him; male and female created he them. Isaiah, 34. 14: the screech owl also shall rest there, and find for herself a place of rest.) Lilith is an embodiment of sensuality, a culmination of Walpurgis Night, of that phase of the Eternal-Womanly which degrades, the extremest opposite of the all-understanding, all-forgiving Virgin at the end of the play.

    German folk-lore ascribed especial power to witches' hair; in the trials of witches therefore their hair was shorn before the proceedings started.

Mephistopheles.   There is no rest today for young or old.
  A new dance starts; come now! let us take hold!
Faust [dancing with THE YOUNG WITCH*]*.
                    Once came a lovely dream to me.
                    I saw therein an apple tree;
                    Two lovely apples on it shone,   *4130*
                    They charmed me so, I climbed thereon.
The Beauty.
                    The little apples man entice
                    Since first they were in Paradise.
                    I feel myself with pleasure glow
                    That such within my garden grow.   *4135*

Mephistopheles [with THE OLD WITCH*]*.
                    Once came a wanton dream to me.
                    I saw therein a riven tree;
                    It had a monstrous hole;
                    'Twas huge, yet I was pleased with it.
The Old Witch.
                    I proffer now my best salute   *4140*
                    To you, the knight with horse's foot!
                    Let me a proper cork prepare,
                    If him a big hole does not scare.

Proctophantasmist.[1]   Accursèd folk! how dare you then?
  Have you not long had proof complete,   *4145*
  A spirit never stands on ordinary feet?
  And now you're dancing like us other men!
The Beauty [dancing].   Why is he at our ball? that fellow there?
Faust [dancing].   Ha! He is simply everywhere.
  He must appraise what others dance.   *4150*
  If over each step he can't make a din,
  The step's as good as if it had not been.
  It irks him most the moment we advance.
  If you'd but turn around in endless repetition
  As he is wont to do in his old mill,   *4155*
  That, to be sure, he'd call not ill,
  Especially if you asked his permission.
Proctophantasmist.   You are still here! This is unheard-of, on my
    word!

[1]The proctophantasmist (rump-visionary) is Friedrich Nicolai, who toward the end
of the eighteenth century made himself ridiculous in advocating dry common-sense in
literature and in opposing new ideas. He had angered Goethe first by writing a parody
of *The Sorrows of Young Werther;* later he attacked Goethe's friend Schiller. Nicolai
then committed an indiscretion. The rumour had gone about in Berlin in 1797 that
ghosts had appeared in the suburb of Tegel, whereupon Nicolai prepared a paper that he
read before the Berlin Academy of Sciences in which he announced that he had been
plagued by ghostly apparitions and had cured himself by applying leeches to his rump.
Goethe now seized an opportunity to even up the score with Nicolai.

Vanish! We brought enlightenment as you have heard!
This devilish crew cares not for rules or books.   *4160*
We are so wise, and yet in Tegel there are spooks!
How long I've swept and swept at this conceit absurd
And can't sweep clean—this is unheard-of, on my word!
The Beauty.   Then do stop boring us in such a place!
Proctophantasmist.   I say it, Spirits, to your face,   *4165*
This spirit despotism I will not endure;
My spirit can not act that way.
      The dancing goes on.
I see that I have no success today;
But anyway I'll take along "A Tour"[1]
And hope still, ere my last step, to subdue   *4170*
The devils and the poets too.
Mephistopheles.   He'll straightway in a puddle set him.
That's how he gets relief, of solace well assured.
When leeches, feasting on his rump, beset him,
Of spirits and of spirit he is cured.   *4175*
      To FAUST *who has left the dance.*
Why do you let the pretty maiden go
Who sang so sweetly as you danced along?
Faust.   Ugh! in the very middle of her song
A mouse sprang from her lips—'twas small and red.
Mephistopheles.   That's quite all right. There's naught in that to
      dread.   *4180*
It is enough you did not find the mouse was grey.
Who in a lover's hour will bother anyway?
Faust.   I saw then—
Mephistopheles.   What?
Faust.   Mephisto, see you there—
Far off she stands, alone—a girl so pale and fair?
She drags herself but slowly from that place.   *4185*
She seems to move with shackled feet.
I must confess, I thought it was the face—
That she looks like my Gretchen sweet.
Mephistopheles.   Do let that be! That is of good to none.
It is a magic image, lifeless eidolon.   *4190*
It is not well to meet that anywhere;
Man's blood grows frigid from that rigid stare;
And he is turned almost to stone.
The story of Medusa you of course have known.
Faust.   In truth, the eyes of one who's dead are those,   *4195*
Which there was no fond, loving hand to close;
That is the breast that Gretchen offered me,
That is the body sweet that I enjoyed.
Mephistopheles.   It's sorcery, you fool, you're easily decoyed!
She seems to each as though his love were she.   *4200*

[1]Nicolai's *Description of a Tour through Germany and Switzerland,* in twelve volumes.

Faust.   What rapture! Ah, what misery!
   Yet from this vision I can't turn aside.
   How strange that such a lovely neck
   A single band of crimson must bedeck!
   A knife's edge scarcely seems less wide.   *4205*
Mephistopheles.   Quite right! I see it likewise, it is true!
   And she can bear her head twixt side and elbow too,
   For Perseus struck it off for her—
   I vow, illusion's still bewitching you!
   Do come on up the little height!   *4210*
   The Prater[1] is not livelier;
   And if someone has not bewitched me quite,
   I truly see a theatre.
   What's going on?
Servibilis.   They're starting now. The play
   Will be the last of seven, one that's new;   *4215*
   To give so many is the usual way.
   A dilettante wrote the play
   And dilettanti will enact it too.
   Excuse me, gentlemen, if I must disappear;
   With dilettant delight I raise the curtain.   .   *4220*
Mephistopheles.   I find that all is well, to find you here;
   Your proper place is on the Brocken, that is certain.

WALPURGIS NIGHT'S DREAM

OR, OBERON AND TITANIA'S GOLDEN WEDDING

INTERMEZZO

Theatre Manager.
        Now for once we'll rest today,
        Valiant sons of Mieding.[2]
        Misty vale and mountain grey   *4225*
        Are all the scene we're needing!

Herald.
        Golden wedding cannot be
        Till fifty years have vanished;
        And yet golden is 't to me
        When the strife is banished.   *4230*

Oberon.
        Are ye spirits to be seen,
        Come forth and show it duly!
        Fairy king and fairy queen,
        They are united newly.

---

[1] A park in Vienna.

[2] Mieding was Goethe's right-hand man in the presentation of plays in Weimar until Mieding's death in 1782.

Puck.

> Now comes Puck and whirls about   4235
> And slides his foot a-dancing;
> After come a hundred out,
> Themselves and him entrancing.

Ariel.

> Ariel awakes the song
> With pure and heavenly measure;   4240
> Many frights he lures along,
> And fair ones too, with pleasure.

Oberon.

> Spouses who would live in peace,
> Learn from our example!
> When a pair would love increase,   4245
> To separate them's ample.

Titania.

> Sulks the husband, carps the wife,
> Just seize them quickly, harry
> Her away far to the south
> And him to far north carry.   4250

Orchestra Tutti [fortissimo].

> Snout of fly, mosquito-bill,
> With kin of all conditions,
> Frog in leaves and crickets shrill,
> These are the musicians!

Solo.

> See, here comes the bagpipe's sack!   4255
> Soapbubble-like, it's blowing.
> Hear the snecke-snicke-snack
> Through its snub nose flowing!

A Spirit that is just taking form.

> Spider's foot and paunch of toad
> And wings the wight doth grow him!   4260
> True, a beastie 'twill not be
> But yet a little poem.

A Little Couple.

> Short step here and high leap there
> Through honey-dew and sweetness;
> Yet you'll soar not through the air,   4265
> With all your tripping fleetness.

Inquisitive Traveller.

> Is that not mummers' mocking play?
> Shall I trust to my vision?
> Fair god Oberon today
> Is here on exhibition?   4270

Orthodox.[1]

> Claws or tail I do not see
> And yet, beyond a cavil,
> Just like "The Gods of Greece" is he
> Likewise a very devil.

Northern Artist.

> What I may grasp today may be   4275
> But sketches of this tourney,
> Yet I'm betimes preparing me
> For my Italian Journey.

Purist.

> Woe! bad luck has led me here.
> How decency they're mocking!   4280
> Of all the witches' host, dear! dear!
> But two are powdered! Shocking!

Young Witch.

> Powder is like a petticoat,
> For grey hags hoddy-doddy;
> So I sit naked on my goat   4285
> And show a strapping body.

Matron.

> We are too well-behaved by far,
> With you to snarl a lot here;
> Yet, young and tender as you are,
> I hope that you will rot here.   4290

Leader of the Orchestra.

> Snout of fly, mosquito-bill,
> Don't swarm around the naked!
> Frog in leaves and cricket shrill,
> Do mark the time and take it!

Weather-Vane [*turning in one direction*].

> The comp'ny's all one can wish for,   4295
> Each one a bride, I swear it!
> And man by man a bachelor,
> Most prom'sing, I declare it!

Weather-Vane [*turning in the other direction*].

> And will the ground not open out
> To swallow all who're dancing,   4300
> Then I will swiftly leave this rout
> And straight to Hell go prancing.

Xenia.[2]

> See us here as insects! Ha!
> Each one with sharp shears on her,

---

[1]Count Ferdinand Leopold von Stolberg, who accused Schiller of blasphemy when Schiller wrote his poem, *The Gods of Greece.*
[2]Goethe and Schiller wrote many Xenia.

That Lord Satan, our papa,   4305
We fittingly may honour.

Hennings.[1]

Just see them all, a crowding throng,
Naïvely jesting, playing!
That they had kind hearts all along,
They'll in the end be saying.   4310

"Leader of the Muses."

Amid this witches' host, indeed,
One's way one gladly loses;
For, sure, I could these sooner lead
Than I can lead the Muses.

The Quondam "Spirit of the Times."

With proper folk one can all do.   4315
Come, cling close, none can pass us!
The Blocksberg has a broad top too,
Like Germany's Parnassus.

Inquisitive Traveller.

What's the name of that stiff man?
He goes with haughty paces;   4320
He snuffles all he snuffle can.
"He scents the Jesuits' traces."

Crane.

If water clear or muddy be,
I fish with pleasure, really;
That's why this pious man you see   4325
With devils mixing freely.

Worldling.[2]

By pious people, I speak true,
No vehicle's rejected;
Conventicles, more than a few,
On Blocksberg are erected.   4330

Dancer.

Another chorus now succeeds!
I hear a distant drumming.
"Don't be disturbed! It's, in the reeds,
The herons' changeless booming."

Dancing Master.

How each his legs kicks up and flings!   4335
Somehow gets on, however!
The clumsy hops, the crooked springs,
And how it looks, ask never!

[1]August von Hennings, who had published a book of poems called *Leader of the Muses* and edited a journal called *Spirit of the Times* (later *Spirit of the Nineteenth Century,* hence "Quondam"), had attacked the Xenia.
[2]Goethe himself.

Fiddler.

>They hate each other well, that crew,
>And they would like to rend them. 4340
>As Orpheus' lyre the beasts all drew,
>The bagpipe here will blend them.

Dogmatist.

>I'll not let screams lead me to war
>With doubts and critic-cavils.
>The Devil must be something, or 4345
>Else how could there be devils?

Idealist.

>For once, as I see phantasy,
>It is far too despotic.
>In truth, if I be all I see,
>Today I'm idiotic. 4350

Realist.

>This riot makes my torture sheer
>And greatly irks me surely;
>For the first time I'm standing here
>On my feet insecurely.

Supernaturalist.

>With much delight I join this crew 4355
>And share with them their revels;
>For that there are good spirits too
>I argue from these devils.

Skeptic.

>They go to track the flamelets out
>And think they're near the treasure. 4360
>Devil alliterates with Doubt,
>So I am here with pleasure.

Leader of the Orchestra.

>Frog in leaves and cricket shrill,
>Cursed dilettants! Perdition!
>Fly-snout and mosquito-bill, 4365
>You're each a fine musician!

The Adroit.

>Sans-souci, we call us so,
>Gay creatures free from worry;
>We afoot no more can go,
>So on our heads we hurry. 4370

The Ne'er-Do-Wells.

>We once sponged many a bite, 'tis true,
>God help us! That is done now!
>We've danced our shoes entirely through,
>On naked soles we run now.

Will-o'-the-Wisps.

From the marshes we come out,   4375
Where we arose from litter;
Yet here in dancing roundabout
We're gallants all a-glitter.

A Falling Star.

From the heights above plunged I,
With star- and fire-light o'er me;   4380
Crookèd now in grass I lie,
Who'll to my feet restore me?

The Heavy Ones.

Room! more room! All round us too!
Thus downward go the grasses.
Spirits come and they, it's true,   4385
Are clumsy, heavy masses.

Puck.

Bloated, enter not the fray,
Like elephant-calves about one!
And the clumsiest today
Be Puck himself, the stout one!   4390

Ariel.

If kind Nature gave you wings,
If them Mind uncloses,
Follow my light wanderings
To yon hill of roses!

Orchestra [*pianissimo*].

Cloud and mist drift off with speed,   4395
Aloft 'tis brighter growing.
Breeze in leaves and wind in reed,
And all away is blowing.

A DISMAL DAY.   A FIELD.
FAUST.   MEPHISTOPHELES.

Faust.   In misery! Despairing! Long pitiably astray upon the earth and
now imprisoned! That lovely, ill-starred creature locked up in a prison
as a criminal, to suffer horrible tortures. To that has it come! to that!—
Treacherous, contemptible spirit, and that you have concealed from me!
—Stay, then, stay! Roll your devilish eyes ragingly in your head! Stay
and defy me with your intolerable presence! Imprisoned! In irrepara-
ble misery! Delivered up to evil spirits and to condemning, feelingless
mankind! And me, meanwhile, you cradle in insipid diversions, hide
from me her increasing wretchedness, and let her, helpless, go to ruin!
Mephistopheles.   She's not the first one.
Faust.   Dog! Detestable monster! Turn him, Thou Spirit Infinite, turn
the worm back into his dog's-form, as at night it often pleased him to trot
along before me, to roll in a heap before the feet of the innocent wanderer, and as he fell, to spring upon his shoulders. Turn him back into

his favourite form, that he may crawl on his belly, before me in the sand, that I may trample him beneath my feet, the outcast!—Not the first one! —Woe! Woe! that no human soul can grasp it, that more than one creature has sunk down into the depths of this misery, that the first one, in writhing, deathly agony, did not atone for the guilt of all the others in the sight of the Eternal Pardoner! The misery of this single one pierces the marrow of my life; and you are calmly grinning at the fate of thousands!

Mephistopheles.   Now we are again at our wits' end, there where the reason of you mortals snaps from over-stretching. Why do you enter into fellowship with us if you can not carry it through? Will you fly and are not safe from dizziness? Did we force ourselves on you, or you on us?

Faust.   Bare not so your greedy fangs at me! It fills me with loathing! Great, glorious Spirit, Thou who didst deign to appear to me, Thou who knowest my heart and my soul, why fetter me to the infamous comrade who feeds on mischief and slakes his thirst in destruction?

Mephistopheles.   Have you ended?

Faust.   Save her! or woe to you! The most hideous curses be on you for thousands of years!

Mephistopheles.   I can not loose the bonds of the avenger, nor undo his bolts. Save her! Who was it that plunged her into ruin? I or you?

FAUST *looks around wildly.*

Mephistopheles.   Will you reach for the thunder? 'Tis well that it was not given to you miserable mortals! To smash to pieces the man who blamelessly answers back, that is the tyrant's way of venting himself when embarrassed.

Faust.   Take me to her! She shall be free!   .

Mephistopheles.   And the danger to which you will expose yourself? Know that the guilt of blood, from your hand, still lies upon the town. Over the spot where a man was slain, avenging spirits hover and lie in wait for the returning murderer.

Faust.   That too from you? The murder and death of a world be upon you, monster! Lead me to her, I say, and set her free!

Mephistopheles.   I will lead you, and what I can do, hear! Have I all power in Heaven and on earth? The warder's senses I will becloud; make yourself master of the keys and lead her forth with human hand. I'll watch! The magic horses are ready, I will carry you away. That I can do.

Faust.   Up and away!

NIGHT.   AN OPEN FIELD.

FAUST *and* MEPHISTOPHELES *storming along on black horses.*

Faust.   What weaving are they round the Ravenstone?

Mephistopheles.   I know not what they are brewing and doing.   4400

Faust.   Hovering up, hovering down, bending low, bowing down.

Mephistopheles.   A witches' guild.

Faust.   They strew and dedicate.

Mephistopheles.   On! On!

A PRISON

Faust [with a bunch of keys and a lamp, in front of an iron wicket].

A long-unwonted shudder over me falls,   *4405*
The woe of human lot lays hold on me.
Here then she dwells, within these humid walls,
And all her crime was a fond fantasy.
You hesitate to go to her? You fear
Again to see her near?   *4410*
On! Your faltering brings death lingering here!
    He grasps the lock.
Someone is singing [inside].

                    My mother, the whore,
                    She has murdered me!
                    My father, the rogue,
                    He has eaten me,   *4415*
                    My sister, so small,
                    My bones, one and all,
                    In a cool place did lay.
                    A forest bird fair I became that day;
                    Fly away! Fly away!   *4420*

Faust [unlocking the wicket].
    She does not dream her lover listens, near again,
    And hears the rustling straw, the clanking chain.
        He steps in.
Margaret [hiding herself on her pallet].
    Woe! Woe! They come! How bitter 'tis to die!
Faust [softly].   Hush! Hush! I come to set you free!
Margaret [grovelling at his feet].
    If you're a man, then feel my misery!   *4425*
Faust.   You will wake the warders with your cry!
        He takes hold of the chains, to unlock them.
Margaret [on her knees].   Who, headsman, ever had this power
    Over me to give?
    You fetch me at the midnight hour!
    Be merciful and let me live!   *4430*
    Will it not be soon enough when the matin's rung?
        She stands up.
    Ah! I am still so young, so young!
    And now to die!
    It was my ruin that so fair was I.
    My love was near, now he is far;   *4435*
    Torn lies the wreath, scattered the flowers are.
    Seize me not thus so violently!
    What have I done to you? Oh, pity me!
    Let me not in vain implore!
    I've never, my life long, seen you before!   *4440*

Faust.   Can I survive this misery?

Margaret.   You now have power over me.
  Let me but nurse my baby once again.
  I fondled it the livelong night;
  They took it from me, just to give me pain,   4445
  And now they say I murdered it outright.
  I never shall again be glad.
  They're singing songs about me! That is bad
  Of people! An old story ends just so.
  Who bids them tell it of me, though?   4450

Faust [throws himself down].
  Here at your feet a lover lies,
  To loose the bondage of these miseries.

Margaret [throws herself beside him].
  Oh, let us kneel, call on the saints to hear us!
  See! under these steps near us
  And the threshold's swell,   4455
  Seething all Hell!
  The Devil,
  In fearful brawling,
  Holds awful revel!

Faust [loudly].   Gretchen! Gretchen!   4460

Margaret [listening attentively].
  That was my lover calling!
    She springs up. The chains fall off.
  Where is he? I heard him calling! I am free!
  No one shall hinder me.
  To his neck will I fly,
  On his bosom lie!   4465
  He called "Gretchen!" He stood at the door of my cell.
  Through the midst of the howl and clatter of Hell,
  Through the anger and scorn of the devilish crew,
  The tones of that sweet, loving voice I knew.

Faust.   It's I!

Margaret.   It's you! Oh, say it once again!   4470
    Embracing him.
  It's he! It's he! Where's all my misery?
  And where the anguish of the gaol? the chain?
  It's you! You've come to save me!
  And I am saved!
  The very street is here anew   4475
  Where for the first time I saw you,
  And the cheerful garden too
  Where I and Martha wait for you.

Faust [urging her to go].   Come! Come with me!

Margaret.   Oh, tarry!
  So gladly do I tarry where you tarry!   4480
    Caressing him.

Faust.   Hurry!
  Unless you hurry,
  We must pay for it dearly.
Margaret.   What? And can you kiss no more! Is this
  My love, away from me a short while merely,   *4485*
  And yet forgotten how to kiss?
  Why do I cling about your neck so fearfully?
  When once but at a glance, a word, from you,
  All Heaven swept me through and through,
  And you kissed me as if you'd smother me.   *4490*
  Kiss me! Do!
  Or I'll kiss you!
    She embraces him.
  Oh, woe! Your dear lips are so cold,
  Are still!
  Where has your loving   *4495*
  Been roving?
  Who did me this ill?
    She turns away from him.
Faust.   Come! follow me, love, have courage, be bold!
  I'll press you to my heart with warmth a thousandfold;
  I only beg you now to follow me!   *4500*
Margaret [*turning toward him*].
  And is it you, then? You, quite certainly?
Faust.   It's I! Come with me!
Margaret.   You unlock the chain,
  You take me in your lap again!
  How is it that you do not shrink from me?
  And do you know, my love, whom you set free?   *4505*
Faust.   Come! come! The depths of night already wane.
Margaret.   My mother I have slain.
  My child I've drowned! It's true!
  Was it not given to me and you?
  To you as well! It's you! I scarce can deem   *4510*
  It real. Give me your hand! It is no dream!
  Your darling hand! But ah, it's wet!
  Quick wipe it off! It seems that even yet
  I see blood run.
  Ah, God! What have you done?   *4515*
  Oh, put away
  The sword, I pray!
Faust.   Let what is done and over, over be!
  You're killing me.
Margaret.   No, you must stay alive, you must indeed!   *4520*
  I'll tell you how the graves must be.
  For them you must take heed
  Tomorrow morn for me.
  The best place give to my mother,

And close beside her my brother,   4525
Me a little to one side,
A space—but not too wide!
And put the little one here on my right breast.
No one else will lie beside me!
Ah, in your arms to nestle and hide me,   4530
That was a sweet, a lovely bliss!
But now, much as I try, it seems to go amiss.
It seems to me as if I must
Force myself on you and you thrust
Me back, and yet it's you, so kind, so good to see. 4535

Faust.   If you feel it is I, then come with me!

Margaret.   Out there?

Faust.   To freedom!

Margaret.   If the grave's out there,
Death lurking near, then come with me!
From here to the eternal bed of rest   4540
And no step further—No!
You go away now? Henry! Oh, that I could go!

Faust.   You can! Just will it! Open stands the door.

Margaret.   I dare not go; for me there's no hope any more.
Why flee? They'll surely lie in wait for me.   4545
It is so wretched to beg one's way
And with an evil conscience too.
It is so wretched, in unknown parts to stray,
And they will seize me anyway.

Faust.   I shall remain with you.   4550

Margaret.   Quick! Quick! Begone!
Save your poor child! On! On!
Keep to the way
Along the brook,
Over the bridge   4555
To the wood beyond,
To the left where the plank is
In the pond.
Quick! Seize it! Quick!
It's trying to rise,   4560
It's struggling still!
Save it! Save it!

Faust.   Collect your thoughts! And see,
It's but one step, then you are free!

Margaret.   If we were only past the hill!   4565
There sits my mother upon a stone,
My brain is seized by cold, cold dread!
There sits my mother upon a stone,
And to and fro she wags her head;
She becks not, she nods not, her head's drooping lower, 4570
She has slept long, she'll wake no more.

She slept and then we were so glad.
Those were happy times we had.

Faust.   No prayers help here and naught I say,
So I must venture to bear you away.   *4575*

Margaret.   Let me alone! No, I'll not suffer force!
Don't pounce so murderously on me!
I have done all for love of you.

Faust.   My darling! See!
The day is dawning! Darling!

Margaret.   Day! Yes, day is dawning! The last day breaks for me!   *4580*
My wedding-day this was to be!
Tell no one you have been with Gretchen.
My wreath's gone forever!
It is gone and in vain.
We'll see one another again,   *4585*
But at dances never.
The crowd comes surging, no sound it makes,
The street and square
Cannot hold all there.
The death-bell tolls, the white wand breaks.   *4590*
How they seize me, bind me with lashes!
Away and to the block I'm sped.
Each neck is wincing at the flashes
As swift the keen blade flashes over my head.
Hushed lies the world as the grave.   *4595*

Faust.   Oh! had I never been born!

Mephistopheles [*appears outside*].   Off! or you're lost and lorn.
What vain delaying, wavering, prating!
My shivering steeds are waiting,
The morning twilight's near.   *4600*

Margaret.   What rises up from the threshold here?
He! He! Thrust him out!
In this holy place what is he about?
He seeks me!

Faust.   You shall live!

Margaret.   Judgment of God! My all to thee I give!   *4605*

Mephistopheles [*to* FAUST].
Come! Come! Along with her I will abandon you.

Margaret.   Thine am I, Father! Rescue me!
Ye angels! Ye heavenly hosts! Appear,
Encamp about and guard me here!
Henry! I shrink from you!   *4610*

Mephistopheles.   She is judged!

A Voice [*from above*].   She is saved!

Mephistopheles [*to* FAUST].   Here to me!
     He disappears with FAUST.

A Voice [*from within, dying away*].   Henry! Henry!

The Second Part

OF THE TRAGEDY

❧❧❧❧❧❧❧❧

ACT I

A PLEASING LANDSCAPE

TWILIGHT

FAUST, *reclining on flowery turf, weary, restless, trying to sleep.*
SPIRITS, *charming little figures forming a circle, hovering about.*

Ariel [*song accompanied by Aeolian harps*].

When in spring the rain of flowers
Hovering sinketh over all,
When the meadows, bright with showers,   4615
Unto all the earth-born call,
Tiny elves with souls propitious
Haste to help where help they can;
Be he blameless, be he vicious,
They lament the luckless man.   4620

Hovering around this head in circles airy,
Look that ye show the noble law of fairy:
Appease the furious conflict in his heart!
Draw out the burning arrows of remorse,
From suffered horrors cleanse his inmost part!   4625
Four pauses makes the night upon its course:
Hasten to fill them with your kindly art!
His head upon a cooling pillow lay,
Then bathe him in the dew from Lethe's stream!
His limbs, cramp-stiffened, soon will freely play   4630
When rest has made him strong for morn's new beam.
Perform the fairest elfin rite,
Restore him to the holy light!

Chorus [*singly, or two or more, alternating and together*].

When the breezes, warmth exhaling,
Fill the green-encircled plain,   4635
Twilight sinks its mists enveiling,
Brings sweet fragrance in its train,
Softly whispers peace to mortals,
Rocks the heart to childlike rest,
Closes eyelids, daylight's portals,   4640

Of the weary and oppressed.
   Night already sinks and darkles,
Holy follows star on star,
Light now bright, now fainter sparkles,
Glitters near and gleams afar,   *4645*
Glitters, in the lake reflecting,
Gleams in night's clear canopy;
Deepest slumber's bliss perfecting,
Reigns the moon's full majesty.
   Now the hours are passed and over,   *4650*
Pain and bliss have fled away.
Feel it now! Thou wilt recover!
Trust the gleam of new-born day!
Vales grow green and hills are swelling,
Lure to bowers of rest again;   *4655*
Harvest's coming now foretelling,
Roll the silvery waves of grain.
   If thou every wish wouldst gain thee,
Gaze at yonder glory wide!
Lightly do the bonds restrain thee;   *4660*
Sleep's a shell, cast it aside!
Be the crowd faint-hearted, quailing,
Falter not, but be thou bold!
All is his who never-failing
Understands and swift lays hold.   *4665*

A tremendous tumult announces the approach of the sun.

Ariel.   Hark! The storm of hours is nearing!
Sounding loud to spirit-hearing,
Is the new-born day appearing.
Rocky portals grate and shatter,
Phoebus' wheels roll forth and clatter.   *4670*
What a tumult Light brings near!
Trumpets, trombones are resounding,
Eyes are blinking, ears astounding;
The unheard ye shall not hear.
Slip into a flowery bell   *4675*
Deeper, deeper; quiet dwell
Under the leaf, in the cliff,
If it strikes you, ye are deaf.

Faust.   Refreshed anew life's pulses beat and waken
To greet the mild ethereal dawn of morning;   *4680*
Earth, through this night thou too hast stood unshaken
And breath'st before me in thy new adorning,
Beginst to wrap me round with gladness thrilling,
A vigorous resolve in me forewarning,
Unceasing strife for life supreme instilling.—   *4685*
Now lies the world revealed in twilight glimmer,
The wood resounds, a thousand voices trilling;

The vales where mist flows in and out lie dimmer,
But in the gorges sinks a light from heaven,
And boughs and twigs, refreshed, lift up their shimmer   4690
From fragrant chasms where they slept at even;
Tint upon tint again emerges, clearing
Where trembling pearls from flower and leaf drip riven:
All round me is a Paradise appearing.

  Look up!—The peaks, gigantic and supernal,   4695
Proclaim the hour most solemn now is nearing.
They early may enjoy the light eternal
That later to us here below is wended.
Now on the alpine meadows, sloping, vernal,
A clear and lavish glory has descended   4700
And step by step fulfils its journey's ending.
The sun steps forth!—Alas, already blinded,
I turn away, the pain my vision rending.

  Thus is it ever when a hope long yearning
Has made a wish its own, supreme, transcending,   4705
And finds Fulfilment's portals outward turning;
From those eternal deeps bursts ever higher
Too great a flame, we stand, with wonder burning.
To kindle life's fair torch we did aspire
And seas of flame—and what a flame!—embrace us!   4710
Is it Love? Is it Hate? that twine us with their fire,
In alternating joy and pain enlace us,
So that again toward earth we turn our gazing,
Baffled, to hide in youth's fond veils our faces.

  Behind me therefore let the sun be blazing!   4715
The cataract in gorges deeply riven
I view with rapture growing and amazing.
To plunge on plunge in a thousand streams it's given,
And yet a thousand, downward to the valleys,
While foam and mist high in the air are driven.   4720
Yet how superb above this tumult sallies
The many-coloured rainbow's changeful being;
Now lost in air, now clearly drawn, it dallies,
Shedding sweet coolness round us even when fleeing!
The rainbow mirrors human aims and action.   4725
Think, and more clearly wilt thou grasp it, seeing
Life is but light in many-hued reflection.

THE EMPEROR'S PALACE
The throne-room

The State Council awaiting the EMPEROR. *Trumpets. Cour-*
tiers of all kinds enter, splendidly dressed. The EMPEROR
ascends the throne, at his right hand the ASTROLOGER.
Emperor.   I greet you, faithful friends and dear,

Assembled here from far and wide.
I see the wise man at my side,   4730
But wherefore is the Fool not here?
A Squire.   A pace behind your mantle's sweep
There on the stairs he fell in a heap;
They bore away that load of fat,
But dead or drunk? No one knows that.   4735
A Second Squire.   Now at a swift, amazing pace
Another's pushing to his place.
He's quaintly primped, in truth, and smart,
But such a fright that all men start.
The guards there at the doorway hold   4740
Their halberds crosswise and athwart—
But here he is. The Fool is bold!
Mephistopheles [*kneeling before the throne*].
What is accursed and welcomed ever?
What's longed for, ever chased away?
What's always taken into favour?   4745
What's harshly blamed, accused each day?
Whom don't you dare to summon here?
Whose name hears gladly every man?
What to your throne is drawing near?
What's placed itself beneath your ban?   4750
Emperor.   Your words you may at present spare!
The place for riddles is not here;
They are these gentlemen's affair.
Solve them yourself! I'd like to hear.
My old fool's gone far, far away, I fear me;   4755
Take you his place and come and stand here near me.
     MEPHISTOPHELES *mounts the steps and stations himself on the left.*
Murmurs of the Crowd.
               A brand-new fool—new pains begin—
               Whence did he come?—how came he in?—
               The old one fell—he's spent and done—
               A barrel he—a lath this one—   4760
Emperor.   And so, ye faithful whom I love,
Be welcome here from near and far.
Ye meet beneath a favouring star;
Fortune is written for us there above.
Yet wherefore in these days, oh, say,   4765
When all our cares we'd thrust away
And wear the mummer's mask in play
And gaiety alone enjoy,
Why should we let state councils us annoy?
But since the task seems one we may not shun,   4770
All is arranged, so be it done.
Chancellor.   The highest virtue like an aureole
Circles the Emperor's head; alone and sole,

He validly can exercise it:
'Tis justice!—All men love and prize it;   4775
'Tis what all wish, scarce do without, and ask;
To grant it to his people is his task.
But ah! what good to mortal mind is sense,
What good to hearts is kindness, hands benevolence,
When through the state a fever runs and revels,   4780
And evil hatches more and more of evils?
Who views the wide realm from this height supreme,
To him all seems like an oppressive dream,
Where in confusion is confusion reigning
And lawlessness by law itself maintaining,   4785
A world of error evermore obtaining.
　　This man steals herds, a woman that,
Cross, chalice, candlestick from altar;
For many years his boastings never falter,
His skin intact, his body sound and fat.   4790
　　Now plaintiffs crowd into the hall,
The judge, encushioned, lords it over all.
Meanwhile in billows, angry, urging,
A growing tumult of revolt is surging.
Great crimes and shame may be the braggart's token,   4795
On worst accomplices he oft depends;
And "Guilty!" is the verdict often spoken
Where Innocence only itself defends.
To pieces is our world now going,
What's fitting loses all its might;   4800
How ever shall that sense be growing
Which, only, leads us to the Right?
At last will men of good intent
To briber, flatterer incline;
A judge who can impose no punishment,   4805
At last with culprits will combine.
I've painted black, and yet a denser screen
I'd rather draw before the scene.
　　Pause.
Decisions cannot be evaded;
When all do harm and none are aided,   4810
Majesty too becomes a prey.
Commander-in-Chief.　In these wild days what riots quicken!
Each strikes and he in turn is stricken,
And no command will men obey.
The citizen behind his wall,   4815
The knight upon his rocky nest,
Have sworn to last us out, and all
Maintain their power with stubborn zest.
The mercenaries, restless growing,
Blusteringly demand their pay,   4820

And if to them no more were owing,
They would be quick to run away.
Let one forbid what all men fain expect,
He's put his hand into a hornet's nest;
The empire which they should protect 4825
Lies plundered, desolate, and waste.
This furious riot no one is restraining,
Already half the world's undone;
Outside the realm kings still are reigning,
But no one thinks it his concern—not one. 4830

Treasurer.   Who will depend upon allies!
The funds they pledged as subsidies,
Like leaking pipe-borne water, do not flow.
Then, Sire, of these wide states—yours by succession—
Who now has come into possession? 4835
A new lord rules wherever one may go,
Insist on living independently;
How he keeps house, we must look on and see.
Of rights we've given up so many,
We're left without a claim to any. 4840
And as to parties, of whatever name,
There's been no trust in them of late;
They may give praise or they may blame,
Indifferent are their love and hate.
To rest them well from all their labour 4845
Lie hidden Ghibelline and Guelph.
Who is there now who'll help his neighbour?
Each has enough to help himself.
Barred are the gates where gold is stored,
And all men scratch and scrape and hoard, 4850
And empty all our coffers stay.

Steward.   What ills I too must learn to bear!
We want each day to save and spare,
And more we're needing every day,
And daily do I see new trouble growing. 4855
The cooks lack nothing, they've no woes;
For boars and stags and hares and roes
And fowls, geese, ducks, and turkeys too,
Allowances-in-kind, sure revenue,
They still are not so badly flowing. 4860
The flow of wine? That, to be sure, is slowing.
Where once in cellars cask on cask was nuzzling,
The best of brands and vintages befuzzling,
Our noble lords' eternal guzzling
Is draining every last drop out. 4865
The City Council's store must now be opened up.
A basin, bowl, is seized as drinking-cup
And under the table ends the drinking-bout.

Now I'm to pay, give each his wages.
The Jew will spare me no outrages,   4870
He'll make advances which for ages
Will put our revenues to rout.
The swine are no more fatten fed,
Pawned is the pillow on the bed,
At table we eat bread for which we owe.   4875
Emperor [*after some reflection, to* MEPHISTOPHELES].
Say, Fool, can you not add a tale of woe?
Mephistopheles.   Indeed, not I! I see this ambient splendour,
Yourself and yours!—Should one his trust surrender
Where Majesty holds undisputed sway
And ready might sweeps hostile force away?   4880
Where honest purpose holds command
And wisdom guides the active hand?
What can the powers of evil do, combining
To make a darkness where such stars are shining?
Murmurs.

> That is a rogue—full well he knows—   4885
> Sneaks in by lying—while it goes—
> I know for sure—what lurks behind—
> What then?—he has some scheme in mind—

Mephistopheles.   Where in this world does not some lack appear?
Here this, there that, but money's lacking here.   4890
One can not pick it off the floor, that's sure,
But what lies deepest, wisdom can procure.
In veins of mountains, walls far underground,
Gold coined and uncoined can be found;
And do you ask me who'll bring it to light?   4895
A man endowed with Mind's and Nature's might!
Chancellor.   Nature and Mind—don't talk to Christians thus!
Men burn up atheists, fittingly,
Because such speeches are most dangerous.
Nature is sin, and Mind is devil,   4900
They nurture doubt, in doubt they revel,
Their hybrid, monstrous progeny.
That's not for us!—Our Emperor's ancient land
Has seen arise two castes alone
Who worthily uphold his throne: 4905
The saints and knights. Firm do they stand,
Defying every tempest day by day
And taking church and state in pay.
In rabble minds that breed confusion
Revolt arises like a tide.   4910
Heretics, wizards! Imps of delusion!
They ruin town and country-side.
Them will you now with brazen juggle

Into this lofty circle smuggle,
While in a heart depraved you snuggle. 4915
Fools, wizards, heretics are near allied.
Mephistopheles. I see the learnèd man in what you say!
What you don't touch, for you lies miles away;
What you don't grasp, is wholly lost to you;
What you don't reckon, you believe not true; 4920
What you don't weigh, that has for you no weight;
What you don't coin, you're sure is counterfeit.
Emperor. That's not the way to help or aught determine.
What do you mean now with this Lenten sermon?
I'm sated of this endless "If" and "How." 4925
There is no money. Well, then, get it now!
Mephistopheles. I'll furnish what you wish and more. It's true,
It is a light task, yet the light's a burden too.
The gold lies there and yet to win it,
That is the art—who knows how to begin it? 4930
Recall those fearful times when roving bands
Poured like a deluge drowning men and lands,
How many men, so greatly did they fear,
Concealed their dearest treasure there and here.
So it was of old when mighty Rome held sway, 4935
So it was till yesterday, aye, till today.
It all lies buried in the earth, to save it;
The earth's the Emperor's, and he should have it.
Treasurer. Now for a fool, his words are noways trite.
That is, in truth, the old Imperial Right. 4940
Chancellor. Satan is laying his golden nooses;
We're dealing with no right and pious uses.
Steward. If he brings welcome gifts to court, I'm sure,
A little wrong with them I can endure.
Commander-in-Chief. Shrewd fool to promise each what will befit; 4945
Whence it may come, no soldier cares a whit.
Mephistopheles. Perhaps you think I'm trying to betray you;
Well, here's the astrologer; ask him, I pray you.
Circle on circle, hour and house he knows.
Tell us then what the heavenly aspect shows. 4950
Murmurs.
   Two rogues—each to the other known—
   Dreamer and Fool—so near the throne—
   An ancient ditty—worn and weak—
   The Fool will prompt—the Sage will speak—

Astrologer [MEPHISTOPHELES *prompting him*].
The Sun himself is gold of purest ray, 4955
The herald Mercury serves for love and pay;
Dame Venus has bewitched you all, for she,
In youth and age, looks on you lovingly.

Chaste Luna has her humours whimsical;
The strength of Mars, though striking not, threats all; 4960
And Jupiter is still the fairest star.
Saturn is great, small to our eyes and far;
Him as a metal we don't venerate,
Little in worth but heavy in his weight.
Ah, when with Sol chaste Luna doth unite, 4965
Silver with gold, the world is glad and bright.
It's easy then to get all that one seeks:
Parks, palaces, and breasts and rosy cheeks.
All these procures the highly learnèd man
Who can perform what one of us never can. 4970
Emperor. All that he says I hear twice o'er,
And yet I'm not convinced the more.
Murmurs.

> What's all this smoke—a worn-out joke—
> Astrology—or alchemy—
> An oft-heard strain—hope stirred in vain— 4975
> If he appear—a rogue is here—

Mephistopheles. They stand around and gape in wonder;
They won't believe that a great prize is found.
Of mandrakes one appears to maunder,
Another of the sable hound. 4980
What though one's wit make others prickle,
Another cry out: "Sorcery!"—
If still he sometimes feels his sole a-tickle
And his stride is not what it used to be!
You feel the secret operation 4985
Of Nature's endless ruling might,
And from earth's undermost foundation
A living trace steals up to light.
When in your limbs you're feeling twitches,
When something lays uncanny hold, 4990
Be swift to delve, dig up the riches,
There lies the fiddler, lies the gold!
Murmurs.

> My foot's like lead, can't move about—
> Cramp's in my arm—that's only gout—
> A tickle's jerking my big toe— 4995
> All down my back it hurts me so—
> From signs like these it should be clear
> The richest gold-preserve is here.

Emperor. Make haste! You shan't escape today.
Prove now your scummy, lying phrases 5000
And show at once those noble spaces.
My sword and sceptre I will put away;

If you're not lying, I will lend
My own exalted hands, this work to end,
But if you're lying, I'll send you to hell!   5005
Mephistopheles.   That pathway I could find full well!
But I've not words enough to tell
What, ownerless, is waiting everywhere.
The farmer, ploughing furrows with his share,
Turns with the clods a pot of gold;   5010
He seeks saltpetre in a clay wall, and
He finds a golden, golden roll to hold,
Scared and rejoiced, in his own wretched hand.
Who would explore the earth-hid wonder,
What vaultings must he burst asunder,   5015
What dark ways burrow through and under
Near neighbouring on the world below!
In cellars vast, preserved of old,
Plates, dishes, beakers too, of gold
He sees displayed there, row on row.   5020
There goblets, made of rubies, stand,
And if he'll put them to a use,
Beside them is an ancient juice.
Yet—you'll believe my master-hand—
The wooden staves are long since rotten;   5025
A cask of tartar has the wine begotten.
Not only gold and jewels rare,
Proud wines of noble essences are there,
Enveiled in horror and in gloom.
The wise seek here without dismay.   5030
A fool can recognize a thing by day;
In darkness mysteries are at home.
Emperor.   What is the gain of dark? You can have that!
If aught has value, it must come to light.
Who can detect a rogue in dead of night?   5035
All cows are black, and grey is every cat.
The pots down there, heavy with golden freight—
Drive your plough on, unearth them straight.
Mephistopheles.   Take hoe and spade yourself, dig on!
You'll grow great, through this peasant-toil.   5040
A herd of golden calves[1] anon
Will wrench their way out of the soil.
Then with delight, without delay,
Yourself you can, you will your love array.
A jewel in which light and colour dance   5045
Both Majesty and Beauty can enhance.
Emperor.   Be quick, be quick! How long are we to wait?
Astrologer [*as above*].   Such urgent longing, Sire, pray moderate!
Let first the motley, joyous play proceed,

[1]Cf. Exodus, 32. 3-4.

To no fair goal can minds distracted lead.   *5050*
First, penance in a calm mood doth behoove us,
Earn what's beneath us by what is above us.
Who wishes good, should first be good,
Who wishes joy, should mollify his blood,
Who asks for wine, the ripe grape should he press,   *5055*
Who hopes for miracles, more faith possess.
Emperor.   So let the time in merriment be spent!
   Ash-Wednesday's coming to our heart's content.
   Meanwhile we'll celebrate, whate'er befall,
   All the more merrily mad Carnival.   *5060*
     Trumpets, exeunt.
Mephistopheles.   How closely linked are Luck and **Merit,**
   Is something fools have never known.
   Had they the Wise Man's Stone, I swear it,
   There'd be no Wise Man for the Stone.

A SPACIOUS HALL

With adjoining apartments decorated and adorned for a masquerade.

Herald.   Don't think ye'll here see German revels,   *5065*
   A Dance of Death, of Fools and Devils!
   A cheerful festival awaits you here.
   Our ruler, when to Rome he went campaigning,
   His profit and your pleasure gaining,
   The perils of the Alps disdaining,   *5070*
   Won for himself a realm of cheer.
   First, at the holy feet bowed down,
   A grant of power he besought,
   And when he went to fetch his crown,
   The fool's-cap too for us he brought.   *5075*
   Now we are all new-born in years,
   And every well-sophisticated man
   Happily draws it over head and ears.
   Akin to crazy fools he now appears,
   Under it acting wisely as he can.   *5080*
   I see the crowds are coming yonder,
   Some pair in love, some swing asunder,
   Crowd presses crowd, like youth let out of school.
   Come in or out, let naught be daunting!
   Now too as ever holds the rule: *5085*
   A hundred thousand follies vaunting,
   The world remains one great, big fool!
Flower Girls [*song accompanied by mandolins*].
          That ye may approval tender
          We're adorned tonight in sport;
          Florentines, we joined the splendour   *5090*
          Of this festive German court.

Flowers in our chestnut tresses
We are wearing gay and bright,
Silken threads and silken jesses
Also play their part tonight; 5095
    For we think we are deserving
All your praises full and clear.
See the flowers we made, preserving
All their bloom throughout the year.
    Scraps of every tint we've taken, 5100
Each with due symmetric form;
Though each may your wit awaken,
See the whole and feel its charm.
    Fair are we in every feature,
Flower maidens gay of heart; 5105
For the ways of women's nature
Are so near akin to art.

Herald.

Let us see your baskets' riches;
Head and arms bear lovely treasure,
Bear gay beauty that bewitches. 5110
Let each choose what gives him pleasure.
Hasten till we see appearing
Gardens in each nook and alley.
Pedlars, wares, such beauty bearing,
Well the throng may round them rally. 5115

Flower Girls.

Barter in these cheery places,
But don't haggle as ye go!
And in brief and pithy phrases,
What he has, let each one know.

An Olive Branch with Fruits.

Flowery sprays I do not covet, 5120
Strife I shun, I am above it;
To my nature it is strange.
Yet I am the nation's marrow,
Pledge secure 'gainst spear and arrow,
Sign of peace where men may range. 5125
And today I'm hoping, fleetly
To adorn a fair head meetly.

A Wreath of Golden Ears.

To bedeck you, gifts of Ceres
Will be lovely, sweet, and rare;
What for us most wished and dear is 5130
Be for your adornment fair.

A Fancy Wreath.

Mallow-like, these gay-hued flowers,
From the moss, a wondrous bloom!

They are rare, in Nature's bowers,
But Dame Fashion gives them room. 5135

A Fancy Nosegay.

Name me? Theophrastus[1] never
Would a name for me assever!
If to some scarce worth a penny,
Still I hope I may please many
If she'll take whom she possesses, 5140
If she'll twine me in her tresses,
Or the fairest fate deciding,
On her heart grant me abiding.

Rosebuds, a Challenge.

Let fantastic gaudy flowers
Bloom as Fashion oft empowers, 5145
Wondrous-strange and finely moulded,
Such as Nature ne'er unfolded.
Green stalks, gold bells, look entrancing
From rich locks, their charm enhancing!
But we hide from mortal eyes. 5150
Happy he who us espies!
When anew the summer beameth
As the rosebud, kindling, gleameth,
From such bliss who'd be abstaining?
Sweet the promise and attaining 5155
Which in Flora's fair domain
Rule over vision, heart, and brain.

Under green, leafy arcades the FLOWER GIRLS *adorn their wares daintily.*

Gardeners [song accompanied by theorbos].

See the flowers sprout unhasting,
Charms around your head they're weaving!
Fruits lead not astray, deceiving; 5160
One enjoys them in the tasting.
Sun-burnt faces offer gladly
Cherries, royal plums, and peaches.
Buy! The tongue, the palate, teaches
That your eye can judge but badly. 5165
Come! The ripest fruit entices,
Eat it, with glad relish smitten;
Over a rose one poetizes,
But an apple must be bitten.
Grant us, prithee, to be mated 5170
With your youth so flowery-fair!
Neighbourly so decorated
Be our plenteous ripe ware.
Under garlands gay that wind them

---

[1]Theophrastus (born about 390 B.C.) has been called the father of botany.

In adorned and leafy bowers,   *5175*
All are here for you to find them:
Buds and leaves and fruit and flowers.

*Midst alternating songs, accompanied by guitars and theorbos,
both choruses continue to set their wares out attractively in
tiers and to offer them for sale.*

MOTHER AND DAUGHTER.

Mother.

Maiden, when thou cam'st to light,
Little caps I wove thee:
Body tender, face so bright,   *5180*
How they made me love thee!
Thought of thee as quickly won,
Wedded to the richest son,
Thought as wife wouldst prove thee.
Ah, already many a year   *5185*
Hence, unused, has fleeted;
Motley host of wooers here
Swiftly past has speeded.
With the one didst nimbly dance,
Gav'st the other nudge and glance   *5190*
Which he might have heeded.
Every fête that we might plan,
Vain it was to match one;
Forfeit games and "Hindmost Man,"
Naught availed to snatch one.   *5195*
Each fool wears today his cap;
Darling, open now thy lap,
Haply wilt thou catch one.

*Girl playmates, young and fair, join the group; a confidential
chatter is heard. Fishers and fowlers with nets, fishing-rods,
limed twigs, and other gear enter and mingle with the pretty
girls. Reciprocal attempts to win, catch, escape, and hold fast
give opportunity for the most agreeable dialogues.*

Woodcutters [*enter boisterously and boorishly*].

Make room! A clearing!
Spaces for revel!   *5200*
Trees that we level
Crash in their falling;
And when we're hauling,
We hit what's nearing.
Our praises grudge not,   *5205*
This truth pray nourish:
Did rough folk drudge not
In every county,

Could fine folk flourish,
Come by their bounty,   5210
However they fretted?
Learn this in season!
For ye'd be freezing,
Had we not sweated.

Pulcinelli[1] [awkward, almost silly].

Oh, fools that ye are,   5215
Born bent, and we are
The really clever,
Loads bearing never.
Our caps and jackets
And rags are packets   5220
Quite light to carry.
And we are merry,
Forever lazy,
In slippers easy,
In them to shuffle   5225
Through market and scuffle,
To gape at the pother,
Croak at each other.
Heeding the racket,
Through crowds that pack it,   5230
Like eels we're slipping,
Together tripping,
All mad together.
We care not whether
Ye blame or praise us,   5235
Nothing can faze us.

Parasites [fawningly lustful].

Of you, stout porters,
And your supporters,
The charcoal-burners,
We are not spurners.   5240
For all the bending
And nods assenting,
Phrases too flowing,
And two-ways blowing,
They're warming and chilling   5245
Just as one's feeling,
Yet what the profit?
Heaven might send fire,
Enormous, dire,
But, then, what of it,   5250
Were there no billets
Or coal in barrows
To grill your skillets

[1]Clowns.

Through to their marrows?
There's sizzling, broiling,   5255
There's bubbling, boiling.
True taster, picker,
The platter-licker,
He smells the roasting,
He sniffs the fishes,   5260
With gusto accosting
His patron's dishes.

A Drunken Man [*maudlin*].

'Sdeath today to all my worry!
For I feel so frank and free;
Fresh delight and ditties merry,   5265
These I brought along with me.
So I'm drinking, drink ye, drink ye!
Clink your glasses, clink ye, clink ye!
Ye behind there, now come on!
Clink your glasses, so it's done.   5270
    Angrily my wife shrieked loudly,
Sneering at my piebald suit,
And although I swaggered proudly,
"Scarecrow, scarecrow!" did she hoot.
Yet I'm drinking, drink ye, drink ye!   5275
Clink your glasses, cling ye, clink ye!
Clink them, scarecrows, every one!
Clinking, clinking, so it's done.
    Say not that my way I'm losing,
I am where my worries fade.   5280
If mine host lend not, refusing,
Hostess lends, or eke the maid.
Still I drink on! Drink ye, drink ye!
Up, ye others! Clink ye, clink ye!
Each to each! Thus on and on!   5285
Now methinks that it is done.
    How and where I'm pleasure plying,
Still may it always be at hand.
Let me lie where I am lying,
For I can no longer stand.   5290

Chorus.

Brothers all, now drink ye, drink ye!
Toast ye gaily, clink ye, clink ye!
Sit ye firm on bench and board!
Under the table lies one floored.

The HERALD *announces various poets, poets by nature, courtly
and knightly minstrels, sentimentalists as well as enthusiasts.
In the throng of competitors of all kinds no one allows another
to begin a speech. One slips past with a few words.*

Satirist.

Know ye what my soul as poet   5295
Chiefly would delight and cheer?
Sing and say, if I dared do it,
That which none would like to hear.

*The poets of night and churchyards excuse themselves, because
they are just engaged in a most interesting conversation with a
newly-arisen vampire, and from it a new school of poetry may
perhaps arise; the* HERALD *is obliged to accept their apologies
and meanwhile he calls forth Greek mythology which, in modern masks, loses neither its character nor its charm.*

THE GRACES.

Aglaia.

Charm we're bringing into living,
So be charming in your giving!   5300

Hegemone.

Charming be ye in receiving!
Lovely is desire's achieving.

Euphrosyne.

And when peacefully ye're living,
Be most charming your thanksgiving!

THE FATES.

Atropos.

I, the eldest Fate, from yonder   5305
For the while to spin am bidden.
Much to think of, much to ponder,
In life's tender thread is hidden.
    Finest flax I winnow featly
That your thread be supple, tender;   5310
Fingers shrewd will twirl it neatly,
Make it even, smooth, and slender.
    Ye who, warm with dance and pleasure,
All too wanton, snatch a token,
Think that this thread has a measure,   5315
Have a care! It might be broken.

Clotho.

    Know ye that the shears were lately
Given to my care to ply;
For our Ancient's conduct greatly
Did, in truth, none edify.   5320
    She drags on most useless spinnings
On and on in air and light,
Promise of most glorious winnings

Clips and drags to realms of night.
    Yet when I was young and reigning,   *5325*
I, too, erred oft in those years;
Now I yield to curb restraining,
In their case I keep the shears.
    So I gladly wear a bridle,
And this scene with joy survey.   *5330*
In these hours so gay and idle,
    Revel, riot, sport, and play!

Lachesis.

    Unto me, alone discerning,
Was the thread's control decreed;
For my reel, forever turning,   *5335*
Never erred through too great speed.
    Threads are coming, threads are reeling,
Each one in its course I guide;
None may slip from spindle wheeling,
Each must in its orbit glide.   *5340*
    Could I once forget in leisure,
For the world I'd fear with pain;
Hours, they count, and years, they measure,
And the Weaver takes the skein.

Herald.   Those coming now, ye'd never recognize them,   *5345*
However learned ye were in ancient letters.
To look at them—the world's worst ill-abettors—
Ye'd call them welcome guests and prize them.
    They are the Furies, no one will believe us.
Fair are they, well-made, friendly, young moreover;   *5350*
But if ye lend them ear, ye will discover
How serpent-like such doves can wound and grieve us.
    Malicious are they—true!—and with effront'ry,
But now when each fool boasts his reputation,
They too ask not angelic exaltation;   *5355*
They know they are the pests of town and country.

THE FURIES.

Alecto.   What boots it? For to trust us ye'll not stickle,
For each is young and fair, a coaxing kitten.
If one among you by a girl is smitten,
We shall not cease, his ears to scratch and tickle,   *5360*
    Until we dare to tell him, to his loathing,
That for this man and that one she is primping,
Crooked in her back, all wit doth lack, and limping,
And if betrothed to him, she's good-for-nothing!
    And the betrothed—we know the way to sting her.   *5365*
Why scarce a week ago her precious lover
To such-and-such a girl spoke basely of her;
Though they be reconciled, a sting will linger.

Megaera.   That's but a jest! For when they once are married,
  I go to work in every case to fritter   5370
  The fairest bliss away with fancies bitter.
  The moods of men are varied, hours are varied.
    None holds embraced what his desire has chosen,
  But seeks a More-desired with foolish yearning
  And from long-wonted, highest blessings turning,   5375
  Flees a warm love and tries to warm a frozen.
    I'm skilled in managing such household troubles,
  And Asmodeus,[1] comrade true, I summon
  To scatter strife betimes twixt man and woman;
  Thus I destroy the human race in couples.   5380
Tisiphone.
        Poison, steel—not words malicious—
        Mix I, whet I, for the traitor.
        Lov'st thou others? Sooner, later,
        Overwhelms thee ruin vicious.
        What the sweetest moment offers,   5385
        Turns perforce to wormwood galling!
        Here no haggling, pulling, hauling;
        As one sins, one always suffers.
        None shall sing about forgiving!
        To the rocks my cause I'm crying.   5390
        Echo, hark! "Revenge!" replying.
        For the unstable, death! not living!

Herald.   Now, if it please you, stand aside a pace,
  For what comes now is not your kind or race.
  Ye see a mountain pressing through the throng,   5395
  Its flanks with brilliant housings proudly hung,
  A head with long tusks, snake-like snout below.
  A mystery! but soon the key I'll show.
  A dainty woman on his neck is sitting
  And with her wand subjects him to her bidding;   5400
  Another stands aloft, sublime to see,
  Girt by a radiance dazzling, blinding me.
  Beside them chained, two noble women near,
  Fearful the one, the other blithe of cheer.
  One longs for freedom and one feels she's free.   5405
  Let each declare now who she be.
Fear.
        Lamps and lights and torches smoking
        Through this turmoil gleam around;
        Midst these faces, shamming, joking,
        I, alas, in chains am bound.   5410
        Hence, ye throngs absurdly merry!
        I mistrust your grins with right;

[1] A spirit of strife; cf. Tobit, 3. 8.

Every single adversary
Presses nearer in this night.
   Friend turned foe would here bewray me,   *5415*
But his mask I know well. Stay,
Yonder's one who wished to slay me;
Now revealed, he slinks away.
   Through the wide world I would wander,
Following every path that led,   *5420*
But destruction threatens yonder,
Holds me fast twixt gloom and dread.

Hope.   Hail, belovèd sisters, hail!
Though today and yesterday
Ye have loved this maskers' play,   *5425*
Yet tomorrow ye'll unveil.
This I know of you quite surely.
If beneath the torches' flaring
We can't find our special pleasure,
Yet in days of cheerful leisure,   *5430*
As our will doth bid us purely,
Now in groups, now singly faring,
We'll roam over lovely leas,
Resting, doing, as we please,
In a life no cares assailing,   *5435*
Naught forgoing, never failing.
Everywhere as welcome guest
Let us enter, calm in mind,
Confident that we shall find
Somewhere, certainly, the best.   *5440*

Prudence.

Two of man's chief foes, behold them,
Fear and Hope, in fetters mated;
From this crowd I'll keep and hold them.
Room, make room! Ye're liberated.
   I conduct the live colossus,   *5445*
See the burden that it carries,
And the steepest pass it crosses,
Step by step, and never wearies.
   But upon the summit of it
Yonder goddess with her pinions   *5450*
Broad and agile, seeking profit,
Turns to spy all man's dominions.
   Girt is she by splendour glorious
Shining far along all courses,
Victory her name! Victorious   *5455*
Goddess of all active forces.

Zoïlo-Thersites.[1]   Ho, ho! Just right I've reached this spot,

---

[1]Goethe combines in one figure Zoilus, who defamed Homer, and Thersites, who defamed Agamemnon (see *Iliad*, ii).

We're one and all a wretched lot!
And yet the goal I've chosen me
Is she up there, Dame Victory.   *5460*
She with her snowy wings spread out
Thinks she's an eagle, past all doubt,
And wheresoever she may stir,
Thinks men and lands belong to her.
But when some glorious deed is done,   *5465*
At once I put my armour on.
Up with the low, down with the high,
The crookèd straight, the straight awry—
That, only, makes me feel aglow,
And on this earth I'll have it so.   *5470*
Herald.   Then take thou that, a master-blow
From my good staff, thou wretched hound,
Then straightway writhe and twist around!—
How swift the two-fold dwarfish clump
Balls up into a loathsome lump!—   *5475*
But see! lump turns to egg—a wonder!
Puffs itself up and bursts asunder.
Thence comes a pair of twins to earth,
Adder and bat—a wondrous birth!
On in the dust one crawls and creeps,   *5480*
The black one round the ceiling sweeps,
And where they haste to join again,
To be the third I am not fain.

Murmuring.

      Come! they're dancing now back there!—
      No! I want to flee from here—   *5485*
      Feel ye not the ghost-like breed
      Creeping, wheeling, round us speed?—
      Something whizzes past my hair—
      My foot felt a something there—
      Still not one of us is harmed—   *5490*
      But we all have been alarmed—
      Now all ruined is our fun—
      This, the beasts! they wanted done.

Herald.   Since on me, when masquerading,
Herald's duties ye've been lading,   *5495*
Stern I guard the portal, wary
Lest into your revels merry
Aught may slink of harmful savour;
Neither do I shrink nor waver.
Yet I fear lest spectres erring   *5500*
Through the windows may be faring;
If black arts and spooks beset you,

From them I could never get you.
Of the dwarf we were suspicious.
Lo! Back there a pageant issues!   5505
As a herald, it's my duty
To explain those forms of beauty,
But what's past all comprehending,
For that I've no explanation.
Help ye, all, my education!—   5510
See what hitherward is tending!
Lo! a four-yoked chariot splendid
Through the crowd its way has wended,
Yet the crowd it does not sunder;
I can see no crushing yonder.   5515
In the distance colours shimmer,
Stars gay-coloured beam and flimmer,
Magic-lantern-like they glimmer.
All storm on as to assault.
Clear the way! I shudder!
A Boy Charioteer.   Halt!   5520
Steeds, let now your wings fall idle,
Feel the well-accustomed bridle;
Master self as you I master;
When I thrill you, on! and faster!
Let us honour now these spaces!   5525
Look around at all the faces;
More and more admirers cluster.
Herald, up! Take wonted muster!
Ere we flee, tell thou our stories,
Name us and describe and show us;   5530
For we all are allegories,
Therefore thou shouldst surely know us.
Herald.   There's no name I could ascribe thee,
But I rather might describe thee.
Boy Charioteer.   Try it then!
Herald.   I must avow,   5535
Firstly, young and fair art thou.
A half-grown boy thou art; but women rather
Would see thee full-grown altogether.
It seems that thou wilt be a fickle wooer,
Right from the start a real undoer.   5540
Boy Charioteer.   That's well worth hearing! On with thee,
Discover now the riddle's happy key.
Herald.   Thy flashing ebon eyes, locks black and glowing,
More radiant from the jewelled diadem!
And what a graceful robe doth stream   5545
From shoulder down to buskin flowing,
With glittering gaud and purple hem!
Now might we flouting "Maiden!" deem thee,

Yet, good or ill as it might be,
Already maidens would esteem thee.   5550
They'd teach thee soon thine A B C.
Boy Charioteer.   And yonder one, in splendour glowing,
Who proudly sits on chariot throne?
Herald.   A king he seems, of wealth o'erflowing;
Happy the man who has his favour won!   5555
He has naught more to earn and capture,
He swift espies where aught's amiss,
And has in giving more pure rapture
Than in possessing and in bliss.
Boy Charioteer.   To stop with this will not avail;   5560
Thou must describe him in far more detail.
Herald.   There's no describing Dignity.
The healthy, full-moon face I see,
The lips so full, the cheeks so blooming
Beneath the turban's beauty looming,   5565
The flowing robe he's richly wearing—
What shall I say of such a bearing?
He seems a ruler known to me.
Boy Charioteer.   Plutus,[1] the god of wealth, is he.
Hither he comes in gorgeous trim;   5570
Sorely the Emperor longs for him.
Herald.   Now thine own *What* and *How* relate to me!
Boy Charioteer.   I am Profusion, I am Poesy!
The poet who's attained his goal
When he's poured out his inmost soul.   5575
I too am rich with untold pelf
And value me the peer of Plutus' self,
Adorn, enliven, make his revels glow;
And what he lacks, that I bestow.
Herald.   Bragging becomes thee charmingly,   5580
But now thine arts, pray, let us see.
Boy Charioteer.   Here see me snap my fingers. Lo!
Around the chariot gleam and glow!
And now a necklace of pearls appears!
      Continuing to snap his fingers in every direction.
Here spangled gold for neck and ears   5585
And flawless comb and coronet
And rings with precious jewels set.
Flamelets I scatter too in turn,
Waiting to see where they may burn.
Herald.   How the dear mob is snatching, seizing,   5590
Even the giver almost squeezing!
Dream-like he's scatt'ring gems where all
Are snatching in the spacious hall.
But what is this? A brand-new juggle!

[1]Faust, so disguised.

However busily one snatch and struggle,　　　　　5595
His trouble really does not pay;
The gifts take wing and fly away.
The pearls are loosened from their band
And beetles scrabble in his hand;
He shakes them off, the poor biped,　　　　　5600
And then they hum around his head.
Others, instead of solid things,
Catch butterflies with flimsy wings.
How much he promises, the knave!
Glitter of gold was all he gave.　　　　　5605

Boy Charioteer.
Of masks, I note, thou canst proclaim each feature.
Beneath the shell to fathom out the nature
Is not the herald's courtly task;
A keener eye for that we ask.
But feuds I shun, if only in suggestion;　　　　　5610
To thee, lord, I address my speech and question.
　　　Turning to PLUTUS.
Didst thou not give me charge supreme
Over the four-yoked, whirlwind team?
Guide I not happily as thou leadest?
Am I not everywhere thou biddest?　　　　　5615
And on bold pinions did I not for thee
Bear off the palm of victory?
However oft for thee as I've contended,
Success was ever my portion; and when now
The laurel decorates thy brow,　　　　　5620
Did not my hand and art entwine and blend it?

Plutus.　If need be that I testify, then hear it!
I say with joy: Thou art spirit of my spirit!
Thy deeds are ever after my own will;
Rich as I am, thou art richer still.　　　　　5625
Thy service to reward in fitting measure,
The laurel more than all my crowns I treasure.
This truth in all men's hearts I would instil:
In thee, dear son, I have much pleasure.

Boy Charioteer [*to the crowd*].
The greatest gifts my hand deals out,　　　　　5630
Lo! I have scattered roundabout.
On this head and on that one too
There glows a flamelet that I threw.
From one to other head it skips,
To this one cleaves, from that one slips;　　　　　5635
It seldom flares up like a plume,
And swiftly beams in transient bloom.
Ere many its worth recognize,
It burns out mournfully and dies.

Women's Chatter.

There on the chariot sits a man   5640
Who surely is a charlatan,
Hunched up behind, a perfect clown,
By thirst and hunger so worn down
As naught before, and if ye'd pinch,
He has no flesh to feel and flinch.   5645

Starveling.[1]   Away from me, ye odious crew!
Welcome, I know, I never am to you.
When hearth and home were women's zone,
As Avaritia I was known.
Then did our household thrive throughout,   5650
For much came in and naught went out!
Zealous was I for chest and bin;
'Twas even said my zeal was sin.
But since in years most recent and depraving
Woman is wont no longer to be saving   5655
And, like each tardy payer, collars
Far more desires than she has dollars,
The husband now has much to bore him;
Wherever he looks, debts loom before him.
Her spinning-money is turned over   5660
To grace her body or her lover;
Better she feasts and drinks still more
With all her wretched lover-corps.
Gold charms me all the more for this:
Male's now my gender, I am Avarice!   5665
Leader of the Women.
With dragons be the dragon avaricious,
It's naught but lies, deceiving stuff!
To stir up men he comes, malicious,
Whereas men now are troublesome enough.
Women [en masse].

The scarecrow! Box his ears, the japer!   5670
Why does the wooden cross threat here?
As if his ugly face we'd fear!
Dragons are made of wood and paper.
Have at him, crowd him, scoff and jeer!

Herald.   Peace! By my staff! Peace or begone!   5675
And yet my aid's scarce needed here.
In yonder space so quickly won
See the grim monsters moving on,
Swift to unfold their pinions' double pair.
The dragons shake themselves in ire;   5680
Their scaly jaws spew smoke and fire.

[1]Mephistopheles.

The crowd has fled, the place is clear.
   PLUTUS *descends from his chariot.*
Herald. He's stepping down, what royal grace!
  He becks, the dragons move apace;
  Down from the chariot they've borne the chest   5685
  With all its gold, and Avarice thereon.
  There at his feet it stands at rest;
  A marvel how it was ever done.
Plutus [*to the* CHARIOTEER].
  Now art thou rid of thy too heavy burden,
  Free art thou! Off to thine own sphere and guerdon!   5690
  Thy sphere's not here! Here shapes most hideous,
  Distorted, motley, wild, press in on us.
  Where thou see'st naught but lovely clarity,
  Where thine own vision is enough for thee,
  Thither where only Good and Beauty please and wait, 5695
  Away to Solitude! there thine own world create!
Boy Charioteer. Thus I esteem myself a worthy envoy of thee,
  And as my nearest kinsman do I love thee.
  Where thou art, Plenty is; where I remain,
  Each feels himself enriched by glorious gain.   5700
  Oft in the clash of life a man doth waver:
  Shall he in thee or me seek favour?
  Thy followers can idly rest, it's true;
  Who follows me always has work to do.
  My deeds in darkness never are concealed;   5705
  If I but breathe, I am at once revealed.
  And so, farewell! My bliss thou grantest me,
  But whisper low and I am back with thee.
    Exit as he came.
Plutus. It's time now to unloose the precious metals.
  I strike the padlocks with the herald's rod.   5710
  The chest flies open! See in brazen kettles
  A boiling, bubbling up of golden blood.
  First, ornaments of crowns, chains, rings will follow!
  Seething, it threatens all to melt and swallow.

Alternating Cries from the crowd.
        See here! and there! how treasures brim!   5715
        The chest is filling to the rim—
        Vessels of gold are grilling there,
        And coins in rolls are milling there.—
        As if just minted, ducats jump,
        Oh, how my heart begins to thump!—   5720
        All that I want I see and more!
        They're rolling there along the floor.—
        It's yours, they say—appease your itch,
        Just stoop a bit and rise up rich.—

Swift as the lightning, we, the rest,   5725
Will take possession of the chest.

Herald.   What does this mean? Ye silly folk!
It's but a masquerading joke.
Naught more can be desired tonight;
Think ye we give you gold outright?   5730
Verily in this game for such
As ye, yes, vouchers were too much.
Blockheads! A pleasant show, forsooth,
Ye take at once as solid truth.
What's truth to you?—Delusion vain,   5735
Catch where ye can, ye clutch amain.
Plutus, chief mummer, hero of the masque,
Drive from the field this folk, I ask.
Plutus.   Thy staff is apt for it, I see;
Lend it a little while to me.   5740
I'll dip it swift in seething glare.
Now, on your guard, ye masks, beware!
Snaps, sparks, and flashes, see it throw!
Thy staff already is aglow.
Whoever crowds too close to me   5745
I'll straightway singe relentlessly.
And now upon my rounds I'll go.
Cries and Crowding.
       Alas! it's up with us, oh woe!—
       Away, escape! Escape who can!—
       Fall back, fall back, thou hindmost man!   5750
       Hot sparks are flying in my face.—
       I stagger from the glowing mace!—
       Lost are we all, we all are lost!—
       Back, back, ye masquerading host!
       Back, senseless mob, don't come so nigh!   5755
       Had I but wings, away I'd fly!—

Plutus.   Backward the circle round us shrinks,
And no one has been scorched, methinks.
Scattered by fright,
The crowd takes flight.   5760
Yet, symbol of the reign of law,
A ring invisible I'll draw.
Herald.   A glorious deed hast done tonight.
How can I thank thy sapient might?
Plutus.   My noble friend, be patient yet;   5765
Many a tumult still doth threat.
Avaritia.   Here, if we like, we can look on
And view this circle at our leisure;
To stand in front always gives women pleasure

Where gaping or where nibbling's to be done.   5770
Not yet so wholly rusty are my senses
But that a woman fair is always fair;
And since today it costs me no expenses,
We'll go a-courting with an easy air.
Because, though, in such over-crowded places   5775
Not every ear distinctly hears all phrases,
I'll wisely try—I hope not vainly—
In pantomime to show my meaning plainly.
Hand, foot, and gesture will not now suffice,
So I must use a farcical device.   5780
I'll treat the gold as were it mere wet clay;
This metal I can turn in any way.
Herald.   The skinny fool! What is that he began?
Can he have humour, such a starveling man?
He's kneading all the gold to dough;   5785
Beneath his hands it's soft, yet though
He squeeze it, roll it, as he will,
Misshapen is it even still.
He turns to the women there, and they
All scream and want to get away,   5790
With gestures of disgust and loathing.
The mischievous rogue will stop at nothing.
I fear a joyous man is he
When he's offended decency.
Through silence I'll not lend my backing;   5795
Give me my staff to send him packing.
Plutus.   What threatens from without he does not see.
Let him go on with his tom-fooling;
There'll be no room soon for his drooling;
The Law is mighty, mightier Necessity.   5800

Tumult and Song.
              The wild host comes in all its might,
              From woodland dell and mountain height.
              They stride along—resist who can!
              They celebrate their great god Pan.
              They know indeed what none can guess;   5805
              Into the vacant ring they press.

Plutus.   I know you well, you and your great god Pan!
Together ye've performed a daring plan.
I know right well what is not known to all
And ope the circle duly to their call.   5810
Oh, may good fortune be decreed them!
The strangest thing may now befall,
They know not where their steps may lead them;
They have not looked ahead at all.

Savage Song.

5815

Ye folk bedight, ye tinsel-stuff!
They're coming rude, they're coming rough;
In lofty leap, in speedy chase,
They come, a stout and sturdy race.

Fauns.   The faun-host flocks
  In merry round,   5820
  The oak-wreath bound
  On curly locks;
  A pair of finely pointed ears
  Out from the curly head appears,
  A stubby nose, face broad and flat.   5825
  With women no one's harmed by that;
  And if the faun his paw advance,
  The fairest will hardly refuse to dance.

A Satyr.   The satyr now comes hopping in
  With foot of goat and withered shin;   5830
  He needs to have them wiry-thin,
  For chamois-like on mountain heights
  To look around him he delights.
  Braced by the air of freedom then,
  He jeers at children, women, and men,   5835
  Who deep in the valley's smoke and stew
  Fondly imagine they're living too,
  While pure and undisturbed and lone
  The world up there is all his own.

Gnomes.   Tripping, a little crowd appears.   5840
  They do not like to go in pairs;
  In mossy garb, with lamplet bright,
  They move commingling, swift and light,
  Where each his task can best perform,
  Like firefly-ants, a crowding swarm.   5845
  They scurry, busy, here and there,
  Bustling and working everywhere.
    Kinship to kind "Good-men" we own,
  As surgeons of the rocks are known,
  The mountains high, go sapping them,   5850
  The swelling veins, go tapping them;
  Metals we hurl on pile on pile,
  With cheery hail—"Good Luck!"—the while,
  A greeting well-meant through and through.
  We're friends of all good men and true.   5855
  Yet gold we bring and gold reveal
  That men may pander and may steal,
  That iron fail not his proud hand
  Who ever wholesale murder planned.
  He whom these three commandments fail to bother   5860

Will pay no heed to any other.
For all that we are not to blame;
As we are patient, so be ye the same!
Giants.   "The Wild Men of the Woods"—their name,
In the Hartz Mountains known to fame.   5865
In nature's nakedness and might
They come, each one of giant height,
A fir tree's trunk in each right hand,
Around their loins a bulging band,
Apron of twigs and leaves uncouth;   5870
Such guards the Pope has not, in truth.
Nymphs in chorus [surrounding GREAT PAN].[1]
He's really here!—
Of this world-sphere
The All we fête
In Pan the Great.   5875
Ye gayest ones, surround him here,
Dance madly, hov'ring round him here,
For since he's solemn and yet kind,
Man's happiness he has in mind.
Even beneath the azure, vaulted roof   5880
He ever kept slumber far aloof;
Yet purling brooks seek him in quest
And soft airs cradle him to rest.
And when he sleeps at mid of day,
No leaflet stirs upon its spray;   5885
Health-giving plants with balsam rare
Pervade the still and silent air.
Then may the nymph in joy not leap
And where she stood, she falls asleep.
But when at unexpected hour   5890
His voice is heard in all its power,
Like crack of lightning, roar of sea,
Then no one knows which way to flee.
Brave warriors into panic break,
And in the tumult heroes quake.   5895
Hence honour to whom honour's due,
Hail him who led us here to you!

Deputation of Gnomes [to GREAT PAN].
            When the treasure, rich and shining,
            Winds through clefts its thread-like way
            And naught but the rod's divining   5900
            Can its labyrinths display,
               Troglodytes in caverns spacious,
            Under vaulted roofs we bide,
            While in day's pure air thou, gracious,

[1]A mask of the Emperor.

All the treasures dost divide.   5905
  We discover here quite near us
Treasure rich, a fountain vein,
Aptly promising to bear us
More than one could hope to gain.
  This thou mayst achieve at pleasure,   5910
Take it, Sire, into thy care!
In thy hands doth every treasure
Yield the whole world blessings rare.

Plutus [to THE HERALD].
  We must possess ourselves, serene in spirit,
And come what may must confidently bear it.   5915
Still hast thou shown indeed a valiant soul,
But soon a thing most horrible will try it.
Stoutly men now and later will deny it.
Inscribe it truly in thy protocol.

Herald [grasping the staff which PLUTUS keeps in his hand].
  The dwarfs lead Pan, the great god, nigher,   5920
Quite gently, to the well of fire.
It seethes up from the deepest maw,
Then down again the flames withdraw,
And gloomy gapes the open jaw.
The foam and flame roll up again.   5925
Complacent doth Great Pan remain,
Rejoicing in the wondrous sight,
While pearls of foam spurt left and right.
How can he in such wizardry confide?
He stoops down low to look inside.—   5930
But now his beard is falling in!—
Whose can it be, that beardless chin?
His hand conceals it from our gaze.—
A great mishap is taking place.
The beard flies backward, all ablaze,   5935
And kindles wreath and head and breast;
Turned into sorrow is the jest.—
To quench the fire they race and run,
But free from flames there is not one,
And as they slap and beat it too,   5940
They only stir up flames anew;
In fiery flames entangled, caught,
A maskers' group is burned to naught.
  But hark! what news is spreading here
From mouth to mouth, from ear to ear!   5945
O evermore ill-fated Night,
How thou hast turned our bliss to blight!
Tomorrow morn will everywhere
Proclaim what no one likes to hear.
Yet everywhere I'll hear the cry: 5950

"The Emperor suffers agony!"
Oh, would that something else were true!
The Emperor burns, his escort too.
Accursed who led him so astray,
Who bound about them resined spray,   5955
Raging around with boisterous song,
Bringing to ruin all the throng.
O Youth, O Youth, and wilt thou never
Keep within proper bounds thy pleasure?
O Highness, Highness, wilt thou never   5960
Use might and reason in due measure?
    The mimic woods are catching fire,
The tongues of flame lick higher, higher,
Where netted rafters interlace;
A fiery doom threats all the place.   5965
Now overflows our cup of woe,
And who shall save us I don't know.
The ashes of a night will be
All that was once rich majesty.
Plutus.   Terror has enough been spread,   5970
Let us now bring help instead!
Strike, thou hallowed staff, the ground
Till earth quiver and resound!
Fill thyself, O spacious air,
With cool fragrance everywhere.   5975
Hither come, around us streaming,
Mist and clouds with moisture teeming,
Come and veil the rampant flame;
Cloudlets, whirl ye, drizzling, purl ye,
Hither glide ye, softly drenching,   5980
Quelling everywhere and quenching;
Ye, who're moist, allaying, bright'ning,
Change to harmless summer lightning
All this empty fiery game!
And when spirits threat and lower,   5985
Then let Magic show its power!

PLEASURE GARDEN
MORNING SUN

EMPEROR. COURTIERS.

FAUST *and* MEPHISTOPHELES, *dressed becomingly, not conspicu-
ously, according to the mode; both kneel.*
Faust.   Pardon you, Sire, the flames and wizardry?
Emperor [*beckoning him to rise*].
Many such pleasantries I would like to see.
Presto! I stood within a glowing zone,

It seemed almost Pluto and I were one.   *5990*
In coal-black night and yet with fires aglow
Lay an abyss. From many a vent below
Thousands of savage flames were upward whirling,
Into a single vault above me swirling,
Licking their tongues of flame against the dome's far height   *5995*
Which now appeared and now was lost to sight.
Far, far away, through spiral shafts of flame
Peoples I saw, in moving files they came,
In a wide circle pressing on and on
And paying homage as they've always done.   *6000*
Courtiers I recognized amid the splendour,
I seemed a prince over many a salamander.
Mephistopheles.   That are you, Sire, since every element
Doth own you absolute to all intent.
Obedient have you now proved fire to be.   *6005*
Where waves heave wildest, leap into the sea!
The pearl-strewn bottom you will scarcely tread
Ere a glorious billowing dome forms overhead.
You'll see there light-green rolling billows swelling,
Their edges purple, forming the fairest dwelling   *6010*
Round you, the centre. Wander at your will,
The palaces attend you even still.
The very walls rejoice in life, in teeming,
Arrowy swarming, hither, thither streaming.
Sea-wonders push and dart along to win   *6015*
The new soft glow but none may enter in.
The dragons, mottled, golden-scaled, are playing;
There gapes the shark but you laugh at his baying.
Though now the court surrounds you in delight,
Still such a throng has never met your sight.   *6020*
Yet long you're not deprived of forms endearing;
The Nereids come curiously nearing
Your splendid palace in the cool of ocean,
The young with fish-like, shy, and wanton motion,
The old ones prudent. Thetis learns of this,   *6025*
Gives her new Peleus hand and mouth to kiss.—
The seat, then, on Olympus' wide domain . . .
Emperor.   Over the air I leave to you to reign;
Quite soon enough does one ascend that throne.
Mephistopheles.   Earth, Lord Supreme, already is your own.   *6030*
Emperor.   What brought you here to ravish us with sights
Directly out of the Arabian Nights?
If like Scheherazade you are inventive,
Be sure of every favour and incentive.
Be near whenever—as is oft the case—   *6035*
I grutch at this poor world of commonplace.
Steward [*enters in haste*].   Ah, Most Serene, in all my life I never

Thought I could give you news of such high favour
As this which richly blesses me
And drives me here almost in ecstasy.   6040
Bill upon bill has now been squared,
The usurers' talons have been pared.
From hellish worry I am free!
In Heaven life can not happier be.
Commander-in-Chief [*follows in haste*].
  Arrears are paid as they were due   6045
  And all the army's pledged anew;
  The soldier feels his blood made over.
  Landlords and wenches are in clover.
Emperor. How free you breathe, with breasts so lightened!
  Your wrinkled foreheads, how they're brightened!   6050
  How you come in with eager speed!
Treasurer [*appears*]. Inquire of these who did the deed.
Faust. It's for the Chancellor to tell the story.
Chancellor [*approaching slowly*].
  I'm blessed enough now when I'm old and hoary.
  So hear and see the fateful, solemn leaf   6055
  Which into joy has transformed all our grief.
    He reads.
  "To all whom it concerns, let it be known:
  Who hath this note, a thousand crowns doth own.
  As certain pledge thereof shall stand
  Vast buried treasure in the Emperor's land.   6060
  Provision has been made that ample treasure,
  Raised straightway, shall redeem the notes at pleasure."
Emperor. I sense a crime, a monstrous, cheating lure!
  Who dared to forge the Emperor's signature?
  Is still unpunished such a breach of right?   6065
Treasurer. Remember, Sire, yourself it was last night
  That signed the note. You stood as mighty Pan,
  The Chancellor came and spoke in words that ran:
  "A lofty festal joy do for thyself attain:
  Thy people's weal—a few strokes of the pen!"   6070
  These did you make, then thousand-fold last night
  Conjurors multiplied what you did write;
  And that straightway the good might come to all,
  We stamped at once the series, large and small;
  Tens, twenties, thirties, hundreds, all are there.   6075
  You can not think how glad the people were.
  Behold your city, once half-dead, decaying,
  Now full of life and joy, and swarming, playing!
  Although your name has blessed the world of yore,
  So gladly was it never seen before.   6080
  The alphabet is really now redundant;
  In this sign each is saved to bliss abundant.

Emperor.   My people take it for good gold, you say?
  In camp, in court, sufficient as full pay?
  Although amazed, still I must give assent.   6085
Steward.   The flight of notes we could nowise prevent;
  Like lightning notes were scattered on the run.
  The changers' shops open wide to everyone;
  And there all notes are honoured, high and low,
  With gold and silver—at a discount, though.   6090
  From there to butcher, baker, tavern hasting,
  One-half the world seems thinking but of feasting,
  The other in new raiment struts and crows;
  The draper cuts the cloth, the tailor sews.
  In cellars "Long live the Emperor!" is the toasting;   6095
  There platters clatter, there they're boiling, roasting.
Mephistopheles.   Who all alone will down the terrace stray
  Perceives the fairest in superb array;
  With her proud peacock-fan she hides one eye
  And looking for a note goes simpering by;   6100
  More swiftly than through eloquence and wit
  Love's richest favour can be gained by it.
  With purse and scrip one is no longer harried.
  A notelet in one's breast is lightly carried;
  With billets-doux quite snugly will it nestle.   6105
  The priest bears it devoutly in his missal.
  The soldier, that he may the faster haste,
  Lightens the girdle quickly round his waist.
  Pardon, Your Majesty, if I may seem
  To mete a lofty work but slight esteem.   6110
Faust.   Treasures in superfluity still sleep
  Within your borders, buried deep,
  And lie unused. Thought in its widest measure
  Gives the most meagre bounds to such a treasure.
  Imagination in its highest flight,   6115
  Strain as it may, can't soar to such a height.
  Yet spirits, fit to fathom the unsounded,
  Have boundless confidence in the unbounded.
Mephistopheles.   Nor gold nor pearls are half as handy as
  Such paper. Then a man knows what he has.   6120
  There is no need of higgling or exchanging;
  In love and wine one can at will be ranging.
  If you want metal, changers are at hand;
  If lacking there, dig for a while the land.
  Goblet and chain are auctioned off and sold;   6125
  Paper redeemed without delay in gold
  Confounds the doubter who had scoffed and taunted.
  This men demand, to metals they are wonted.
  Ready at hand the Emperor's realm will hold
  Henceforth enough of paper, jewels, gold.   6130

Emperor.   Our realm owes you this great prosperity;
   As is the service, the reward should be.
   Our empire's soil be trusted to your care,
   The worthiest guardians of the treasures there.
   You know the vast and well-preservèd hoard,   *6135*
   And when men dig, it's you must give the word.
   Become as one, ye masters of our treasure,
   Fulfil your stations' dignities with pleasure
   Here where in blest accord and unity
   The upper and the lower world agree.   *6140*
Treasurer.   Twixt us no slightest strife shall cause division;
   I love to have as colleague the magician.
      Exit with FAUST.
Emperor.   If now I shall endow each man of you,
   Let each confess what use he'll put it to.
A Page [*receiving*].   I'll joy to live, be glad and gay.   *6145*
Another Page [*likewise*].   My love shall have a chain and rings
   today.
A Chamberlain [*accepting*].
   Wine twice as good shall henceforth down me trickle.
Another Chamberlain [*likewise*].   I feel the dice inside my pocket
   tickle.
A Banneret [*thoughtfully*].   From debt I'll make my lands and castle
   free.
Another Banneret [*likewise*].   I'll add this treasure to my treasury.   *6150*
Emperor.   I hoped for joy and heart for new emprise,
   But knowing you one can your course surmise.
   Well do I see, with all this treasure-store
   You still remain just as you were before.
Fool [*approaching*].   You're scattering favours, grant me some, I
   pray.   *6155*
Emperor.   Alive again? You'd soon drink them away.
Fool.   The magic leaves! I don't quite comprehend—
Emperor.   Of course, for you'd put them to some bad end.
Fool.   Still more drop there, I don't know what to do.
Emperor.   Just pick them up, I let them fall for you.   *6160*
      Exit.
Fool.   Five thousand crowns are mine? How unexpected!
Mephistopheles.   Two-leggèd wineskin, are you resurrected?
Fool.   That happens oft but like this never yet.
Mephistopheles.   You are so glad you're breaking out in sweat.
Fool.   Is that the same as cash? Look, are you sure?   *6165*
Mephistopheles.   What throat and belly want it will procure.
Fool.   And cattle can I buy and house and land?
Mephistopheles.   Of course! Just bid and they will be at hand.
Fool.   Castle with wood, chase, fish-brook?
Mephistopheles.   On my word!
   I'd like to see you as a stern Milord!   *6170*

Fool.   Tonight a landed owner I shall sit!
      Exit.
Mephistopheles [*solus*].   Who still will have a doubt of our fool's
      wit?

A DARK GALLERY

FAUST.   MEPHISTOPHELES.

Mephistopheles.   Why draw me into this dark gallery?
      Is not in there enough of sport,
      Enough of fun and fraud and raillery   6175
      Amid the crowded motley of the court?
Faust.   Don't speak of tricks! Your jests are old and hoary;
      Down to the very soles you've worn that story;
      But now you're going to and fro to flee
      From having any talk with me.   6180
      I am tormented further things to do;
      The Chamberlain is urging and the Steward too.
      The Emperor orders—straightway must it be—
      Both Helena and Paris will he see,
      Of man and woman in their true ideal   6185
      Demands to see the forms distinct and real.
      To work! I gave my word—I must not break it.
Mephistopheles.   A foolish promise—fool you were to make it.
Faust.   Whither your powers lead us, friend,
      You have not well reflected;   6190
      We first have made him rich—no end!
      Now to amuse him we're expected.
Mephistopheles.   You fancy these things easy to arrange.
      Here where we stand, the steps are steeper.
      You grapple with a realm most strange,   6195
      And wantonly will plunge in debt still deeper.
      You think that Helena is summoned here
      As quickly as the paper spectres were.
      With witches' witchery and ghostly ghost,
      With changeling dwarfs I'm ready at my post;   6200
      But devils' darlings, though one may not flout them,
      As heroines no one goes mad about them.
Faust.   There you go harping on the same old chord!
      Into uncertainty you always lead us,
      Sire of all hindrances that can impede us;   6205
      For each new help you want a new reward.
      Mutter a little and the deed is done;
      She will be here ere I can turn me.
Mephistopheles.   The heathen-folk do not concern me.
      They occupy a hell that's all their own.   6210
      But help there is.
Faust.   Quick! Tell its history!

Mephistopheles. Not glad do I reveal a loftier mystery—
  Enthroned sublime in solitude are goddesses;
  Around them is no place, a time still less;
  To speak of them embarrasses. 6215
  They are the *Mothers!*
Faust [*terrified*].   Mothers!
Mephistopheles.   Do you fear?
Faust. The Mothers! Mothers! Strange the word I hear.
Mephistopheles. Strange is it. Goddesses, to men unknown,
  Whom we are loath to name or own.
  Deep must you dig to reach their dwelling ever; 6220
  You are to blame that now we need their favour.
Faust. Whither the way?
Mephistopheles.   No way! To the Unexplorable,
  Never to be explored; to the Unimplorable,
  Never to be implored. Are in the mood?
  There are no locks, no bars are to be riven; 6225
  Through solitudes you will be whirled and driven.
  Can you imagine wastes and solitude?
Faust. I think that you might save yourself such chatter;
  It savours of the witch's-kitchen patter
  After a long, long interlude. 6230
  Was I not forced to live with men?
  Learn the inane, teach the inane?
  If I spoke wisely, true to my conviction,
  Then doubly loud resounded contradiction.
  Indeed, from mankind, so perversely given, 6235
  To solitude and deserts I was driven;
  Till not to be too lone and all-forsaken,
  At last to devil's company I've taken.
Mephistopheles. And had you swum to ocean's farthest verge
  And utter boundlessness beheld, 6240
  Still yonder you'd have seen surge upon surge;
  Although impending doom your fear compelled,
  You'd have seen *something*. Dolphins you'd have seen
  Cleaving the hushèd ocean's emerald-green,
  Have seen the moving clouds, sun, moon, and star. 6245
  Naught will you see in that vast Void afar,
  Nor hear your footstep when it's pressed,
  Nor find firm ground where you can rest.
Faust. You speak as of all mystagogues the chief,
  Whoever brought trustful neophytes to grief; 6250
  Only reversed. Into the Void I'm sent,
  That art and power I may there augment.
  You treat me like the cat's-paw you desire
  To snatch the chestnuts for you from the fire.
  Come, let us fathom it, whatever may befall. 6255
  In this your Naught I hope to find my All.

Mephistopheles.   I praise you, truly, ere you part from me,
  Since that you understand the Devil I can see.
  Here, take this key.
Faust.   That tiny, little thing!
Mephistopheles.   Seize and esteem it, see what it may bring!   6260
Faust.   It's growing in my hand! it flashes, glows!
Mephistopheles.   Will you see now what blessing it bestows?
  The key will scent the right place from all others;
  Follow it down, 'twill lead you to the Mothers.
Faust [*shuddering*].   The Mothers! Like a blow it strikes my ear!   6265
  What is that word that I don't like to hear?
Mephistopheles.   So narrow-minded, scared by each new word?
  Will you but hear what you've already heard?
  Let naught disturb you, though it strangely rings,
  You! long since wonted to most wondrous things.   6270
Faust.   And yet in torpor there's no gain for me;
  The thrill of awe is man's best quality.
  Although the world may stifle every sense,
  Enthralled, man deeply senses the Immense.
Mephistopheles.   Descend, then! I might also tell you: Soar!   6275
  It's all the same. Escape from the Existent
  To phantoms' unbound realms far distant!
  Delight in what long since exists no more!
  Like filmy clouds the phantoms glide along.
  Brandish the key, hold off the shadowy throng.   6280
Faust [*inspired*].   Good! Gripping it, I feel new strength arise,
  My breast expands. On, to the great emprise!
Mephistopheles.   When you at last a glowing tripod see,
  Then in the deepest of all realms you'll be.
  You'll see the Mothers in the tripod's glow,   6285
  Some of them sitting, others stand and go,
  As it may chance. Formation, transformation,
  Eternal Mind's eternal re-creation.
  Images of all creatures hover free,
  They will not see you, only wraiths they see.   6290
  So, then, take courage, for the danger's great.
  Go to that tripod, do not hesitate,
  And touch it with the key!

    FAUST *assumes a decidedly commanding attitude with the key.*

Mephistopheles [*observing him*].   So—it is well!
  'Twill come and like a slave obey your spell.
  Calmly you'll rise, upborne by fortune rare,   6295
  And have the tripod here ere they're aware.
  And when you've brought it hither, you can cite
  Hero and heroine from the realms of night,
  The first to face that deed and venture on it.

It's done and you're the one who will have done it.   6300
Then must the incense-cloud, by magic hand,
Turn into gods, as gods before you stand.
Faust.   And now what?
Mephistopheles.   Downward let your being strain!
   Stamping, sink hence and, stamping, rise again!
      FAUST *stamps and sinks out of sight.*
Mephistopheles.   I only hope he'll profit from the key!   6305
   Will he come back? I'm curious to see.

BRIGHTLY LIGHTED HALLS
EMPEROR *and* PRINCES.

The Court moving about.
Chamberlain [*to* MEPHISTOPHELES].
   The spirit-scene you promised still is owing.
   To work! Impatient is our master growing.
Steward.   A moment since His Grace inquired of me.
   Delay not! Don't disgrace His Majesty!   6310
Mephistopheles.   Upon that errand has my comrade gone;
   He surely knows what's to be done.
   He works secludedly and still,
   And all his powers he perforce engages.
   Who'd raise that treasure, Beauty, at his will,   6315
   Requires the highest art, Magic of Sages!
Steward.   The kind of arts you need, that is all one;
   It is the Emperor's will that it be done.
A Blonde [*to* MEPHISTOPHELES].
   One word, sir! See my face without a spot,
   But thus in tiresome summer it is not!   6320
   Then brownish-red there sprout a hundred freckles
   Which vex my lily skin with ugly speckles.
   A cure!
Mephistopheles.   You radiant darling, what a pity,
   Spotted in May-time like a panther-kitty.
   Take frog-spawn, toads' tongues, cohobate¹ them,   6325
   And carefully, at full moon, distillate them.
   When the moon's waning, spread the mixture on,
   And when the spring has come, the spots are gone.
A Brunette.   To fawn around you, see the crowd advancing!
   I beg a remedy! A chilblained foot   6330
   Hinders me much in walking and in dancing
   And makes me awkward even when I salute.
Mephistopheles.   Pray let me tread upon it with my foot.
Brunette.   Well, I suppose that happens between lovers.
Mephistopheles.   In my tread, child, a greater meaning   6335
   hovers.
      ¹Distil repeatedly.

Like unto like, whatever pain one undergo!
Foot healeth foot, so is it with each member.
Come here! Give heed! Don't *you* tread *me,* remember!
Brunette [*screaming*].   Oh, how that stings! you did tread hard!
    Oh! Oh!
    'Twas like a horse's hoof.
Mephistopheles.   With this cure you can go.   6340
Dance to your heart's content, now you are able,
Or foot it with your sweetheart 'neath the table.
Lady [*pressing forward*].   Let me go through! Too painful are my
    sorrows;
Deep in my heart this anguish burns and burrows.
Till yesterday his bliss hung on *my* glances   6345
But now he turns his back; only *her* talk entrances.
Mephistopheles.   That's serious, but listen carefully.
Press up to him quite softly, take
This bit of charcoal, and then on him make
A mark on sleeve or cloak or shoulder as may be;   6350
Remorse will pierce him to the very core.
The coal, however, you must straightway swallow,
Nor let a drop of wine or water follow;
Tonight you'll have him sighing at your door.
Lady.   It is not poison, is it?
Mephistopheles [*indignant*].   Respect where it is due!   6355
For such a coal you'd travel many a mile;
It comes here from a funeral pile
Such as whose flames we once more fiercely blew.
Page.   I am in love, they do not take me seriously.
Mephistopheles [*aside*].   Whom I am now to listen to, I do not see.   6360
    To the PAGE.
Let not the youngest maid your fancy fetter;
Those on in years know how to prize you better.
    Others crowd up.
Still more and more? It is a brawl, in sooth!
I'll help myself at last with naked truth,
The worst of aids! Great is my misery.—   6365
O Mothers, Mothers! Do let Faust go free!
    Gazing around him.
The lights are burning dimly in the hall,
At once the Court starts forward, one and all.
I see them file according to their grades
Through distant galleries and long arcades.   6370
Now they're assembling in that ample space,
The old Knight's Hall; yet hardly all find place.
The spacious walls with tapestries are rich,
While armour decorates each nook and niche.
Here is no need, methinks, of magic incantation,   6375
Ghosts will come here without an invitation.

HALL OF THE KNIGHTS

Dim illumination. The EMPEROR *and Court have entered.*

Herald.   Mine ancient office of announcing plays
    Is marred by spirits' mystic interference;
    In vain one dares in reasonable ways
    To fathom their mysterious appearance.   *6380*
    The chairs are placed, the seats are ready all;
    The Emperor is seated just before the wall;
    Upon the arras there he may with ease behold
    The glorious battles that men fought of old.
    Now Emperor and Court are seated here;   *6385*
    The benches crowd together in the rear;
    And lovers in this spirit-hour's uncanny gloom
    Have found beside their loved ones lovely room.
    And so, since all have duly taken places,
    We're ready, let the spirits come and face us!   *6390*
        Trumpets.
Astrologer.   Now let the drama start without delay.
    Our Sire commands! Ye walls, give way!
    Naught hinders now. Here magic doth conspire;
    The arras rolls away as if by fire.
    The wall is splitting, turning in the gloom,   *6395*
    A deep stage seems to be appearing,
    A light mysterious to be nearing,
    And I ascend to the proscenium.
Mephistopheles [*rising to view in the prompter's box*]
    I hope for favour here from all and each,
    For promptings are the Devil's art of speech.   *6400*
        To the ASTROLOGER.
    You know the tempo of the stars on high;
    You'll understand my whispering masterly.
Astrologer.   By magic might before us doth appear,
    Massive enough, an ancient temple here.
    Like Atlas who upheld the sky of old,   *6405*
    Columns enough, in rows, you can behold.
    Well for the weight of stone may they suffice,
    Since two could bear a mighty edifice.
Architect.   So that's antique! I can't say I would praise it;
    Top-heavy, clumsy, is the way to phrase it.   *6410*
    Rude is called noble, awkward great; far more
    I love slim shafts that boundless soar.
    High pointed arches lift the soul on high,
    Such edifices most do edify.
Astrologer.   Receive with reverent awe star-granted hours   *6415*
    By magic's spells enthralled be Reason's powers,
    And in its stead, arising far and free,

Reign glorious, daring Phantasy!
What you desired so boldly, be it now perceived;
It is impossible, therefore to be believed.   6420
    FAUST *rises to view on the other side of the proscenium.*
Astrologer.   In priestly robe and wreathed, a wonder-man!
  Who'll now fulfil what he in faith began,
  A tripod with him from the depths below.
  Now from the bowl the incense-perfumes flow.
  He girds himself, the lofty work to bless;   6425
  Henceforth there can be nothing but success.
Faust [*in the grand manner*].
  In your name, Mothers! ye who have your throne
  In boundless space, eternally alone,
  Yet not alone. Around your heads there waver
  Life's images, astir, yet lifeless ever.   6430
  What once has been, in radiance supernal,
  It's stirring there, for it would be eternal,
  And ye allot it, Powers who all things sway,
  To vaulted night, to canopy of day.
  On some the lovely stream of life lays hold,   6435
  Others are sought by the magician bold;
  Boldly in rich profusion he displays
  The marvel whereon each would like to gaze.
Astrologer.   The glowing key doth scarcely touch the bowl,
  Over the prospect misty vapours roll;   6440
  They creep along, then cloud-like on they fare,
  Spread out, round off, entwine, they part, they pair.
  Now note a mystic masterpiece! For lo!
  The vaporous clouds make music as they go.
  Aerial tones bring forth—what can it be?   6445
  While they proceed, all turns to melody.
  The columned shaft, the very triglyph, rings;
  Yea, I believe that all the temple sings.
  The mist is sinking; from the filmy haze
  A handsome youth steps forth with measured pace.   6450
  Here ends my task, I do not need to name him;
  As gentle Paris who would not proclaim him?
    PARIS *steps forth.*
A Lady.   What glorious, blooming youth and strength I see!
A Second Lady.   Fresh as a peach, as full of juice, is he!
A Third Lady.   The finely chiselled, sweetly swelling lip!   6455
A Fourth Lady.   From such a cup how would you like to sip?
A Fifth Lady.   He's handsome, yes, and yet not quite refined.
A Sixth Lady.   A bit more graceful might he be, I find.
A Knight.   I think I see him when a shepherd boy. He's wearing
  No traces of a prince and naught of courtly bearing.   6460
Another Knight.   Oh, well! Half nude the youth is fair to look upon,
  But we must see him with his armour on.

A Lady.   He seats him gently and with easy grace.
A Knight.   You'd find his lap, perchance, a pleasant place?
Another Lady.   He lays his arm so lightly over his head.   6465
A Chamberlain.   That's not allowed! How thoroughly ill-bred!
A Lady.   You lords can always find some fault to cavil at.
Chamberlain.   Before the very Emperor to stretch himself like that!
A Lady.   He's only playing, thinks he's quite alone.
Chamberlain.   A play too should be courteous near the throne.   6470
A Lady.   Sleep captures now the charming youth completely!
Chamberlain.   And now he'll snore, quite properly and meetly!
A Young Lady [*enraptured*].
  What fragrance with the incense-stream is blending,
  Refreshment to my inmost bosom sending!
An Older Lady.   A zephyr pierces deep into my soul, in truth!   6475
  It comes from him.
A Very Old Lady.   It is the bloom of youth,
  Ambrosia-like within the boy distilling
  And all the atmosphere around us filling.
      HELENA *appears.*
Mephistopheles.   So that is she! She'd not disturb my rest;
  Pretty indeed, but still I'm not impressed.   6480
Astrologer.   For me right now there's nothing more to do;
  I see and honourably confess it true.
  The Fair One comes, and had I tongues of fire!—
  Always did Beauty many songs inspire.
  Who sees her is enrapt! and far too blessed   6485
  For human lot the man who her possessed.
Faust.   Have I still eyes? Is Beauty's spring, outpouring,
  Revealed most richly to my inmost soul?
  My dread path brought me to this loftiest goal!
  Void was the world and barred to my exploring!   6490
  What is it now since this my priesthood's hour?
  Worth wishing for, firm-based, a lasting dower!
  Vanish from me my every vital power
  If I forsake thee, treacherous to my duty!
  The lovely form that once my fancy captured,   6495
  That in the magic glass enraptured,
  Was but a foam-born phantom of such beauty!—
  To thee alone I render up with gladness
  The very essence of my passion,
  Fancy, desire, love, worship, madness!   6500
Mephistopheles [*from the prompter's box*].
  Be calm! Don't drop your role in such a fashion!
An Elderly Lady.   Tall, well-formed, but her head's too small for me.
A Fairly Young Lady.   Just see her foot! How could it clumsier be?
A Diplomat.   I have seen princesses of this same kind!
  She's beautiful from head to foot, I find.   6505
A Courtier.   She nears the sleeper, cunningly demure.

A Lady.   How hideous by that form so young and pure!
A Poet.   By her rare beauty he is beamed upon.
A Lady.   A picture! Luna and Endymion!
A Poet.   Quite right! and now the goddess seems to sink,   6510
Bends over him as if his breath to drink.
How enviable!—A kiss!—The cup is full.
A Duenna.   Before the crowd! My word! That is too cool.
Faust.   A fearful favour for the youth!
Mephistopheles.   Be still!
And let the phantom do all that it will.   6515
A Courtier.   She steals away, light-footed. He awakes.
A Lady.   Just as I thought, another look she takes.
A Courtier.   He is astounded, thinks a wonder doth occur.
A Lady.   But what she sees, no wonder is to her.
A Courtier.   She turns around to him with charming grace.   6520
A Lady.   I see, she'll take him now into her school;
Stupid is every man in such a case.
He thinks, I guess, that he's the first—the fool!
A Knight.   She'll pass with me! A fine, majestic air!
A Lady.   The courtesan! How vulgar, I declare!   6525
A Page.   Where he is now, oh, would that I were there!
A Courtier.   In such a net who would not fain be caught?
A Lady.   Through many hands has gone that jewel rare;
Even the gilding's rather worse for wear.
Another Lady.   From her tenth year she has been good for naught.[1] 6530
A Knight.   Each makes the best his own as chance obtains;
I'd be contented with these fair remains.
A Dryasdust Scholar.   I see her plainly and yet, frankly, I can see
That one may doubt if she the right one be.
What's present always causes obfuscation;   6535
I like to cling to written attestation.
And there I read that, soon as she was sighted,
The Trojan greybeards[2] all were most delighted.
Methinks, that fits the case here perfectly.
I am not young and yet she pleases me.   6540
Astrologer.   A youth no more! A man, heroic, brave,
Embraces her who scarce herself can save.
Strong-armed, he lifts her high in air.
Will he, then, bear her off?
Faust.   Rash fool, beware!
You dare? You hear not? Halt! It is too much!   6545
Mephistopheles.   Why, this mad phantom-play, you've made it such!
Astrologer.   But one word more! From all we've seen today,
I call the piece *The Rape of Helena.*
Faust.   What! "Rape"? Fellow, am I for naught here?

---

[1]That is, from the time Theseus is said to have fallen in love with her and to have carried her off.
[2]Cf. *Iliad*, iii. 156-8.

This key do I not hold it in my hand,   6550
I whom through stormy solitudes it brought here,
Through waves of horror to this solid land?
Here do I plant my foot! Realities are here,
Here strife with spirits may the spirit dare
And for itself the great twin-realm prepare.   6555
Though she was far, how can she nearer be?
I'll save her and then doubly mine is she.
I dare! Ye Mothers, Mothers! grant this favour!
Who once has known her can renounce her never!

Astrologer.   What are you doing, Faustus, Faustus! With what might 6560
He seizes her! The form is fading from our sight.
Toward the youth he turns the key, and lo!
He's touching him!—Now! it is done! Ah, woe on woe!

> *Explosion.* FAUST *lies on the ground. The phantoms dissolve in*
> *vapour.*

Mephistopheles [taking FAUST *on his shoulder].*
So there it is! To deal with fools is evil
And in the end it even harms the Devil.   6565

> *Darkness, tumult.*

ACT II

A HIGH-VAULTED, NARROW, GOTHIC CHAMBER

FORMERLY FAUST'S, UNALTERED

Mephistopheles [appears from behind a curtain. As he raises the curtain and looks back, FAUST is seen stretched out on an old-fashioned bed].

Lie there, poor wretch! seduced, unwise,
Scarce to be rescued from Love's chain!
Whom Helena doth paralyze,
His reason he'll not soon regain.
    Looking around him.
I look around and through the glimmer   **6570**
Unchanged, uninjured all appears;
Methinks the coloured window-panes are dimmer,
The cobwebs have increased with years.
The ink is dry, the paper brown and sere,
Yet all is in its place, in very fact;   **6575**
Even the pen's still lying here
Which Faust used when he signed the pact.
Aye, deeper in the pen is lurking still
A trace of blood I lured him on to spill.
To find a relic so unique as this   **6580**
Would be some great collector's highest bliss.
From its old hook the old fur coat's half falling,
Those merry jests of mine recalling
Which once I taught that lad as truth,
Which still may nourish his ingenuous youth.   **6585**
Rough, fur-warm cloak, encased in you,
A great desire comes on me truly
To show off as a proud professor newly,
As men think they've a perfect right to do.
The learnèd know how to attain that level;   **6590**
It is an art long since lost by the Devil.
   He shakes the fur coat which he has taken down. Crickets,
     beetles, and moths fly out.
Chorus of Insects.

               Hail! welcome thy coming,
               Thou patron of yore!
               We're flying and humming
               And know thee once more.   **6595**
               All singly, in quiet,
               Didst plant us, and lo!
               In thousands, O Father,

We dance to and fro.
The rogue in the bosom   6600
Is deeply concealed;
The insects in fur coats
Are sooner revealed.

Mephistopheles.   With what surprising joy this youthful brood I
     view!
Aye, only sow, you'll harvest when the time is due.   6605
I'll give the old fur coat a second clout;
Still here and there another flutters out.
Up and about, ye darlings, helter-skelter,
And quickly in a thousand nooks seek shelter:
Where ancient pasteboard boxes stand,   6610
In yellowed parchment here at hand,
Where dusty shards of old pots lie,
In yonder death's-head's hollow eye.
Amid such trash and mouldering life
Crickets and crotchets must be rife.   6615
     He slips into the fur coat.
Come, cloak my shoulders as of yore,
Head of the house as heretofore.
Yet boots it little so to name me;
Where are the people to acclaim me?
     He pulls the bell which gives out a shrill, penetrating sound,
        making the halls tremble and the doors fly open.

Famulus [*tottering down the long, dark corridor*].
What a clanging! What a quaking!   6620
Stairs are rocking, walls are shaking!
Through the windows' motley quiver
I see summer lightning shiver.
Over me cracks the ancient flooring,
Down come lime and rubbish pouring;   6625
And the door, securely bolted,
Magic power has open jolted.
There! How terrible! A giant
Stands in Faust's old fur, defiant!
At his look, his beck, his winking,   6630
On my knees I'm near to sinking.
Shall I stay? or shall I flee?
Oh, what will become of me?

Mephistopheles [*beckoning*].
Come here, my friend! Your name is Nicodemus.[1]
Famulus.   Most worthy sir! That is my name—Oremus.   6635
Mephistopheles.   That we'll omit!
Famulus.   You know me! What a thrill!
Mephistopheles.   I know you well, old and a student still,
Moss-covered sir! Also a learnèd man

[1]Cf. John, 3. 1-21.

Still studies on since there's naught else he can.
A moderate house of cards one builds him so;   6640
The greatest mind does not complete it, though.
And yet your master! Great his gifts and fame;
Who does not know good Doctor Wagner's name?
First in the learnèd world! 'Tis he alone, they say,
Who holds the world together; every day   6645
He proves that he is wisdom's multiplier.
Hearers and listeners who eagerly aspire
To universal knowledge, round him flock.
None from the rostrum can shine meeter;
He handles keys as doth St. Peter;   6650
Lower and Upper, both he can unlock.[1]
Like his—as Wagner glows and sparkles—
No other's fame can hold its ground.
The very name of Faustus darkles;
Wagner alone has sought and found.   6655
Famulus.   Pardon, good sir, for asking your attention
The while I make an humble intervention:
With what you've said there can be no dissension,
But modesty is his allotted part.
Since that great man's mysterious disappearing   6660
He knows not where to turn in his despairing;
For Faust's return he prays with all his heart,
And thence for weal and solace. None may enter
The room which Doctor Faustus left. Forlorn,
Untouched, it waits its lord's return.   6665
To enter it I scarcely dare to venture.
What aspect of the stars must now appear?
It seemed to me as if the stout walls quivered,
The door-posts trembled, bolts were shivered,
Else you yourself could not have come in here.   6670
Mephistopheles.   Where has the man gone? Where is he?
Lead me to him! Bring him to me!
Famulus.   Ah, sir! Too strict his orders are a bit,
I know not if I dare to venture it.
Month after month to great work he's been giving,   •   6675
In stillest stillness he's been living.
The daintiest of men of learning
Looks now as if he had been charcoal-burning,
His face all black from ears to nose,
His eyes all red from flames he blows.   6680
Each moment for the next he longs;
His music is the clang of tongs.
Mephistopheles.   And shall he entrance now deny me?
I'll speed his luck—just let him try me!
    FAMULUS *goes out,* MEPHISTOPHELES *sits down gravely.*

[1]Cf. Matthew, 16. 19.

Scarce am I settled here at rest,   6685
When yonder stirs a well-known guest.
But now most up-to-date is he;
He'll brag and swagger boundlessly.

Bachelor of Arts [*storming along the corridor*].

Gate and door I find are opeing!
Well, at least one can be hoping   6690
That no more in mould unfitting
Men alive, yet dead, are sitting,
Pining, rotting, mortifying,
And of living still be dying.
Here each wall and each partition   6695
Bends down, sinking to perdition.
If we hence don't soon betake us,
Ruin dire will overtake us.
I am bold, no one can match me,
Yet no farther will one catch me.   6700
But today what am I learning!
Many years ago, a yearning
Freshman, I came hither, fluttering,
Anxious and abashed and stuttering.
Here I trusted long-beards' tattle,   6705
Edified me on their prattle.
Into heavy, dry tomes reaching,
What they knew they lied in teaching,
Taught without themselves believing,
Me, themselves, of life bereaving.   6710
What! there in the cell off yonder,
Dimly-lit, one sits asunder!
Stranger still, as I draw nearer,
Sits he there, the brown fur-wearer,
As I left him, piece for piece,   6715
Still in that old shaggy fleece!
Subtle then he seemed to be,
Not yet understood by me,
But today 'twill not avail him.
Up and on now to assail him!   6720

If, ancient sir, your bald head, sidewards bending,
Has into Lethe's dreary waters not been drawn,
Acknowledge now your pupil hither wending
Who academic rods has quite outgrown.
I find you still as then when I began;   6725
But I am here again, another man!

Mephistopheles.   I'm glad I brought you with my tinkling.
The other time I valued you quite high;
Even in the worm, the chrysalis, an inkling
Is of the future, gaily-coloured butterfly.   6730

Curls and a fine lace-collar wearing,
You showed a child-like pleasure in your bearing.
I guess you never wore a queue?
I see, today cropped like a Swede are you.
You look quite brave and resolute,   6735
But pray don't go home absolute.

Bachelor of Arts.
Old sir! there on the same old desk you're leaning,
But think how time runs on today
And spare your words of double meaning;
We watch now in a very different way.   6740
Then with an honest stripling you were toying,
Succeeded too, but little art employing.
Today no one will venture that, in sooth.

Mephistopheles.   If, unadulterate, one says to youth
What does not please the callow brood—the truth!   6745
And later after many a tide
They learn it painfully on their own hide,
Each fancies then it came from his own head;
"The Master was a fool!" is what is said.

Bachelor of Arts.
Or rogue perhaps! What teacher has the grace   6750
To tell the truth directly to our face?
To simple children each knows what to say,
Add or subtract, now grave, now wise and gay.

Mephistopheles.   There is, indeed, a time to learn;
You're ready now to teach, as I discern.   6755
For many a moon and now and then a sun
A rich experience you have doubtless won.

Bachelor of Arts.   Experience! Mere foam and fluff!
A peer of mind? No trace of that is showing.
Confess: what men have ever known is stuff   6760
And absolutely not worth knowing . . .

Mephistopheles [*after a pause*].
I long have thought so, but I was a fool;
Now to myself I seem right flat and dull.

Bachelor of Arts.   Good! That has a reasonable sound;
A greybeard talking sense at last is found!   6765

Mephistopheles.   I sought a hidden treasure, one of gold;
'Twas hideous coals when all my search was done.

Bachelor of Arts.   Confess it then! Your skull, now bald and old,
Is worth no more than yonder hollow one.

Mephistopheles [*good-humouredly*].
You're ruder, friend, perhaps than you mean quite.   6770

Bachelor of Arts.   In German people lie when they're polite.

Mephistopheles [*moving nearer and nearer toward the proscenium in
his wheeled-chair, to the spectators*].
Here I'm deprived of light and air. I wonder

Could I find refuge with you people yonder?

Bachelor of Arts.   It is presumption that men old and hoar

Seek to be something when they are no more.   6775

Man's life lives in his blood and where, forsooth,

Does blood so stir as in the veins of youth?

Ah, that is living blood, with vigour rife,

Creating newer life from its own life.

There all is stirring, there is something done,   6780

The weak fall out, the capable press on.

While half the world we've brought beneath our sway,

What have you done? Thought, nodded, dreamed away,

Considered plan on plan—and nothing won.

It's certain! Age is but an ague cold,   6785

Chill with its fancies of distress and dread.

Once a man's thirty, he's already old,

He is indeed as good as dead.

'Twere best to kill him right away.

Mephistopheles.   The Devil, here, has nothing more to say.   6790

Bachelor of Arts.   Unless I will it, no devil can there be.

Mephistopheles [*aside*].   The Devil, though, will trip you presently.

Bachelor of Arts.   This is youth's noblest message and most fit!

The world was not till I created it.

'Twas I that led the sun up from the sea;   6795

The moon began its changeful course with me.

The day put on rich garments, me to meet;

The earth grew green and blossomed, me to greet.

At my behest in that primeval night

The stars unveiled their splendour to my sight.   6800

Who, if not I, your own deliverance wrought

From fetters of Philistine, cramping thought?

I, as my spirit bids me, with delight

I follow onward mine own inner light.

Swift I proceed with mine own raptured mind,   6805

Glory before me, darkness far behind.

    Exit.

Mephistopheles.   Original, in all your glory take your way!

How would true insight make you grieve!

What wise or stupid thing can man conceive

That was not thought in ages passed away?   6810

Danger from him will cause us little bother,

He will be changed when a few years have passed;

Though must within the cask may raise a pother,

It turns to wine no less at last.

    To the younger portion of the audience who do not applaud.

I see my words have left you cold;   6815

Good children, I'll not take it evil.

Remember that the Devil's old;

Grow old, to understand the Devil.

LABORATORY

In the style of the Middle Ages; scattered, clumsy apparatus
for fantastic purposes.

Wagner [at the furnace].   The bell resounds with fearful clangour,
  The sooty walls thrill its vibration.   6820
  No longer can remain uncertain
  My great, most earnest expectation.
  Darkness is lifting like a curtain.
  Within the phial's inmost chamber
  It's glowing like a living ember,   6825
  Yea, like a glorious carbuncle, gleaming
  And flashing, through the darkness streaming.
  A clear white light comes into view!
  Oh, may it not escape once more!—
  Ah, God! what's rattling at the door?   6830
Mephistopheles [entering].   Welcome! I mean it well with you.
Wagner [anxiously].   Welcome in this auspicious hour!
    Softly.
  Don't speak or even breathe, though, I implore!
  Achieved is soon a glorious undertaking.
Mephistopheles [more softly].   What is it, then?
Wagner [more softly].   A man is in the   6835
  making!
Mephistopheles.   A man? And, pray, what lovesick pair
  Have you shut in the chimney-flue?
Wagner.   May God forbid! Begetting, as men used to do,
  Both vain and senseless we declare.
  The tender point whence life used to begin,   6840
  The gracious outward urgence from within,
  To take and give, to have its likeness known,
  Near and remote alike to make its own—
  All that has lost its former dignity.
  Whereas delighted with it still the beast may be,   6845
  A man with his great gifts must henceforth win
  A higher, even higher origin.
    Turning toward the furnace.
  It flashes, see! Now truly we may hold
  That if from substances a hundredfold,
  Through mixture—for on mixture all depends—   6850
  Man's substance gently be consolidated,
  In an alembic sealed and segregated,
  And properly be cohobated,
  In quiet and success the labour ends.
    Turning toward the furnace again.
  'Twill be! The mass is working clearer,   6855
  Conviction gathers, truer, nearer.

What men as Nature's mysteries would hold,
All that to test by reason we make bold,
And what she once was wont to organize,
That we bid now to crystallize.   6860
Mephistopheles.   Whoever lives long learns full many things;
By naught in this world can he ever be surprised.
I've seen already in my wanderings
Many a mortal who was crystallized.
Wagner [hitherto constantly attentive to the phial].
It rises, flashes, gathers on;   6865
A moment, and the deed is done.
A great design at first seems mad; but we
Henceforth will laugh at chance in procreation,
And such a brain that is to think transcendently
Will be a thinker's own creation.   6870
      Looking at the phial rapturously.
The glass resounds with lovely might;
It dims, it clears; life *must* begin to be.
A dainty figure greets my sight;
A pretty manikin I see.
What more do we or does the world want **now?**   6875
The mystery's within our reach.
Come, hearken to this sound, and listen how
It turns to voice, it turns to speech.
Homunculus [in the phial, to WAGNER].
Well, Daddy! how are you? It was no jest.
Come, press me tenderly upon your breast,   6880
But not too hard, for fear the glass might **shatter.**
That is the property of matter:
For what is natural the All has place;
What's artificial needs restricted space.
      To MEPHISTOPHELES.
How now, Sir Cousin, rogue, are you here too?   6885
And at the proper moment? Many thanks to you!
You've been led here by some good destiny.
The while I'm living, active must I be.
Fain would I gird me for the work straightway;
You are adroit and can curtail my way.   6890
Wagner.   But one word more! I'm shamed that answers fail me,
When with their problems young and old assail me.
For instance: no one's grasped how, each with either,
Body and soul can fit so well together,
Hold fast as if not to be separated,   6895
Yet each by other daily vexed and hated.
And then—
Mephistopheles.   Stop! I would rather ask if he
Can say why man and wife so ill agree?
This point, my friend, will nevermore be clear.

The little chap wants work to do and it is here.   6900
Homunculus.   What's to be done?
Mephistopheles [pointing to a side door].
                Your talents here you're to
   employ!
Wagner [looking steadfastly into the phial].
   In truth you are the very loveliest boy!
     The side door opens and FAUST *is seen stretched out on the couch.*
Homunculus [astonished].
   Significant!
     The phial slips out of WAGNER's *hands, hovers above* FAUST *and*
     illumines him.
              [1]With beauty girt!—Clear waters moving
In a dense grove and women who undress;
Fairest of forms!—The picture is improving.   6905
But one outshines the rest in loveliness,
From noblest heroes, nay, from gods, descended.
In the translucent pool her foot she laves;
The living flame of her sweet form is blended
With th' cooling, clinging crystal of the waves.   6910
But what a noise of pinions swiftly dashing,
And in the pool what swishing, splashing!
The maidens flee abashed, but she, the queen,
With calm composure gazes on the scene.
With pleasure proud and womanly she sees   6915
The swan-prince[2] nestle fondly at her knees,
Importunate, yet tame. He grows more daring.
But swiftly upward floats a vapour pale
And covers with its closely woven veil
A scene most lovely and beyond comparing.   6920
Mephistopheles.   How many tales you can relate!
Small as you are, in fancies you are great.
I can see naught—
Homunculus.   Of course. You from the North,
In ages dark and drear brought forth,
In all the murk of knighthood and of papistry,   6925
How could your vision, then, be clear and free?
Only in gloom are you at home.
     Looking around.
Bemouldered stone-work, dingy, horrid,
With pointed arches low and florid!
If this man wakes, there'll be new things to dread;   6930
At once upon the spot he will lie dead.
Prophetic dreams of woodland springs beguile him,
Of swans and naked beauties. Here,

---

[1]Lines 6903-20 constitute a reproduction in verse of Correggio's painting of Leda and
the swan.
[2]Zeus.

In such a place, how could he reconcile him,
Which I, the most adaptable, scarce bear?   6935
Now off with him!
Mephistopheles.   Whither I'll hear with pleasure.
Homunculus.   Command the warrior to the fight,
Lead forth the maid to tread a measure;
Then all is fitting, all is right.
Just now—my memory brings to light—   6940
Is Classical Walpurgis Night.
For him could be no happier event
Than to be taken to his element.
Mephistopheles.   Of that I've never chanced to hear.
Homunculus.   How would it come, pray, to your ear?   6945
Only romantic ghosts are known to you;
A ghost that's genuine must be classic too.
Mephistopheles.   But whither, then, are we to travel? Tell me!
Your antique cronies now repel me.
Homunculus.   Satan, northwest is where you're wont to play,   6950
But to the southeast we will sail today.
Along a great plain is Peneus[1] flowing free,
Its silent bays shadowed by bush and tree.
To mountain gorges sweeps the level view,
Above it stands Pharsalus old and new.   6955
Mephistopheles.   Alack! have done! and call not old dissension
'Twixt tyranny and slavery to my attention.
It wearies me, no sooner is it done
When once more is the same old fight begun.
And no one notes that he is but the game   6960
Of Asmodeus who still fans the flame.
They're fighters, so they say, for freedom's rights;
More closely scanned, it's slave with slave that fights.
Homunculus.   Oh, leave to men their fractious being.
Each must defend himself as best he can,   6965
From boyhood up; thus he becomes a man.
To this man's cure we must be seeing.
Come, prove it here if you've a remedy;
If you have not, then leave the cure to me.
Mephistopheles.   Many a Brocken-game I might essay,   6970
But heathen bolts, I'll find, will block my way.
The Greeks were never worth much, it is true,
Yet their free play of senses dazzles you,
The heart of man to happy vices winning.
Gloomy will always seem our ways of sinning.   6975
What now?
Homunculus. I know you're free of squeamish twitches!
And if I touch upon Thessalian witches,
I think I have not talked for naught.
[1]A river in Thessaly.

Mephistopheles [*lustfully*].   Thessalian witches! They are persons—
     well,
     For them I long have asked and sought.   6980
     Night after night with them to dwell
     Is not, I'd say, a pleasant thought;
     Let's spy them, try them, though—
Homunculus.   The mantle there!
     Come, wrap it straightway round the knight!
     As heretofore the rag will bear   6985
     You both upon your novel flight.
     I'll light the way.
Wagner [*anxiously*.] And I?
Homunculus.   Well, you
     Will stay at home, most weighty work to do.
     Open the parchment-sheets, collect
     Life-elements as the recipes direct,   6990
     With caution fitting each to other. Ponder
     The *What*—to solve the *How* still harder try,
     While through a little piece of world I wander
     To find the dot to put upon the *i*.
     Accomplished then will the great purpose be.   6995
     Striving earns high requital: wealth,
     Honour and fame, long life and perfect health,
     Knowledge and virtue too—well, possibly.
     Farewell!
Wagner [*sorrowfully*].   Farewell! My heart is wrung with pain.
     I fear that I will see you never again.   7000
Mephistopheles.   Now to Peneus, quick, descend!
     Sir Coz shall not be meanly rated.
          To the spectators.
     It's true, at last we all depend
     On creatures we ourselves created.

CLASSICAL WALPURGIS NIGHT
PHARSALIAN FIELDS
Darkness

Erichtho.   To this night's awful festival, as oft before,   7005
     I stride in view, Erichtho,[1] I the gloomy one,
     Not so atrocious as the tiresome poet-crew
     Calumniate me to excess . . . They never end
     In praise and censure . . . Even now the vale appears
     Far, over-whitened with the billows of gray tents,   7010
     Spectres of that most dire and most appalling night.
     How oft it has recurred already! Evermore
     It will recur forever . . . No one grants the realm
     Unto another, none to him who through his might

[1] A Thessalian witch.

Has won and rules it. For each one who knows not how   *7015*
To rule his own, his inborn self, is all too fain
To rule his neighbour's will, as prompts his own proud mind . . .
Here was a great example fought even to the end:
How violence opposes greater violence,
How freedom's lovely, thousand-blossomed wreath is rent,   *7020*
And the stiff laurel bends around the ruler's head.
Here of an early budding greatness Pompey dreamed,
There Cæsar by the wavering balance watchful lay!
Strength will they measure. And the world knows now who won.

    The watch-fires glow and flash, diffusing ruddy flames;   *7025*
The ground where blood was shed exhales reflected light;
And by the night's most rare and wondrous splendour lured,
The legion of Hellenic myths assembles here.
Round all the watch-fires fabled forms of ancient days
Hover uncertain to and fro or sit at ease . . .   *7030*
In truth, not fully orbed, yet radiant bright, the moon
Is rising, spreading gentle splendour everywhere;
The tents' illusion vanishes, the lights burn blue.

    But lo! above my head what sudden meteor!
It beams and it illumines a corporeal ball.   *7035*
'Tis life I scent. Becoming is it not for me
That I approach the living, doing harm to them.
That brings me evil fame and benefits me not.
Already it sinks down. Discreetly I withdraw.
    Moves away.
    The AERONAUTS *overhead.*

Homunculus.

                Once again around I hover,   *7040*
                Flames and horrors dire I follow;
                Spectral all that I discover
                In the vale and in the hollow.

Mephistopheles.

                As through my old window looking
                Midst far northern waste and gloom,   *7045*
                Ghosts revolting I see spooking,
                Here as there I am at home.

Homunculus.

                See! a woman tall is stalking
                In long strides before us there.

Mephistopheles.

                As if scared, it seems, she's walking,   *7050*
                Saw us coming through the air.

Homunculus.

                Let her stalk! Set down the burden
                Of your knight, for near at hand
                Are the new life and the guerdon
                That he seeks in fable-land.   *7055*

Faust [*touching the soil*].   Where is she?
Homunculus.   That's a question over-
   tasking,
   But here you'll learn, I think, by asking.
   Make ready, go ere it is day;
   From flame to flame inquiring wander.
   Who to the Mothers dared the way,   7060
   Has nothing more to fear or ponder.
Mephistopheles.   Here I too claim a part to play,
   Yet for our weal naught better can I say
   Than that each one amid the fires
   Should seek his own adventures and desires.   7065
   Then as a sign to reunite us,
   Let, little friend, your lantern sound and light us.
Homunculus.   Thus shall it ring and light display.
   The glass resounds and emits a powerful light.
   Now to new wonders, quick away!
   Exit.
Faust [*alone*].   Where is she?—now no further question make ...   7070
   Though it be not the soil on which she stepped,
   Nor this the wave that to her coming leapt,
   Yet 'tis the air that speaks the tongue she spake.
   Here by a wonder! Here in Grecian land!
   I felt at once the earth on which I stand.   7075
   As, while I slept, new strength my limbs was steeling,
   I rise renewed, Antæus[1] in my feeling.
   And while the strangest things assembled here I find,
   I'll search this labyrinth of flames with serious mind.
   Goes away.

BY THE UPPER PENEUS

Mephistopheles [*peering around*].
   As mid these little fires I wander aimless,   7080
   I find myself quite strange and disconcerted.
   Naked are almost all, some few are shirted;
   The griffins impudent, the sphinxes shameless,
   Winged, curly things—who'll ever dare to name them?
   Seen fore and aft, they're crude enough to shame them ...   7085
   It's true, indecency is our ideal,
   But the antique is too alive and real.
   By modern taste the nude should be controlled
   And overlaid in fashions manifold ...
   A loathsome folk! yet so I must not treat them;   7090
   As new-come guest I should politely greet them ...
   Hail, ye wise grizzlies, hail, ye ladies fair!
A Griffin [*snarling*].   Not grizzlies! Griffins! No one likes to hear

[1] A giant whose strength was renewed in contact with Earth, his mother.

Himself called grizzly. In each word there rings
An echo of the source from which it springs.   7095
Graves, growling, grumpy, gruesome, grim, and grey,
All of one sort in etymology are they,
And put us out of sorts.
Mephistopheles.   Yet—not to leave this thesis—
The *gri* in your proud title *Griffin* pleases.
Griffin [as above and continuously so].
Of course! The kinship has been proved to hold.   7100
'Tis true, it's oft rebuked but oftener extolled.
Let one but *grip* at maidens, crowns, and gold;
Fortune is mostly gracious to the *Gripper* bold.
Ants of the colossal kind.[1]
You speak of gold! In great heaps did we hoard it,
In rocky caverns secretly we stored it;   7105
The Arimaspians[2] have nosed it out,
They bore it off so far they laugh and shout.
Griffin.   We'll bring them to confess their deed.
Arimaspians.   But not in this free night of jubilee.
Ere morning all will squandered be;   7110
This time we'll probably succeed.
Mephistopheles [who has seated himself between the SPHINXES].
How pleasantly I grow familiar here;
I understand them one and all.
A Sphinx.   We breathe our spirit-tones into your ear,
And then you render them material.   7115
Until we know you better, tell your name.
Mephistopheles.   Men think that many a title I may claim.
Are Britons here? Such travellers are they;
Cascades and battlefields they love to trace,
Ruins and many a musty classic place;   7120
A worthy goal they would find here today.
They testified that in the old stage-play
I was seen there as "Old Iniquity."
A Sphinx.   How did they hit on that?
Mephistopheles.   It puzzles even me.
A Sphinx.   Perhaps!—Do you know planets and their power?   7125
What say you to the aspect of the hour?
Mephistopheles [looking upward].
Star courses star, I see the clipped moon glide
And feel quite happy at your cosy side;
I'll warm myself against your lion's-hide.
'Twould hurt to soar up, I'd but go astray.   7130
Propound some riddles or charades to play.
A Sphinx.   Express yourself; that too will be a riddle.
See if your inmost essence you can rede:

[1]These derive from Herodotus, iii. 102.
[2]Cf. ibid., 116; iv, 13. 27.

"What both the pious and the wicked need:
For those a breastplate for ascetic fencing,   7135
For these a comrade, crazy pranks advancing,
Both but the joy of Zeus enhancing."
First Griffin [*snarling*].   I don't like him.
Second Griffin [*snarling more loudly*].   What is it he wants here?
Both.   The nasty wretch belongs not in our sphere!
Mephistopheles [*brutally*].
You think perhaps the guest's nails do not scratch   7140
And with your sharp claws cannot match?
Just try it!
A Sphinx [*gently*].   Here you might forever stay,
But from our midst you'll drive yourself away.
At home you think to do just as you please,
But if I err not, here you're ill at ease.   7145
Mephistopheles.   Right appetizing are you upward from the bosom,
But further down your beastly part is gruesome.
A Sphinx.   These words, you hypocrite, you'll surely rue,
Because our paws are sound; but I can see
That with that shrunken horse's-foot you do   7150
Not feel at ease in our society.
            SIRENS *prelude overhead.*
Mephistopheles.   What birds are they who're cradled yonder
On boughs beside the poplared river?
A Sphinx.   Beware! The best of men have ever
Been led by that singsong to wander.   7155
Sirens.
                Ah, why mar thy taste completely,
                Mid these hideous wonders dwelling?
                Hear our notes accordant swelling,
                See our hosts come singing sweetly
                As becometh sirens meetly.   7160
Sphinxes [*mocking them in the same melody*].
                Force them down! And so reveal them!
                Mid the branches they conceal them;
                Nasty falcon-claws they're wearing
                And will fall on thee, unsparing,
                If thou lendest willing ear.   7165
Sirens.
                Hence with hate, let envy perish!
                We the purest pleasures cherish
                Strewn beneath the sky's blue sphere!
                On the earth and on the ocean
                Let him see in every motion   7170
                Sign of welcome and of cheer.

Mephistopheles.   What novelties and how assuring
When both from string and voice alluring

The tones about each other twine.
But lost on me is all the trilling,   *7175*
Tickling my ears but never thrilling
Down in its depths this heart of mine.
Sphinxes. Speak not of heart! Vain so to call it!
 A shrivelled-up, old leathern wallet
 Would better with your face combine.   *7180*
Faust [approaching]. How strangely satisfying are these creatures!
 Repulsive, yet what big, compelling features!
 I feel now the approach of some good chance;
 Whither is hailing me that earnest glance?
  Referring to the SPHINXES.
 Before such Oedipus once stood his ground;   *7185*
  Referring to the SIRENS.
 Before such did Ulysses writhe, in hemp fast bound;
  Referring to the ANTS.
 By such was noblest treasure once amassed;
  Referring to the GRIFFINS.
 By these 'twas kept inviolate to the last.
 New spirit thrills me when I see all these;
 Great are the figures, great the memories.   *7190*
Mephistopheles. In former times such creatures you'd have scouted
 Which now it seems that you approve;
 Aye, when one seeks his lady-love,
 Monsters themselves are welcome and not flouted.
Faust [to the SPHINXES*].* Ye forms like women, answer me and say: *7195*
 Has anyone of you seen Helena?
Sphinxes. We did not last till Helena's generation;
 Hercules slew the last ones of our nation.
 From Chiron[1] you might get the information.
 This ghostly night he's galloping around;   *7200*
 If he will stop for you, you've gained much ground.
Sirens.

    With us too thou wouldst not miss it! ...
    When Ulysses, with us whiling,
    Sped not past us, unreviling,
    Much he told made bright his visit;   *7205*
    All his tales we'd tell to thee
    If thou camest to renew thee
    To our meadows by the sea.

A Sphinx. Sir, hark not to trickery!
 Whereas Ulysses to the mast,   *7210*
 Let us now with good counsel bind thee.
 If lofty Chiron thou canst find thee,
 What I have sworn, thou wilt learn at last.
  FAUST *goes away.*
[1]The centaur, noted for his vast knowledge.

Mephistopheles [*vexed*].   What croaks on pinions rushing by?
 So fast that they elude the eye?   7215
 Swiftly in single file they fly.
 A hunter tires of such as these.
A Sphinx.   Like to the storm that winter harrows,
 Reached scarcely by Alcides'[1] arrows,
 They are the swift Stymphalides.   7220
 They mean well with their croak-salute,
 Their vulture's-beak, their goose's-foot.
 Here in our midst they'd like to be
 And prove they're of our pedigree.
Mephistopheles [*as if intimidated*].
 Some other things are hissing shrill.   7225
A Sphinx.   For fear of these you need not quake;
 They are the heads of the Lernæan snake;[2]
 Cut from the trunk, they think they're something still.
 But say, what's wrong? why so distressful?
 Why this behaviour so unrestful?   7230
 Where would you go? Be off, good-by!—
 I see, that chorus twists your neck awry.
 Don't force yourself to stay! Go, leave this place,
 Greet yonder many a charming face.
 The Lamiæ,[3] wanton wenches, you'll find there,   7235
 Their foreheads brazen, faces smiling,
 As when the satyrs they're beguiling.
 There all things may a goat's-foot dare.
Mephistopheles.   You'll stay here and I'll find you here again?
Sphinxes.   Yes! Go and mingle with the airy train.   7240
 We long ago are wont, from Egypt coming here,
 To sit enthronèd to the thousandth year.
 Respect to our position you must pay.
 Thus rule we lunar, rule we solar day.

> At the pyramids our station,   7245
> We look on the doom of races,
> War and peace and inundation,
> With eternal changeless faces.

BY THE LOWER PENEUS

PENEUS *surrounded by waters and nymphs.*

Peneus.   Wake and stir, ye whispering bushes,
 Softly breathe, ye reeds and rushes,   7250
 Rustle, willows by the river,

---

[1]Alcides: Hercules. The Stymphalides were monstrous birds of prey, with iron beaks and talons.
 [2]Hercules cut off eight heads of the Lernæan Hydra; the ninth head remained immortal.
 [3]Ghosts with an appetite for human flesh and blood.

Lisp, ye poplar sprays a-quiver,
To my interrupted dream! . . .
Fearful, stirring breezes wake me
And mysterious tremors shake me   7255
From my rippling, restful stream.
Faust [*stepping to the edge of the river*].
If I dare such fancies harbour,
Deep within the tangled arbour
Of these twigs and bushes noises
Sounded as of human voices.   7260
Wave doth seem a very chatter,
Zephyr sounds a jesting patter.
Nymphs [*to* FAUST].

    Ah, best were it for thee
    To lie here, reviving
    In coolness thy members   7265
    Worn out by their striving,
    The rest thus enjoying
    That from thee doth flee;
    We'll rustle, we'll murmur,
    We'll whisper to thee.   7270

Faust. I am awake! Oh, let them stay me,
Those peerless forms, and let them sway me
As mine eye sees them in its quest.
What thrills run through my every member!
Do I but dream? Do I remember?   7275
Ah, once before was I so blessed.
A cooling stream is softly gliding,
Amid the trembling copse half hiding;
It scarcely murmurs in its flow.
From every side, clear and delighting,   7280
A hundred streamlets are uniting
To fill a bath-like pool below.
The fair young limbs of women trouble
The liquid mirror, showing double,
And double so the eye's delight!   7285
Bathing with joy, each other aiding,
Now boldly swimming, shyly wading,
Ending in screams and water-fight.
These should content me, here with pleasure
My sight should be restored at leisure;   7290
Yet toward yonder leafy screen
My vision ever further presses;
The verdant wealth of those recesses
Surely enveils the lofty queen.
    Strange and marvellous! Swans are swimming   7295
From the inlets, hither skimming

In their stately majesty,
Calmly floating, sweetly loving,
Heads and beaks uplifted moving
In proud self-complacency.   7300
But among them one seems peerless,
In his self-love proud and fearless;
Through the throng he sails apace,
Swells his plumage like a pillow,
He, a billow breasting billow,   7305
Speeds on to the sacred place ...
The others to and fro, together,
Swim with unruffled, radiant feather,
Or soon in stirring, splendid fray
Seek to divert each timid beauty   7310
Away from any thought of duty
To save herself if save she may.

Nymphs.

        Sisters, hearken, lend a hearing
        At the river's verdant shore;
        If I err not, more and more   7315
        Sounds of horse's hoofs are nearing.
        Would I knew who in swift flight
        Brings a message to this night!

Faust.   I believe the earth's resounding
    To a steed that's hither bounding.   7320
                Turn there, my glance!
                A most auspicious chance,
                Can it be hither faring?
                O marvel past comparing!
A rider's trotting on toward me.   7325
Spirited, strong, he seems to be;
Borne on a snow-white steed he's nearing ...
I do not err, I know him now,
The famous son of Philyra!—
Halt, Chiron, halt! and give me hearing!   7330

Chiron.   What now? What is it?
Faust.   Check your pace and stay!
Chiron.   I do not rest.
Faust.   Take me along, I pray!
Chiron.   Then, mount! and I can question you at leisure:
    Whither your way? You're standing on the shore
    And I will bear you through the stream with pleasure.   7335
Faust [mounting].   Whither you will, I'll thank you evermore ...
    The noble pedagogue, so great in name,
    Who reared full many a hero, to his fame,
    The troop of Argonauts, renowned in story,
    And all who built the poets' world of glory.   7340

Chiron.   Let us not talk of that. As mentor, none,
   Not Pallas' self, is venerated.
   For, after all, in their own way men carry on
   As if they never had been educated.
Faust.   The doctor who can name each plant, who knows   7345
   All roots, even that which deepest grows,
   Who soothes the wounded, makes the sick man whole,
   You I embrace with all my might and soul.
Chiron.   If at my side a hero felt the smart,
   I knew the aid and counsel to be tendered!   7350
   But in the end all of my art
   To parsons and herb-women was surrendered.
Faust.   Upon a true, great man I gaze!
   Who will not hear a word of praise,
   Modestly strives to shut his ears   7355
   And acts as had he many peers.
Chiron.   You are well-skilled, I see, in idle patter,
   Princes and common folk alike to flatter.
Faust.   At least confess that you have seen
   The greatest men that in your time have been.   7360
   You've with the noblest vied in earnest strife
   And like a demigod have lived your life.
   Of all the figures of heroic mould
   Whom as the ablest did you hold?
Chiron.   Among the Argonauts, superb procession!   7365
   Each one was worthy after his own fashion,
   And by the special power that he possessed,
   Could do what lay beyond the rest.
   Castor and Pollux ever did prevail
   Where youthful bloom and beauty turned the scale.   7370
   In swift resolve and act for others' good
   The sons of Boreas[1] proved their hardihood.
   Reflective, strong and shrewd, in council wise,
   Thus Jason ruled, a joy to women's eyes.
   Then Orpheus, gentle, still, and contemplating,   7375
   But, when he smote the lyre, all subjugating;
   Keen-sighted Lynceus who by day and dark
   Past reef and shallow steered the sacred bark.
   Danger is tested best by banded brothers:
   When one achieves, then praise him all the others.   7380
Faust.   I beg, of Hercules I would be learning!
Chiron.   Oh, woe! Awaken not my yearning! ...
   Phoebus I ne'er had seen, nor yet
   Seen Ares, Hermes, as they're called, in fine,
   When my enraptured vision met   7385
   A form that all men call divine.
   A king by birth as was no other,
   [1]They rescued their sister's husband from the Harpies.

A youth most glorious to view,
A subject to his elder brother
And to the loveliest women too.   7390
His like will Gæa[1] bring forth never
Nor Hebe lead to Heaven again;
Songs struggle in a vain endeavour,
Men torture marble all in vain.

Faust.   Though men may strive in stone and story,   7395
Never has he appeared in all his glory.
You now have spoken of the fairest man;
Tell of the fairest woman all you can!

Chiron.   What! Woman's beauty? That is not worth telling,
Too oft a rigid image do we see;   7400
I praise alone a being welling
With love of life and gaiety.
Self-blest is beauty, cold and listless,
'Tis winsomeness that makes resistless,
Like that of Helena whom once I bore.   7405

Faust.   You bore her?

Chiron.   Aye, upon this back.

Faust.   Was I not crazed enough before?
And here to sit! Such bliss I do not lack!

Chiron.   She also grasped me by the hair,
Seizing it just as you are doing now.   7410

Faust.   I'm losing all my senses! Tell me how,
Whence, whither? Ah, you really did her bear?
She only is my whole desire!

Chiron.   Easy it is to tell what you require.
Castor and Pollux had at that time freed   7415
Their darling sister[2] from base robbers' greed.
The robbers, wonted not to be subdued,
Took heart and in a storm of rage pursued.
Brothers and sister, speeding on their way,
Were checked by swamps that near Eleusis lay;   7420
The brothers waded, but I splashed, swam over;
Then off she sprang, she stroked and pressed me
On my wet mane, thanked and caressed me
Sweetly self-conscious, affectionate and sage.
How charming was she! young, the joy of age!   7425

Faust.   Just ten years old!

Chiron.   The doctors of philology
Have fooled you like themselves, I see.
Peculiar is it with a mythologic dame;
The poet brings her, as he needs, to fame;
She never grows adult and never old,   7430
Always of appetizing mould,

[1]Earth.
[2]Helen, held captive by Theseus.

Ravished when young, still wooed long past her prime.
Enough, the poet is not bound by time.
Faust.   Then, here too, be no law of time thrown round her!
On Pheræ's isle indeed Achilles found her   *7435*
Beyond the pale of time. A happiness, how rare!
In spite of fate itself love triumphed there.
Is it beyond my yearning passion's power
To bring to life the earth's most perfect flower?
That deathless being, peer of gods above,   *7440*
Tender as great; sublime, yet made for love!
You saw her once, *today* I've seen her too,
Charming as fair, desired as fair to view.
My captured soul and being yearn to gain her;
I will not live unless I can attain her.   *7445*
Chiron.   Strange person! As a man you feel an ecstasy,
But to us spirits you seem mad to be.
Now, as it haps, good fortune meets you here,
Since for some moments every year
I'm wont to Manto to repair   *7450*
Who, Aesculapius' child, in silent prayer
Implores her father, for his honour's gain,
To throw some light in the physicians' brain
That from rash slaughter may their hands refrain ...
I love her most of all the guild of sybils,   *7455*
Gentle and kind, nor prone to shifty quibbles.
If but a while you stay, her art secure
By powerful roots will work your perfect cure.
Faust.   I'm sound in mind. A cure is not my aim;
Else, like to others, I'd be base and tame.   *7460*
Chiron.   The noble fountain's cure, neglect it not!
Be quick, dismount! We've reached the spot.
Faust.   Say, whither have you in this gruesome night
Borne me through pebbly waters in our flight?
Chiron.   Here[1] Rome and Greece each bearded each in fight,   *7465*
Olympus on the left, Peneus on the right.
The greatest realm that ever was lost in sand;
The monarch flees, the conquering burghers stand.
Look up! Here stands, significantly near,
The eternal temple in the moonlight clear.   *7470*

Manto [*dreaming, within*].
                        From horse-hoofs bounding
                        The sacred stairs are resounding;
                        Demigods are drawing near.
Chiron.
                        Quite right!
                        Raise your eyes; behold who's here!   *7475*

[1]At Pydna, where the Romans defeated King Perseus of Macedonia (168 B.C.).

Manto [*awakening*].   Welcome! I see you do not fail to come.
Chiron.   Likewise for you still stands your temple-home.
Manto.   Are you still roaming, never weary?
Chiron.   Well, you abide in stillness eerie,
   The while I circle joyously.   7480
Manto.   I wait here, time encircles me.
   And this man?
Chiron.   Him hath this ill-fated night
   Caught in its whirl and brought here to your sight.
   Helena, go his wits a-spinning,
   Helena he has dreams of winning,   7485
   But knows no way to make beginning,
   Most worthy, Aesculapian cure to prove.
Manto.   Who yearns for the impossible I love.
    CHIRON *is already far away.*
Manto.   Enter, audacious one, glad shall you be;
   The gloomy way leads to Persephone.   7490
   Within Olympus' cavern foot
   She lists in secret for prescribed salute.
   Here did I smuggle Orpheus in of old.
   Use your turn better! Quick! be bold!
    They descend.

BY THE UPPER PENEUS

Sirens [*by the upper Peneus as before*].
            Plunge ye in Peneus' flood!   7495
            Meetly splashing, swimming, fording,
            Linking songs in tones according,
            For these ill-starred people's good.
            Without water weal is none!
            If our goodly bands were faring   7500
            To the Aegean, swift repairing,
            Every joy would then be won.
   Earthquake.
Sirens.
            Back the foaming wave is going,
            Down its bed no longer flowing;
            Quakes the ground, the waters choke,   7505
            Shores and pebbles crack and smoke.
            Let us flee! Come, all! Come on!
            For this marvel profits none.
            Hence! Ye noble guests and merry,
            To the ocean revel hurry,   7510
            Glittering where the waves are twinkling,
            Heaving gently, shores besprinkling,
            There where Luna twofold gloweth,
            Holy dew on us bestoweth.

There a life astir and cheerful,   7515
Here an earthquake dire and fearful.
Hence, ye prudent, haste away!
For this place strikes with dismay.

Seismos[1] [*growling and blustering in the depths*].
Shove again with shoulders straining,
Stoutly all your strength arraigning!   7520
Upper regions we'll be gaining,
Where to us must all give way.

Sphinxes.

What a most unpleasant quivering,
What a hideous, fearsome shivering!
What a wavering, what a shocking,   7525
Surging to and fro and rocking!
An unbearable affray!
But we shall not change our places,
Though all hell bursts in our faces.

Now a dome—behold the wonder!—   7530
Is arising. Ah, 'tis yonder
Very Ancient, long since hoar,
Who built Delos' isle of yore,
Drove it upward from the billow
For a travailing woman's pillow.[2]   7535
He, with straining, pressing, rending,
Rigid arms and shoulders bending,
Like an Atlas in his gesture,
Heaves up earth and all its vesture,
Loam and stone and sand and gravel,   7540
Quiet shores and calm beds' level.
Thus the valley's placid bosom
Rends he with a power gruesome,
Still most strenuous, never sated,
A colossal caryatid,   7545
Bears an awful weight of boulders,
Buried still up to his shoulders.
But 'twill not come near these spaces;
Sphinxes now are in their places.

Seismos.   I, only, wrought this little matter   7550
As men will finally declare;
But for my batter and my clatter
How would this world be now so fair?
How would your mountains stand above there

[1]Earthquake.

[2]Poseidon, at the instigation of Zeus, thrust up Delos from the sea so that Leto might give birth to Apollo and Diana, her offspring by Zeus. Hera had vowed that the pregnant goddess should not give birth in any place the sun had ever shone upon.

In clear and splendid ether-blue,   7555
If them I had not worked to shove there?
A picturesque, entrancing view!
Whenas (the primal sires surveying,
Chaos and Night) I saw my honour lost,
I, with the Titans joined in playing,   7560
Hurled Ossa, Pelion too, as balls are tossed.
Thus we raged on in youthful passion
Till vexed and weary at the last
Both mountains we, in wanton fashion,
Like twin peaks on Parnassus cast . . .   7565
Apollo gladly lingers yonder
There in the muses' blest retreat.
For Jove himself and for his bolts of thunder
I heaved on high his lofty seat.
Thus I, by strainings superhuman,   7570
Pushed from the depths to upper air,
And dwellers glad I loudly summon
New life henceforth with me to share.

Sphinxes.   Surely one would call primeval
What so burg-like looms today,   7575
But we saw the earth give way
To the straining, vast upheaval.
A bushy wood is spreading up the side,
While rocks on rocks still roll on like a tide.
A sphinx will never let such things perturb her,   7580
Nor in her sacred seat will aught disturb her.

Griffins.   Gold a-spangle, gold a-flitter,
Through the chinks I see it glitter.
Let none rob you of the prize:
Up and claw it, emmets! Rise!   7585

Chorus of Ants.
                    Whereas the giant ones
                    Upward could shove it,
                    Ye nimble, pliant ones,
                    Swift speed above it!
                    Scurry ye out and in!   7590
                    In each cranny
                    Is every crumb ye win
                    Wealth for the canny.
                    Ye must discover it,
                    The slightest treasure,   7595
                    Swiftly uncover it
                    In every fissure.
                    Toil like the busy bees,
                    Ye swarms, retrieve it.
                    Gold only shall ye seize!   7600
                    What's oreless, leave it!

Griffins.   Come, come! Bring in a heap of gold!
   Beneath our claws fast will we hold.
   They're bolts none others can excel,
   They guard the greatest treasure well.   7605
Pygmies.   We are in our places truly,
   Know not how it did befall.
   Whence we came, don't ask unduly,
   For we're here now once for all.
   As a joyous place to settle,   7610
   Suitable is every land;
   If a rocky rift shows metal,
   Straightway is the dwarf at hand.
   Male and female, busy, ready,
   Exemplary is each pair;   7615
   We know not if once already
   This the case in Eden were.
   Our lot gratefully we treasure,
   For we find things here are best;
   Mother Earth brings forth with pleasure   7620
   In the east as in the west.
Dactyls.

               Hath in a night the Earth
               The little ones brought to birth,
               The smallest she will create too,
               They will find each his mate too.   7625
Eldest Pygmies.

               Hasten, in spaces
               Pleasant take places!
               Haste, the work heeding,
               Not strong but speeding!
               Peace is still with ye,   7630
               Build ye the smithy
               For troops to shapen
               Armour and weapon.

               All ye ants, cluster,
               Busily fluster,   7635
               Metals to muster!
               Dactyls conforming,
               Tiny but swarming,
               Our orders hear ye
               And firewood bear ye!   7640
               Heap in a pyre
               Smothering fire!
               Charcoal prepare ye!
Generalissimo.

               With bow and arrow
               Foes will we harrow!   7645

Herons that wander
By that pond yonder,
Numberless nesting there,
Haughtily breasting there,
Shoot them straightway,   7650
All them together,
In helm and feather
Us to array.

Ants and Dactyls.

Who now will save us!
Iron we're bringing,   7655
Chains to enslave us.
Chains we're not springing,
Not yet's the hour;
Heed, then, their power!

The Cranes of Ibycus.

Cries of murder, moan of dying!   7660
Fearful pinions fluttering, flying!
What a groan and moan and fright
Pierces upward to our height!
All have fallen in the slaughter,
Reddened with their blood the water.   7665
Greedy lust, misshapen, cruel,
Steals the heron's noble jewel.
On the helmet now it waves,
Oh, these fat-paunched, bow-legged knaves!
Comrades with our host in motion,   7670
Serried wanderers of the ocean,
Summon we, for vengeance mated,
In a case so near related.
Let none spare his strength or blood!
Hate eternal to this brood!   7675

They disperse in the air, croaking.

Mephistopheles [*on the plain*].
The northern witches I command, but these,
Spirits so alien, make me ill at ease.
The Blocksberg's a convenient place to roam;
Wherever you are, you find yourself at home.
Dame Ilsa watches for us on her Stone,   7680
Wakeful is Henry on his lofty Throne;
The Snorers snort, in truth, in Elend's ears,
But all remains unchanged a thousand years.
But who knows here, if, where he stand or go,
The ground will not heave upward from below? . . .   7685
I wander through a level dale quite happily,
And then behind me rises suddenly
A mountain—scarce a mountain, yet in height
Enough to block the sphinxes from my sight.

Here, down the valley, many a fire is glaring, 7690
Its light on these strange scenes and figures flaring . . .
Still, knavishly confusing, lo! the amorous crew
Flutter and dance before me, flee and woo.
But softly now! Though used to many savours,
Wherever they be, one still seeks novel flavours. 7695

Lamiæ [*drawing* MEPHISTOPHELES *after them*].
                    Quicker and quicker!
                    And never tarry!
                    Then hesitating,
                    Chatting and prating.
                    It is so merry, 7700
                    The ancient tricker
                    To lure behind us
                    To penance dreary.
                    Foot-stiff and weary,
                    On he comes hobbling, 7705
                    After us wobbling;
                    He drags his foot,
                    Hasting to find us.
                    Vain is his suit.

Mephistopheles [*standing still*].
Cursed fate! Men are but women's fools! 7710
From Adam down, becozened tools!
Older we grow but who grows wise and steady?
Were you not fooled enough already?
    We know that wholly worthless is this race
With pinched-in waist and painted face; 7715
Naught's wholesome in a folk so misbegotten;
Grasp where you will, in every limb they're rotten.
We know it, see it, we can feel it,
And still we dance if but the vile jades reel it!

Lamiæ [*pausing*].   Halt! See him ponder, hesitate, delay! 7720
Turn back to meet him lest he slip away!

Mephistopheles [*striding forward*].   Go on! nor in the web of doubt
Let yourself be entangled foolishly;
For if no witches were about,
Why, who the devil would a devil be! 7725

Lamiæ [*most winsomely*].   Round this hero circle we;
Surely soon within his breast
Love for one is manifest.

Mephistopheles.   True, in this uncertain gleam,
Pretty wenches do you seem, 7730
And you'll hear no slurs from me.

An Empusa[1] [*intruding*].   Nor slur me! A maiden too,
Let me join your retinue.

[1]A shape-changing spook.

Lamiæ.   In our group she'll never fit,
    And our sport? she ruins it.   *7735*
Empusa [*to* MEPHISTOPHELES].   From ass-foot Coz Empusa, greeting!
    The trusty one whom now you're meeting.
    You only have a horse's foot;
    Still, take, Sir Coz, my best salute!
Mephistopheles.   Strangers alone were here by expectations,   *7740*
    But now, alas! I'm finding near relations.
    Indeed, an ancient book doth tell us:
    Everywhere cousins from the Hartz to Hellas.
Empusa.   I'm swift in acting with decision,
    In many forms could meet your vision;   *7745*
    But honour due you I would pay
    And so the ass's head I've donned today.
Mephistopheles.   I note, with people of this sort
    Kinship is stuff of great import;
    But come what may, it's all the same,   *7750*
    The ass's head I'd fain disclaim.
Lamiæ.   Avoid this hag! She doth but scare
    Whatever lovely seems and fair;
    What fair and lovely was before,
    She comes, and see! it is no more!   *7755*
Mephistopheles.   These cousins too, slim and delicious,
    Of one and all I am suspicious;
    Behind such darling cheeks of roses
    I have a fear of metamorphoses.
Lamiæ.   Just try it, do! We are not few.   *7760*
    Lay hold! and if the game's luck favours you,
    Grab for yourself the first, great prize.
    What means this lustful, droning tune?
    What sort of way is this to spoon?
    You strut along and act so wise!   *7765*
    Into our group now see him stride!
    Lay one by one your masks aside
    And show your nature to his eyes.
Mephistopheles.   The fairest I have chosen me . . .
    Clasping her.
    Oh, woe! A withered broomstick, she!   *7770*
    Seizing another.
    And this one? . . . Hideous face! Oh, what a lot!
Lamiæ.   Do you deserve things better? Think it not!
Mephistopheles.   The little one I'd like to clasp . . .
    A lizard's slipping from my grasp!
    And snake-like is her slippery braid.   *7775*
    Well, then, a tall one I will catch . . .
    And now a thyrsus-pole I snatch !
    Only a pine-cone as its head.
    Where will this end? . . . Let's try a fat one.

Perhaps I'll find delight in that one.   7780
A last attempt! Then it will do!
So flabby, fubby, worth a treasure
As Orientals such things measure . . .
But ah, the puff-ball bursts in two!
Lamiæ.   Scatter asunder, flicker around him,   7785
Like lightning, in black flight surround him.
The interloping witch's son!
Ye bats, in horrid, changeful reeling,
Whirl ye, on noiseless pinions wheeling!
He'll get off cheap when all is done.   7790
Mephistopheles [*shaking himself*].
I have not grown much wiser, that seems clear.
The North's absurd, absurd it's also here;
Ghosts here and there are a confounded crew,
Tasteless the people and the poets too.
A masquerade is here, I swear,   7795
A sensual dance as everywhere.
At lovely rows of masks I grasped
And shuddered at the things I clasped . . .
I gladly lend myself to cheating
But ask to have it not so fleeting.   7800
       Losing himself among the rocks.
Where am I? Where does this lead out?
There was a path, now stone-heaps roundabout.
I came along on level ways,
And rubble-stuff now meets my gaze;
I clamber up and down in vain.   7805
My sphinxes—where find them again?
I'd not have dreamed so mad a sight,
Aye, such a mountain in one night!
"A witch-ride" would not name it wrong;
They bring their own Blocksberg along.   7810
Oread [*from a natural rock*].   Come up to me! My mount is old
And still has its primeval mould.
Revere these cliff-paths steep ascending
And Pindus' last spur far extending!
Unshaken, thus I reared my head   7815
When over my shoulders Pompey fled.
Beside me here this phantom rock
Will vanish at the crow of cock.
Such fairy-tales I often see arise
And perish in like sudden wise.   7820
Mephistopheles.   Honour to thee, thou honoured head!
With mighty oaks engarlanded.
Moonbeams, however clear and bright,
Never can pierce thy sable night.—
But by the bushes there I see   7825

A light that's glowing modestly.
How strange that all must happen thus!
In truth, it is Homunculus.
Whence do you come, you little rover?
Homunculus.   From place to place I flit and hover   *7830*
And wish that in the best sense I might *be*.
My glass I long impatiently to shatter;
Only from what I've seen and see,
I do not like to venture on this matter.
But I'll tell you quite confidentially: *7835*
I've tracked two sages whom I've overheard
Say "Nature!" "Nature!"—'twas their only word.
I will not part me from them, seeing
That they must know this earthly be-ing;
And in the end I'll doubtless learn   *7840*
Whither most wisely I'm to turn.
Mephistopheles.   Accomplish that in your own way.
Wherever ghosts may be appearing,
The sage finds welcome and a hearing;
And that his art and favour may elate,   *7845*
A dozen new ghosts he'll at once create.
You'll not gain sense, except you err and stray!
You'll come to birth? Do it in your own way!
Homunculus.   Good counsel, though, a man should never scout.
Mephistopheles.   Proceed, then, and we'll see how things turn out.   *7850*
    They separate.
Anaxagoras [*to* THALES].   You will not let your rigid mind be bent.
Is aught more needed to make you assent?
Thales.   To every wind the wave bows fain enough,
But from the rugged rock it holds aloof.
Anaxagoras.   Through flaming gas arose this rock we're seeing.   *7855*
Thales.   In moisture came organic life to being.
Homunculus [*between the two*].
Ah, by your side to go, pray, suffer me!
I'm yearning to begin to be.
Anaxagoras.   Have you, O Thales, even in one night
Brought such a mountain out of slime to light?   *7860*
Thales.   Nature with all her living, flowing powers
Was never bound by day and night and hours.
By rule she fashions every form, and hence
In great things too there is no violence.
Anaxagoras.   But here there was! Plutonic, savage fire,   *7865*
Aeolian vapours' force, explosive, dire,
Broke through the ancient crust of level earth
And a new mountain straightway came to birth.
Thales.   The hill is there; so much at least is gained.
But what is thereby furthered and attained?   *7870*
Both time and leisure in such strife one poses

And only leads the patient rabble by their noses.
Anaxagoras.   Quickly with Myrmidons the hill is teeming,
  They occupy the clefts; and now come streaming
  Pygmies and ants and fingerlings[1]   *7875*
  And other active little things.
      To HOMUNCULUS.
  After the great you never have aspired
  But hermit-like have lived retired;
  If you can wont yourself to sovereignty,
  Then crowned as king I'll have you be.   *7880*
Homunculus.   What says my Thales?
Thales.   That I won't advise.
  With little people little deeds arise;
  Among the great, the little man grows great.
  See there! The cranes, the swarthy cloud,
  They menace the excited crowd   *7885*
  And they would menace thus the king.
  With beaks sharp-pointed, talons fierce,
  The little ones they tear and pierce;
  Already doom comes thundering.
  Herons had suffered impious slaughter,   *7890*
  Standing about the tranquil water.
  But from that rain of murd'rous engines
  Has sprung a blessèd, bloody vengeance;
  It stirs the rage of brotherhood
  And lust for pygmies' impious blood.   *7895*
  Shield, helmet, spear—how profit these?
  What use to dwarfs the heron feather?
  How ant and dactyl hide together!
  The host now wavers, breaks, and flees.
Anaxagoras [after a pause, solemnly].
  If till now subterranean I praised,   *7900*
  In this case be my prayer to Heaven raised . . .
  O Thou on high, the same eternally,
  In name and form threefold supernally,
  By all my people's woe I cry to Thee,
  Diana, Luna, Hecate!   *7905*
  Thou breast-expanding One, most deeply pensive **One,**
  Thou peaceful seeming One, mighty intensive **One,**
  Break from the glooms of Thy dark chasm clear,
  And without magic let Thine ancient might appear!
      Pause.
                        Am I too quickly heard?   *7910*
                        Hath my prayer
                        To yonder sphere
                        The ordered course of Nature stirred?
  And greater, ever greater, draweth near
  [1]The Dactyls of lines 7622-5.

The goddess' throne, her full-orbed sphere—   7915
To gaze upon, appalling, dire!
And ruddier, redder glows its fire . . .
No nearer! threatening orb, I pray,
Lest Thou wilt sweep us, land, and sea away!
  Thessalian witches? Can it then be true   7920
That Thee once from Thy proper path they drew,
By spells of impious magic sung,
And fatal gifts from Thee so wrenched and wrung? . . .
The brilliant shield, behold, it darkles!
And now it splits and flares and sparkles!   7925
What clattering! What hissing yonder!
And midst it what wild hurricane and thunder!
Humbly I kneel here at Thy throne!
Forgive! I have invoked it, I alone!
  He throws himself on his face.

Thales. What has this man not seen and heard!   7930
I know not rightly what occurred;
Nor yet like him have I experienced it.
They're crazy hours, let us admit.
And Luna's swaying comfortably
In her old place as formerly.   7935

Homunculus. Look at the pygmies' seat! I vow,
The hill was round, it's pointed now.
I seemed to feel an awful shock;
Down from the moon had plunged a rock;
At once, without a question, too,   7940
Both friend and foe it squashed and slew.
High arts like these I have to praise,
Which, by some great creative might,
Working above, below, could raise
This mountain-pile in but one night.   7945

Thales. Be calm! 'Twas but like thought in rapid flight.
Let them be gone, the nasty brood!
That you were not their king is good.
Now to the sea's glad fête let us repair.
They hope and honour rare guests there.   7950
  Exeunt.

Mephistopheles [*climbing up on the opposite side*].
Up steep rock stairways I am forced to fag me,
Through stubborn roots of ancient oak trees drag me!
Up in my Hartz there is a resinous savour
With hints of pitch, and that enjoys my favour
Almost like brimstone . . . In this Grecian place,   7955
Of scents like these there's scarcely any trace.
I'm curious to know and would inquire
Wherewith they feed hell's torments and hell's fire.

A Dryad. At home be wise as it befits you there;

Abroad you have no cleverness to spare.   7960
Homeward you should not turn your thoughts while here;
You should the sacred oaks' high worth revere.
Mephistopheles.   We think of what behind us lies;
  What we were used to seems a Paradise.
  But say: What cowers in the cavern there,   7965
  Threefold in form and dimly lighted?
A Dryad.   The Phorkyads! [1] Approach them if you dare
  And speak to them if you are not affrighted.
Mephistopheles.   Why not?—I see a something and I wonder.
  I must confess although it hurts my pride: 7970
  The like of them I've never yet espied.
  Why, worse than mandrakes, they look yonder . . .
  How can the Deadly Sins then ever be
  Considered ugly in the least degree
  If one has seen this monstrous trinity?   7975
  We would not suffer it to dwell
  Upon the threshold of our grimmest hell.
  Here in the land of beauty it is rooted,
  The classic, antique land reputed . . .
  They seem to scent me now and stir and chitter;   7980
  Like vampire bats they peep and twitter.
A Phorkyad.   Give me the eye, my sisters, to espy
  Who to our temple dares to come so nigh.
Mephistopheles.   Most honoured! I approach you, with your leave,
  That I your threefold blessing may receive.   7985
  I come, though as a stranger, be it stated,
  Yet, if I err not, distantly related.
  Gods ancient and revered I've seen ere now,
  To Ops and Rhea made my deepest bow.
  The Fates, your sisters too, whom Chaos bore,   7990
  I saw them yesterday—or else the day before.
  But others like yourselves I've never sighted,
  And I stand mute, amazed, delighted!
The Phorkyads.   Intelligent this spirit seems to be.
Mephistopheles.   That no bard sings your praise amazes me.   7995
  And say! How came it, how could it have been?
  Your likeness, worthy ones, I've never seen!
  On you the chisel should try out its art,
  And not on Juno, Pallas, Venus, and that sort.
The Phorkyads.   Immersed in stillest night and solitude,   8000
  We Three have never felt that thought intrude.
Mephistopheles.   How should it? Since withdrawn from earthly view,
  Here you see none, nor anyone sees you.
  But choose in other places to reside
  Where art and splendour equally preside,   8005

[1]Daughters of Phorkyas (darkness), grey old women with one eye and one tooth in common.

Where daily in quick time from marble blocks
Heroes leap into life in flocks,
Where—
The Phorkyads.   Silence! Stir in us no longings new!
What would it profit if we better knew?
We, born in night, akin to night alone,   *8010*
Are almost to ourselves, to others quite, unknown.
Mephistopheles.   In such a case there is not much to say.
To others, though, one can one's self convey.
One eye, one tooth, suffices for you three,
So it would tally with mythology   *8015*
If into two the being of you three were blended
And your third form to me were lended
For a brief time.
One Phorkyad.   What think you? Should we try?
The Other Phorkyads.   Let's try it! But without the tooth or eye.
Mephistopheles.   Take these away? The essence then you'll take,   *8020*
For it's the perfect image that they make.
One Phorkyad.   Press one eye to—quite easily it's done—
And of your tusks show only one;
At once you will attain our profile meetly
And sisterly resemble us completely.   *8025*
Mephistopheles.   Much honour! Be it so!
The Phorkyads.   So be it!
Mephistopheles [*in profile like a* PHORKYAD].   Done!
Here stand I, Chaos' well-belovèd son!
The Phorkyads.   Daughters of Chaos we, by undisputed right!
Mephistopheles.   Oh, shame! They'll call me now hermaphrodite!
The Phorkyads.   What beauty in the sisters' triad new!   *8030*
We have two eyes, our teeth are two.
Mephistopheles.   From all eyes I must hide this visage well
To fright the devils in the pool of Hell.
     Exit.

ROCKY COVES OF THE AEGEAN SEA
Moon tarrying in the zenith.

Sirens [*couched around on the cliffs, fluting and singing*].
                    If of yore, by spells nocturnal,
                    Did Thessalian hags infernal   *8035*
                    Draw thee down, a crime intending,
                    Gaze thou where night's arch is bending
                    Down with calmness never-ending
                    On the billowy, twinkling ocean,
                    And illumine the commotion   *8040*
                    Rising from the billowing sea!
                    To thy service vowed are we,
                    Lovely Luna, gracious be!

Nereids and Tritons [*as wonders of the sea*].

<blockquote>

With a louder, shriller singing,
Through the breadth of ocean ringing,   8045
Summon here the deep's gay throng!
From the cruel tempest's riot
Fled we to the deepest quiet,
Hither lured by lovely song.

Here behold us decorated   8050
With gold chains and high elated;
Crowns and jewels do ye capture,
Brooches, girdles that enrapture.
All this harvest is your prey.
To us here these shipwrecked treasures   8055
Ye have brought with your sweet measures,
Ye, the magnets of our bay.

</blockquote>

Sirens.

<blockquote>

Well we know, in cool seas biding,
How the fishes, smoothly gliding,
Joy in life, from trouble far;   8060
Yet, ye festive hosts quick moving,
We today would see you proving
That ye more than fishes are.

</blockquote>

Nereids and Tritons.

<blockquote>

We, before we hither wandered,
Thought of that and deeply pondered.   8065
Sisters, brothers, swiftly fare!
Needs today but little travel
Proof to show past any cavil
That we more than fishes are.

</blockquote>

    They disappear.

Sirens.

<blockquote>

Away they speed and race   8070
Straight toward Samothrace;
With kindly wind gone are they far.
What mean they to do in the eerie
Domain of the Mighty Cabiri? [1]
They're gods, and stranger were never;   8075
They beget their like ever and ever
And never know what they are.

Linger thou on thy height,
Lovely Luna, stay thy light,
That the night may not vanish   8080
Nor the day may us banish.

</blockquote>

[1]Originally Phœnician gods, they were worshipped on Lemnos and later on Samothrace. They now were said to have been the rulers of earth and sea.

Thales [*on the shore, to* HOMUNCULUS].
   To ancient Nereus I would lead the way;
   We're not far distant from his cave today,
   But hard and stubborn is his pate,
   Contrary, sour, old reprobate.   8085
   Nothing of mortal humankind
   Is ever to that grumbler's mind.
   The future, though, is known to him,
   Wherefore men hold him in esteem
   And honour him where he holds sway.   8090
   Kind has he been to many a one.
Homunculus.   Let's try it then and see. Come on!
   My glass and flame 'twill not cost me straightway.
Nereus.   Are they men's voices that my ear has heard?
   How quick with wrath my inmost heart is stirred!   8095
   These creatures would be gods by sheer endeavour,
   Yet damned to be like their own selves forever.
   In days of old I could divinely rest,
   Yet I was oft impelled to aid the Best,
   But when at last I saw what they had done,   8100
   'Twas quite as if I had not counselled one.
Thales.   Yet people trust you, greybeard, ocean seer;
   You are the Sage; oh, drive us not from here!
   Gaze on this flame, like to a man, indeed;
   Your counsel only will it hear and heed.   8105
Nereus.   Counsel! With men has counsel once availed?
   Vain are shrewd warnings to a fast-closed ear.
   Oft as their deeds proved, men have grimly failed;
   Self-willed are they still as they always were.
   How I warned Paris with a father's trust   8110
   Before another's wife ensnared his lust!
   Upon the Grecian shore he stood up bold,
   And what I saw in spirit I foretold:
   The reeking air above, a ruddy glow,
   Rafters ablaze, murder and death below: 8115
   Troy's Judgment Day, held fast in noble rhyme,
   A horror famous to the end of time.
   Reckless he laughed at all that I could tell;
   He followed his own lust and Ilion fell—
   A giant corpse, stark when its torments ceased,   8120
   To Pindus' eagles a right welcome feast.
   Ulysses too! Told I not him erewhiles
   Of Cyclops' horrors and of Circe's wiles?
   His dallying, his comrades' thoughtless vein,
   And what not all—but did it bring him gain?   8125
   Till, late enough, a favouring billow bore
   The long-tossed wanderer to a friendly shore.
Thales.   Of course such action gives a wise man pain;

Still, if he's kind, he'll try it once again.
An ounce of thanks will in its bliss outweigh,   *8130*
Yes, tons of thanklessness for many a day.
And nothing trifling to implore have we:
The boy here wisely wants to come to be.
Nereus.   Don't spoil my rarest mood, I pray!
Far other things await me here today: *8135*
My daughters all I've summoned here to me,
The Dorides, the Graces of the Sea.
Olympus not, nor yet your soil, can bear
A form that is so dainty and so fair.
From dragons of the sea, all in most winsome motion,   *8140*
They leap on Neptune's coursers; in the ocean,
Their element, so tenderly at home
They seem to float upon the very foam.
    On Venus' radiant, pearly chariot drawn,
Comes Galatea, lovely as the dawn.   *8145*
Since Cypris[1] turned from us her face,
She reigns in Paphos in the goddess' place.
And so, long since, the gracious one doth own,
As heiress, templed town and chariot-throne.
Away! It spoils a father's hour of pleasure,   *8150*
Harshness of tongue or hate of heart to treasure.
Away to Proteus! Ask that wondrous elf:
How one can come to be and change one's self.
    He goes off toward the sea.
Thales.   We have gained nothing by this stay.
Though one finds Proteus, straight he melts away;   *8155*
And if he stops for you, he'll say at last
Things that confuse you, make you stand aghast.
But, after all, such counsel do you need;
Let's try it and pursue our path with speed.
    They go away.

Sirens [*above on the rocks*].
                    What's that far off, half hiding,   *8160*
                    Through ocean's billows gliding?
                    As if, to breezes bending,
                    White sails were hither wending.
                    Bright beam they over waters,
                    Transfigured ocean's daughters!   *8165*
                    Let us climb down! They're singing!
                    List to the voices ringing!

Nereids and Tritons.

                    What we escort and carry
                    Shall make you glad and merry.

[1]Aphrodite.

Chelone's shield gigantic[1]   8170
Gleams with stern figures antic;
They're gods whom we are bringing.
High songs must ye be singing.

Sirens.

Little in height,[2]
Potent in might   8175
Who shipwrecked men deliver,
Gods old and honoured ever.

Nereids and Tritons.

We're bringing the Cabiri
To the peaceful pageant cheery,
For where they rule auspicious   8180
Neptune will be propitious.

Sirens.

We give way to you:
With resistless power
Ye save the perishing crew
In dire shipwreck's hour.   8185

Nereids and Tritons.

We have brought three only,
The fourth one tarried lonely;
He said he must stay yonder
Since he for all must ponder.

Sirens.

One god the other god   8190
Can jeer and prod.
Their good deeds revere ye!
All their ill ones fear ye!

Nereids and Tritons.

To seven ye should be praying.

Sirens.

Where are the three delaying?   8195

Nereids and Tritons.

For that we've no suggestion,
But on Olympus question;
Haply the eighth's there biding,
Not thought-of yet, and hiding.
In favours to us steady,   8200
Yet are they all not ready.

Peerless, unexplainable,
Always further yearning,
With desire and hunger burning
For the unattainable.   8205

[1]Chelone, a nymph changed into a tortoise because she ridiculed the marriage of Zeus and Hera.

[2]The Cabiri were pictured as a clay-pot with a head superimposed.

Sirens.

> Such our ways:
> Where power most sways,
> Worship we raise,
> Sunward, moonward: it pays!

Nereids and Tritons.

> How brightly shines our fame! behold!   *8210*
> Leading this pageant cheery!

Sirens.

> The heroes of olden time
> To such fame don't climb,
> Where and how it unfold,
> Although they've won the Fleece of Gold,   *8215*
> Ye've won the Cabiri!

> *Repeated in full chorus.*

> Although they've won the Fleece of Gold,
> We! Ye! the Cabiri!

> NEREIDS *and* TRITONS *move past.*

Homunculus.   These shapeless forms I look upon,
> As poor clay-pots I take them;   *8220*
> Their hard heads wise men often run
> Against them and there break them.

Thales.   That's just the thing that men desire;
> The rusty coin is valued higher.

Proteus [*unperceived*].   This pleases me, an ancient fabler!   *8225*
> The odder 'tis, the respectabler.

Thales.   Where are you, Proteus?

Proteus [*ventriloquizing, now near, now far*].   Here! and here!

Thales.   I pardon you that ancient jeer;
> But with a friend such idle words forgo!
> You speak from some false place, I know.   *8230*

Proteus [*as if from a distance*].   Farewell!

Thales [*softly to* HOMUNCULUS].   He is quite near. Shine
>   brilliantly!
> As curious as a fish is he;
> Assume what form and place he may, be sure,
> Flames are for him unfailing lure.

Homunculus.   At once a flood of light I'll scatter,   *8235*
> Discreetly, though, for fear the glass might shatter.

Proteus [*in the form of a giant tortoise*].
> What beams so winsome, fair, and dear?

Thales [*concealing* HOMUNCULUS].
> Good! If you wish, you can observe it near.
> Don't let the little effort worry you,
> Appear on two feet just as humans do.   *8240*
> It's with our will and by our courtesy
> That what we now conceal, who wills may see.

Proteus [*in a noble form*].
    In clever, worldly pranks you still have skill.
Thales.   You change your form with pleasure still.
    He has uncovered HOMUNCULUS.
Proteus [*astonished*]. A radiant dwarflet! Such I never did   *8245*
    see!
Thales.   He asks advice and fain would come to be.
    He has, he told me, come to earth
    But half-way formed, a quite peculiar birth.
    He has no lack of qualities ideal
    But lacks too much the tangible and real.   *8250*
    Till now the glass alone has given him weight;
    He'd like forthwith to be incorporate.
Proteus.   You are a virgin's son, yea, verily:
    You are before you ought to be!
Thales [*softly*].   And from another angle things seem critical;   *8255*
    He is, methinks, hermaphroditical.
Proteus.   Success must come the sooner in that case;
    As soon as he arrives, all will fit into place.
    But here there is not much to ponder:
    Your start must be in that wide ocean yonder!   *8260*
    There on a small scale one begins,
    The smallest things is glad to swallow,
    Till step by step more strength he wins
    And forms himself for greater things to follow.
Homunculus.   Here stirs a soft and tender air,   *8265*
    What fragrant freshness and what perfume rare!
Proteus.   Dearest of urchins! I believe your story.
    Farther away, it grows more ravishing;
    The air upon that narrow promontory
    Is more ineffable, more lavishing;   *8270*
    There, near enough, the host we'll see
    Now floating hither over the sea.
    Come with me there!
Thales.   I'll come along. Proceed!
Homunculus.   A threefold spirit striding—strange, indeed!
    TELCHINES OF RHODES *on hippocampi[1] and sea-dragons, wielding*
      Neptune's trident.
Chorus.   The trident of Neptune we've forged which assuages   *8275*
    The wildest of billows when old Ocean rages.
    When in the dense cloud-banks the Thund'rer is grumbling,
    It's Neptune opposes the horrible rumbling;
    However forked lightning may flash and may glow,
    Still wave upon wave dashes up from below,   *8280*
    And all that between them in anguish has wallowed,
    Long hurled to and fro, by the depths all is swallowed;

---

[1]The Telchines, sons of the sea, first created statues to the gods. The hippocampi combined the forepart of a horse and the tail of a dolphin.

Wherefore he has lent us his sceptre today.
Now float we contented and lightly and gay.
Sirens.

> You, to Helios dedicated,   8285
> You, to bright day consecrated,
> Greet we in this stirring hour
> When all worship Luna's power!

Telchines.   O loveliest goddess in night's dome appearing!
The praise of thy brother with rapture art hearing.   8290
To Rhodes ever blessèd an ear thou dost lend,
For there doth a pæan eternal ascend.
He begins the day's course, with keen, radiant gaze,
When finished the journey, our troop he surveys.
The mountains, the cities, the wave, and the shore   8295
Are lovely and bright to the god we adore.
No mist hovers round us, and if one appear,
A beam and a zephyr—the island is clear!
Phoebus there sees his image in forms hundredfold,
As giant, as youth, as the Gentle, the Bold.   8300
We first, it was we who first nobly began
To shape the high gods in the image of man.
Proteus.

> Oh, leave them to their boasting, singing!
> To sunbeams, holy and life-bringing,
> Dead works are but an idle jest.   8305
> They melt and mould in tireless rapture,
> And when in bronze a god they capture,
> They deem it great and swell their breast.
> What end comes to these haughty men?
> Their forms of gods, so great and true,   8310
> Long since an earthquake overthrew,
> And they were melted down again.
>
> All life on earth, whatever it be,
> Is never aught but drudgery;
> In water life has far more gain.   8315
> I'll bear you to the endless main,
> I, Proteus-Dolphin.

He transforms himself.

>   Now it's done!
> There where the happiest fates are leading
> I'll take you on my back and speeding
> I'll wed you to the ocean. On!   8320

Thales.   Yield to the worthy aspiration
And at its source begin creation,
Ready for life's effective plan!

There you will move by norms unchanging;
Through forms a thousand, myriad, ranging,   *8325*
You will, in time, become a man.
    Homunculus *mounts upon* Proteus-Dolphin.
Proteus.   Come, spirit, seek the realm of ocean;
At once, unfettered every motion,
Live here and move as you would do.
But let not higher orders lure you,   *8330*
For once a man, I can assure you,
Then all is at an end with you.
Thales.   That's as may be; yet it's not ill
A man's role in one's time to fill.
Proteus [*to* Thales].   Well, one of your kind, to be sure!   *8335*
For quite a while they do endure;
For midst your pallid phantom-peers
I've seen you now for many hundred years.
Sirens [*on the rocks*].
          See yon cloudlets, how they mingle
          Round the moon, how fair a ring!   *8340*
          Doves they are, with love a-tingle,
          White as light is every wing.
          Paphos sent them as her greeting,
          Ardent, radiant, they appear,
          Thus our festival completing,   *8345*
          Fraught with rapture full and clear!

Nereus [*approaching* Thales].
    Though night-wanderer make a pother,
    Call yon ring an apparition,
    Still we spirits take another,
    Take the only right position.   *8350*
    They are doves that are attending
    On my daughter's pearly car;
    Taught long since, in times afar,
    Wondrously they're hither wending.
Thales.   Since it gives a real man pleasure,   *8355*
    I too hold that as the best
    When a sacred, living treasure
    Finds in him a still, warm nest.
Psylli and Marsi[1] [*on sea-bulls, sea-calves, and sea-rams*].
    In Cyprus' rugged vaults cavernal
    By sea-god never battered,   *8360*
    By Seismos never shattered,
    Fanned by the zephyrs eternal,
    And, as in days long departed,
    In conscious quiet glad-hearted,
    The chariot of Cypris we've guarded,   *8365*

[1]Psylli and Marsi: snake-charmers.

Through murmuring night's soft vibration,
Over waves and their lovely pulsation,
Unseen by the new generation,
The loveliest daughter we lead.
Our duty we're quietly plying,   *8370*
From no Eagle¹ nor Wingèd Lion² flying,
Nor from Cross nor Moon,
As each dwells upon its throne,
Now swaying, now essaying,
Driving forth and now slaying,   *8375*
Harvest and towns in ashes laying.
Thus on, with speed,
Hither the loveliest mistress we lead.
Sirens.

      Lightly moving, hasting never,
      Round the chariot, line on line,   *8380*
      Now ring twines with ring, to waver
      In a series serpentine.
      Come, ye vigorous Nereides,
      Sturdy women, pleasing, wild,
      Bring, ye delicate Dorides,   *8385*
      Galatea, her mother's child:
      Earnest, like the gods, a woman
      Meet for immortality,
      Yet like women gently human,
      Of alluring charm is she.   *8390*

Dorides [in a chorus, all mounted on dolphins, passing by NEREUS].
      Light and shadow, Luna, lend us,
      On this flower of youth shine clear!
      To our father we present us,
      Pleading bring we bridegrooms dear.
  To NEREUS.

      They are boys we saved from dreaded   *8395*
      Gnashing of the angry main;
      On the reeds and mosses bedded,
      Warmed we them to light again.
      Here, with kisses warm and tender,
      Loyal thanks must they now render;   *8400*
      May the Good thy favour gain!

Nereus.   Great is the gain to win a twofold treasure:
  Pity to show and in the show take pleasure.
Dorides.

      Father, laudst thou our endeavour,
      Grant us joy deserved, in truth;   *8405*

¹The Romans.
²The Venetians.

Let us hold them fast forever
To the deathless breast of youth.

Nereus.   You may delight in your fair capture.
Fashion to men the youthful crew;
Not mine to lend an endless rapture,   *8410*
That only Zeus can grant to you.
The wave that surges and that rocks you,
Allows to love no constant stand,
And when this fancy fades and mocks you,
Then set them quietly on land.   *8415*

Dorides.

Your love, sweet boys, doth us inspire,
Yet sadly we needs must sever;
Eternal the troth that we desire,
But gods will suffer it never.

The Youths.

We're sailor-boys of gallant mood,   *8420*
Pray further kindly tend us!
We've never had a life so good,
Nor can fate better send us.

GALATEA *approaches in her shell chariot.*

Nereus.   It is you, my darling!
Galatea.   O Sire, the delight!
Linger, ye dolphins! Entrancing the sight!   *8425*
Nereus.   They're gone already, they draw us apart,
Wider and wider the circles sweep.
What do they care for the pain of my heart?
Would they but take me out over the deep!
Yet only one glance is so dear   *8430*
That it pays for the whole long year.
Thales.   Hail! Hail again!
How blooms my joy amain!
By Truth and Beauty I'm penetrated ...
From water first was all created!   *8435*
And water is the all-sustaining!
Ocean, continue forever thy reigning.
If thou the clouds wert sending not,
Wert swelling brooks expending not,
Here and there rivers wert bending not,   *8440*
And streams beginning, ending not,
Where then were the world, the mountains, and plain?
'Tis thou who the freshest of life dost maintain.
Echo [*chorus of all the circles*].
'Tis thou from whom freshest of life wells again.
Nereus.   Wheeling afar, they turn apace,   *8445*
No more meet us face to face;

In lengthened chains extended,
In circles festively blended,
In countless companies they career.
But Galatea's sea-shell throne   *8450*
I see ever and anon.
It shines like a star
The crowd among!
My loved one beams through all the throng,
However far,   *8455*
Shimmers bright and clear,
Ever true and near.

Homunculus.

    In this dear water brightens
    All that my lamplet lightens,
    All wondrous fair to see.   *8460*

Proteus.

    This living water brightens
    Where first thy lamplet lightens
    With glorious harmony.

Nereus. What mystery new to our wondering eyes
 Do I see in the midst of these bevies arise?   *8465*
 What flames round the sea-shell, at Galatea's feet?
 Now mighty it flares up, now lovely, now sweet,
 As if with love's pulsing 'twere touched and arrayed.

Thales. Homunculus is it, by Proteus swayed. . . .
 The symptoms are those of a masterful yearning,   *8470*
 Prophetic of agonized throbbing and burning.
 He'll shatter himself on the glittering throne.
 See it flame, now it flashes, pours forth—it is done!

Sirens. What marvel of fire in the billows is flashing
 That sparkling against one another are crashing?   *8475*
 It beams and hitherward wavers, and bright
 All forms are aglow on the pathway of night,
 And roundabout all is by fire overrun.
 Now Eros be ruler who all hath begun!

    Hail, ye waves! Hail, sea unbounded,   *8480*
    By the holy fire surrounded!
    Water, hail! Hail, fire's glare!
    Hail to this adventure rare!

All Together.

    Hail, thou gently blowing breeze!
    Hail, earth rich in mysteries!   *8485*
    Hail, fire, sea, whom we adore,
    Hail, ye elements all four!

ACT III

BEFORE THE PALACE OF MENELAUS IN SPARTA

HELENA. PANTHALIS, LEADER OF THE CHORUS.

HELENA *enters with a* CHORUS *of captive Trojan women.*

Helena. I, much admired and much upbraided Helena,
Come from the strand where we but now have disembarked,
Still giddy from the restless rocking of the waves   *8490*
Which with Poseidon's favour and the strength of Eurus bore
Us on their high reluctant backs from Phrygia's plain
Returning to our native bays and fatherland.
There on the shore with all his bravest warriors
King Menelaus knows the joy of safe return.   *8495*
But thou, O lofty dwelling, bid me welcome now,
Thou whom, when he came home again from Pallas' hill,
My father Tyndareus built near the slope and then
Adorned supremely, more than all of Sparta's homes,
The while, as sisters do, with Clytemnestra I—   *8500*
With Castor, Pollux too—grew up in happy play.
And ye, wings of the brazen portal, you I hail!
Yet wider once ye opened to greet a welcome guest
When Menelaus, one from many singled out,
Shone as a radiant bridegroom there before my gaze.   *8505*
Open thy wings again that I the king's behest
May faithfully fulfil as doth become the wife.
Let me go in and everything remain behind
That hitherto hath stormed about me, threatening doom.
For since, by care untroubled, I departed hence   *8510*
For Cytherea's fane, as sacred duty bade,
And there a robber seized me, he, the Phrygian,
Since then has happened much that mankind far and wide
So fain relate but not so fain is heard by him
Of whom the waxing legend hath a fable spun.   *8515*

Chorus.

     O lady glorious, do not disdain
     Honoured possession of highest estate!
     For to thee alone is the greatest boon given:
     The fame of beauty transcending all else.
     The hero's name resounds ere he comes,   *8520*
     Hence proudly he strides,
     Yet bows at once the stubbornest man
     At the throne of Beauty, the all-conquering.

Helena. Enough! I've sailed together with my consort here
And now before him to his city am I sent;   *8525*

But what intent he harbours, that I can not guess.
Do I come here as wife? do I come here as queen?
Come I as victim for the prince's bitter pain
And for the adverse fate the Greeks endured so long?
Conquered I am but whether captive I know not!   *8530*
For truly the immortal gods ambiguously
Ordained my fame and fate, attendants dubious
For Beauty's person; and on this very threshold now
They stand in gloomy threatening presence at my side.
For rarely did my husband cast a glance at me   *8535*
There in the hollow ship, nor spake he heartening word.
As if he brooded mischief, facing me he sat.
But now when drawing near Eurotas' [1] deep-bayed shore
The foremost ships scarce touched their beaks against the land
In greeting, he spake as if by Zeus himself inspired: *8540*
"Here will my warriors in due order disembark;
I'll muster them drawn up along the ocean-strand,
But thou, proceed, go up Eurotas' holy stream
Along its fruit-abounding shore, and ever on,
Guiding the coursers on the moist, bejewelled mead,   *8545*
Until what time thou comest to the beauteous plain
Where Lacedæmon, once a wide and fruitful field,
By solemn mountains close-engirdled, has been built.
Then enter in the lofty-towered, princely house
And muster me the maids whom there I left behind,   *8550*
And with them summon too the wise old stewardess.
Let her display before thee all the treasure-hoard,
Just as my father left it and what I myself
Since then have added to the pile in war and peace.
All wilt thou find there in due order standing, for   *8555*
It is the prince's privilege on coming home
That he find all in faithful keeping in his house
And each thing in its place just as he left it there.
For of himself the slave has power to alter naught."
Chorus.

     Now quicken with the glorious wealth,   *8560*
     The ever-increased, thine eyes and thy breast;
     For the grace of chain, the glory of crown,
     Rest in their pride and hold themselves rare;
     But enter in and challenge them all.
     They quickly will arm.   *8565*
     I joy in the conflict when beauty vies
     With gold and with pearls and with jewels of price.

Helena.   Thereafter followed further mandate from my lord:
   "Now when thou hast reviewed in order everything,
   Then take as many tripods as thou thinkst to need   *8570*

[1]Eurotas: the chief river of Lacedæmon.

And vessels manifold which for the sacrifice
The priest desires when he performs the sacred rite,
The cauldrons and the bowls, the round and shallow plate;
The purest water from the holy fountain be
At hand in ewers high, and ready keep dry wood   8575
As well, that rapidly accepts and feeds the flame;
And be not wanting finally a sharpened knife.
But to thy care alone I now resign the rest."
So spake he, urging me be gone, but not a thing
That breathes with life did he, the orderer, appoint   8580
Which he, to honour the Olympians, wishes slain.
Dubious it is, but further worry I dismiss,
And let all be committed to the lofty gods
Who evermore fulfil as seemeth good to them;
Men may esteem it evil or esteem it good,   8585
But we who are but mortals must accept and bear.
Ere now full oft the sacrificing priest has raised
The heavy axe to consecrate the earth-bowed beast
And yet he could not finish it, for he was checked
By nearing foes or by an intervening god.   8590
Chorus.

        Thou canst not imagine what will come next;
        Queen, we beg, enter and be
        Of good cheer.
        Evil and good still come
        Unexpected to mortals;   8595
        Though foretold, we credit it not.
        Truly, did Troy burn; truly, we saw
        Death before us, shamefullest death;
        And are we not here
        Joined with thee, serving gladly,   8600
        Seeing the dazzling sun in the heavens,
        Also thee, the earth's fairest,
        Gracious to us happy ones?

Helena.   Be it as it may! What may impend, me it beseems
That I at once ascend into the royal house,   8605
The long-renounced, much yearned-for, well-nigh forfeited,
Which stands again before mine eyes, I know not how.
My feet do not with so much spirit bear me up
The high steps I sped over lightly as a child.
    Exit.
Chorus.

        Cast now, O sisters, ye   8610
        Captives who mourn your fate,
        All your sorrows far from you;
        Share in our mistress' joy,
        Share ye in Helena's joy,

Who to her father's hearth and house   8615
—True, with tardily homeward-turned
But with so much the firmer foot—
Draweth joyfully nearer.
  Praise ye the ever holy,
Happy establishing   8620
And home-bringing Immortals!
How the unfettered one
Soars as on eagle-wings
Over the roughest! while in vain
Doth the sad captive yearningly   8625
Over the prison's high parapets
Spread his arms abroad and pine.
  But a god laid hold on her,
Her the exile,
And from Ilion's ruins   8630
Hither he bore her again
To the ancient, the newly adornèd
Father-house,
From unspeakable
Raptures and torments,   8635
Days of early youth
New-refreshed to remember.

Panthalis [*as leader of the* CHORUS].
 But now forsake ye the joy-encompassed path of song
 And turn your gaze toward the portal's open wings.
 Sisters, what do I see? Does not the Queen return   8640
 Again to us here with swift and agitated step?
 What is it, O great Queen, that here within the halls
 Of this thy house, instead of greeting from thine own,
 Could meet and shake thee thus? Conceal it thou canst not;
 For on that brow of thine I see aversion writ,   8645
 A noble anger that is battling with surprise.

Helena [*who has left the wings of the door open, agitated*].
 A vulgar fear beseemeth not the child of Zeus,
 No lightly fleeting hand of terror touches her;
 But that grim Fright, that from the womb of ancient Night
 Rose at the first beginning and still multiform,   8650
 Like glowing clouds out of the mountain's fiery throat,
 Rolls upward, might make even heroes' breasts to quake.
 In such appalling wise today the Stygians
 Have marked my entrance to the house that I am fain
 To leave this threshold often trod and wished-for long,   8655
 Turning my steps away as of a guest dismissed.
 But no! I have retreated hither to the light
 And ye'll not drive me further, Powers, be who ye may!
 I'll plan some consecration and then, purified,
 May glowing hearth bid lord and mistress welcome home.   8660

Leader of the chorus.   Disclose, O noble lady, to thy serving-maids,
   To us who aid and honour thee, what has occurred.
Helena.   What I have seen, ye too with your own eyes shall see
   Unless old Night indeed has forthwith swallowed up
   Her creature in the fearful depths of her dark womb.   *8665*
   But yet that ye may know, I'll tell it you in words.
   When through the sombre courtyard of the royal house
   I stepped with reverence, my nearest task in mind,
   I marvelled at the drear and silent corridors.
   No sound of busy going to and fro fell on   *8670*
   Mine ear, no diligent swift hasting met my gaze.
   Before me there appeared no maid, no stewardess,
   They who are wont to greet each stranger as a friend,
   But when I now drew near to the bosom of the hearth,
   Beside the tepid glimmering embers there I saw   *8675*
   What huge, veiled form! a woman seated on the ground,
   Not like to one asleep but one far lost in thought.
   With sharp, commanding words I summon her to work,
   Supposing her the stewardess whom there perhaps
   My husband prudently had stationed ere he left;   *8680*
   But in her mantle's folds she still sits motionless;
   And only at my threat her right arm doth she move,
   As if from hearth and hall she'd motion me away.
   Angry I turn from her and forthwith hasten on
   Toward the steps on which aloft the thalamos[1]   *8685*
   Rises adorned, the treasure-chamber near thereto;
   But swiftly now the monster starts up from the floor,
   Imperiously it bars the way to me and shows
   Its haggard height, its hollow eyes bedimmed with blood,
   A form so strange, such as confuses eye and mind.   *8690*
   Yet to the winds I speak, for all in vain do words
   Essay to build up forms as if they could create.
   There see herself! She even ventures forth to light!
   Here we are master till the lord and monarch comes.
   The grisly births of night doth Phoebus, Beauty's friend,   *8695*
   Drive far away to caverns or he binds them fast.
      phorkyas *appears on the sill between the door-posts.*
Chorus.
               Much have I lived through, although my tresses
               In youthful fashion flow round my temples!
               Many the horrors that I have witnessed,
               Woe of dire warfare, Ilion's night   *8700*
               When it fell.
                  Through the beclouded, dust-raising tumult,
               Warriors crowding, I heard th' Immortals
               Terribly shouting, I heard the brazen
               Accents of Strife that clanged through the field   *8705*

[1]Sleeping-chamber.

Rampart-ward.
    Ah, still standing were Ilion's
Ramparts then, but the glowing flames
Soon from neighbour to neighbour ran,
Hence and thence spreading out   *8710*
With the gust itself had made
Over the city in darkness.
    Fleeing I saw through smoke and glow
And the fluttering tongues of flame
Ghastly presences, wrathful gods,   *8715*
Wondrous forms, great as giants,
Striding on through sinister
Vapours illumined by fire.
    Saw I this or was it my
Mind that, anguish-torn, bodied forth   *8720*
Such made confusion? I'll never say
That it was, but yet that I
See with mine eyes this horrid thing,
Certainly this I do know;
I could indeed lay hold on it,   *8725*
But that fear is restraining me,
From the perilous keeps me.
    Which one of Phorkys'
Daughters, then, art thou?
For to that family   *8730*
Thee would I liken.
Art thou perchance of those born hoary,
With but one eye and but one tooth,
Sharing them alternately,
Art thou one of the Graiæ?   *8735*
    Darest thou, monster,
Here beside beauty
Under the eye of great
Phoebus to show thee?
Come, only step forth, notwithstanding,   *8740*
For the hideous sees he not,
As his holy eye has not
Yet alighted on shadow.
    But a sorrowful adverse fate
Us poor mortals doth force, alas!   *8745*
To the unspeakable pain of eyes
Which the detestable, ever accursed, on
Beauty's lovers doth still inflict.
    Yea, then hearken, if thou darest
Meet and defy us, hear the curse,   *8750*
Hear the menace of each rebuke,
Out of the cursing mouths of the happy ones
Formed and fashioned by very gods.

Phorkyas.   Old is the word, yet high and true remains the sense,
That Modesty and Beauty never, hand in hand,   *8755*
Pursue their way along the verdant paths of earth.
Deep-rooted dwells in both of them an ancient hate,
That wheresoever on the way they chance to meet,
Each on the other turns her back in enmity.
Then each one hastens on with greater vehemence,   *8760*
Modesty sad but Beauty insolent of mood,
Till Orcus' hollow night at last envelops them,
Unless old age has fettered them before that time.
You find I now, ye wantons, here from foreign lands,
Your insolence outpouring, like a flight of cranes   *8765*
Proceeding high overhead with hoarse and shrilling screams,
A drawn-out cloud that earthward sends its croaking tones,
Which lure the quiet wanderer to lift his gaze
And look at them; but they fly onward on their way,
He goes on his, and so with us too will it be.   *8770*
      Who are ye then, that round the high house of the king
Like Mænads wild or like Bacchantes dare to rave?
Who are ye then to meet the house's stewardess
With howling as a pack of dogs howls at the moon?
Dream ye 'tis hidden from me of what race ye are,   *8775*
Thou callow, war-begotten, slaughter-nurtured brood?
Man-crazy, thou, seducing as thou art seduced,
Wasting the strength of warrior and of burgher too.
To see you in your crowd, a swarm of locusts seems
To have swooped down, hiding the verdant harvest-field.   *8780*
Devourers, ye, of others' toil! Ye parasites,
Destroyers, in the bud, of all prosperity,
Thou ravished merchandise, bartered and marketed!
Helena.   Who in the presence of the mistress chides the **maids**,
Doth boldly overstep the mistress' household right;   *8785*
For her alone 'tis meet to praise the laudable
As it is hers to punish what there is to blame.
And I am well contented with the service that
They rendered when the lofty power of Ilion
Beleaguered stood and fell and lay, and not the less   *8790*
When on our erring course the grievous, changeful woe
We bore, where commonly each thinks but of himself.
Here also I expect the like from this blithe throng;
Not what the slave is, asks the lord, but how he serves.
Therefore be silent, grin and jeer at them no more.   *8795*
Hast thou the palace of the king kept well till now,
In place of mistress, to thy credit shall it stand;
But now that she has come in person, step thou back
Lest punishment be thine, not merited reward.
Phorkyas.   To threaten her domestics doth remain the right   *8800*
The which the heaven-blest ruler's lofty consort earned

Indeed through many a year of prudent governance.
Since thou, now recognized, dost tread thine ancient place
Anew and once again as mistress and as Queen,
Lay hold upon the reins long-slackened, govern now,   8805
Take in thy keep the treasure, all of us thereto.
But first of all protect me now, the older one,
Against this crowd that by thy swan-like beauty are
Only a meanly-wingèd lot of cackling geese.

Leader of the CHORUS.   How ugly, near to beauty, ugliness appears!   8810
Phorkyas.   How senseless, near to wisdom, seems the want of sense!
   From here on, members of the CHORUS *respond in turn, stepping
      forth singly from the* CHORUS.

The First Chorister.   Of Father Erebus tell us, tell us of Mother
   Night!
Phorkyas.   Then speak of Scylla, thine own flesh's kith and kin!
The Second Chorister.
   There's many a monstrous shoot on thine ancestral tree.
Phorkyas.   Away to Orcus! There seek out thy kindred tribe!   8815
The Third Chorister.
   They who dwell there, in sooth, are far too young for thee.
Phorkyas.   Go to Tiresias the Old, make love to him!
The Fourth Chorister.
   Great-great-granddaughter to thee was Orion's nurse.
Phorkyas.   Harpies, I fancy, fed thee up on filthiness.
The Fifth Chorister.
   With what dost nourish thou such cherished meagreness?   8820
Phorkyas.   'Tis not with blood for which thou all too lustful art!
The Sixth Chorister.   Greedy for corpses, thou, a loathsome corpse
   thyself!
Phorkyas.   The teeth of vampires glitter in thy shameless maw.
Leader of the CHORUS.   That maw of thine I'll stop if I say who
   thou art.
Phorkyas.   First do thou name thyself! The riddle then is solved. 8825
Helena.   Not angry but in sorrow I step in between,
   Forbidding all such turbulent alternate strife!
   For naught more harmful can befall the ruling lord
   Than faithful servants' secret festering dispute.
   The echo of his commands returneth then no more   8830
   To him in swift accomplished deed accordingly.
   No! roaring wilfully around him raves the storm
   While he, himself bewildered, chides, but all in vain.
   Not this alone! Ye have in wrath unmannerly
   Evoked the dreadful figures of unhallowed forms   8835
   Which crowd around me till I feel me torn away
   To Orcus in despite of these my native fields.
   Is it memory? Was it delusion seized on me?
   Was I all that? and am? shall I in future be
   The phantom horrible of town-destroying men?   8840

The maidens shudder, but the eldest, thou, I see,
Dost stand unmoved. Speak to me then some word of sense!
Phorkyas.   Who many years of fortune manifold recalls,
To him divinest favour seems at last a dream.
But thou, so highly favoured, past all bound and aim,   *8845*
Sawst midst the living only men inflamed by love,
Quick kindled to each kind of boldest enterprise.
Thus Theseus, roused by greed, laid hands upon thee first,
A man of glorious form, as strong as Heracles.
Helena.   He bore me off, a ten-year-old and slender roe,   *8850*
And shut me in Aphidnus' tower in Attica.
Phorkyas.   But then by Castor and by Pollux soon released,
Thou wert engirt by chosen heroes courting thee.
Helena.   Yet most my secret favour—as I own with joy—
Patroclus won; he was Pelides' counterpart.   *8855*
Phorkyas.   Thy father wedded thee to Menelaus, though,
The bold sea-rover and sustainer of his house.
Helena.   To him he gave his daughter, gave the kingdom's sway,
And from our marriage union sprang Hermione.
Phorkyas.   But whilst afar he wrested heritage in Crete,   *8860*
To thee, left solitary, came too fair a guest.
Helena.   Wherefore recall that time of semi-widowhood?
And hideous ruin that sprang out of it for me?
Phorkyas.   That voyage for me too, a free-born maid of Crete,
Brought hateful capture, brought me lasting slavery.   *8865*
Helena.   At once he did install thee here as stewardess,
Entrusting much, castle and treasure boldly won.
Phorkyas.   Which thou forsookst, turning to Ilion's tower-girt town,
Lured by the joys of love, the inexhaustible.
Helena.   Remind me not of joyance! An infinity   *8870*
Of all too bitter woe perfused by breast and brain.
Phorkyas.   Yet men say thou appeardst a phantom duplicate,
In Ilion beheld, in Egypt too wert seen.
Helena.   Confuse not wholly my distraught and clouded mind.
Here even, who I am indeed, I do not know.   *8875*
Phorkyas.   And, then, they say: from out the hollow realm of shades
Achilles, fired by passion, joined himself to thee!
Who earlier loved thee spite of all decrees of fate.
Helena.   To him the phantom I a phantom bound myself.
It was a dream, indeed the words themselves say so.   *8880*
I vanish hence, become a phantom to myself.
    Sinks into the arms of half of the CHORUS.
Chorus.
            Silence, silence!
        False seeing one, false speaking one, thou!
        From such horrible, single-toothed mouth,
        What will breathe forth from it,   *8885*
        Such a fearful and loathsome gorge?

For the malignant, benevolent appearing,
Wolfish wrath under sheep's woolly fleece,
To me is more terrible far than Hell's
Three-headed monster's gullet.   *8890*
Anxious, watching, we stand here,
When, how, where will it break forth,
Lurking monster,
Lurking deeply with malice so great?
   Well, then, instead of word freighted with comfort,   *8895*
Lethe-sprinkling, most mild, friendly and fair,
Stirrest thou up more of the past's worst ills
Than of the good we suffered,
And thou darken'st at once
Both the present moment's sheen   *8900*
And the future's
Kindly glimmering light of hope.
  Silence, silence!
That the soul of our lady,
Even now ready to flee,   *8905*
Still may hold fast, hold firmly
Loveliest form, the form of all forms,
On which the sunlight ever has shone.
     HELENA *has revived and again stands in the centre.*

Phorkyas.
From the floating clouds move forward now, high sun of this bright
   day,
When veiled, thou didst us enrapture; blinding now in splendour
   reign!   *8910*
As the world looks bright before thee, dost thou look with lovely
   gaze.
Though as ugly they revile me, well I know the beautiful.

Helena.   Tottering from out the void which in my swoon engirdled
   me,
Gladly would I rest again, for so weary are my limbs;
But for queens it is becoming—yea, all men it doth become—   *8915*
To compose one's self, take courage, whatsoever threat astound.

Phorkyas.   Standing in thy greatness, in thy beauty here and now,
If thy glance says thou commandest, what dost thou command?
   Declare!

Helena.
For your strife's neglect disgraceful be prepared to make amends;
Haste a sacrifice to order as the king commanded me.   *8920*

Phorkyas.   In the house is all now ready: bowl and tripod, sharpened
   axe,
For the sprinkling, for the incense; show the destined sacrifice.

Helena.   That the king did not determine.

Phorkyas.   Spake it not? Oh, word of
   woe!

Helena.   What the woe that overcomes thee?

Phorkyas.   Queen, it is thyself art
   meant.

Helena.   I?

Phorkyas.   And these.

Chorus.   Oh, woe and sorrow!

Phorkyas.   Thou wilt fall beneath
   the axe.   8925

Helena.   Frightful! yet foreboded! Ah, me!

Phorkyas.   Unavoidable it seems.

Chorus.   Ah! and us? What will befall us?

Phorkyas.   She will die a noble death;
   But within from lofty rafters which support the gabled roof,
   Like the thrushes in a bird-trap, ye shall dangle in a row.

   HELENA *and the* CHORUS *stand, astounded and frightened, in a*
      significant, well-arranged group.

Phorkyas.
   Phantoms! . . . Like forms grown rigid are ye standing there,   8930
   Fearing to quit the life to which ye have no claim.
   Men likewise—all of them are phantoms just as ye—
   Renounce not willingly the glorious shining sun.
   Yet no one begs them free or saves them from the end.
   All know it well, and nevertheless it pleases few.   8935
   Enough, ye all are lost! So quickly to the work!

   PHORKYAS *claps her hands; thereupon masked dwarfish figures*
      appear at the door who execute at once and with alacrity the
      commands which PHORKYAS *utters.*

   Hither, thou swarthy, roly-poly, goblin throng,
   Trundle along, there's harm to do here as one will.
   The altar, golden-horned, bring forth and give it place,
   And let the glittering axe lie on the silver rim;   8940
   Fill all the water-jugs that one can wash away
   The black gore's horrible, polluting blemishment.
   Spread out the carpet sumptuously here in the dust
   That so the victim may kneel down in royal wise
   And in it wrapped at once, although with severed head,   8945
   May still be sepulchred with fitting dignity.

Leader of the CHORUS.
   The Queen, absorbed in thought, is standing at one side,
   The maidens wither like to new-mown meadow grass;
   Methinks that I, the eldest, by sacred duty bound,
   Should speak a word with thee, thou primal eldest one.   8950
   Thou art experienced, wise, seem'st well disposed to us,
   Although this brainless troop, misjudging, struck at thee.
   Say, then, what rescue thou mayst know as possible.

Phorkyas.   'Tis easy said! Upon the queen alone it rests
   If she will save herself, you adjuncts too with her.   8955
   Determination's needful and the speediest.

Chorus.   Most revered of all the Parcæ, wisest of the sibyls, thou,
 Hold the golden shears wide open, then proclaim us life and health;
 For we feel our precious limbs already swinging, swaying, dangling
 Undelightfully, for they in dancing rather would delight them, *8960*
 Resting then on lover's breast.
Helena.   Let these be anxious! Pain I feel but naught of fear;
 But if thou know'st of rescue, grateful be 't received.
 For to the wise, far-seeing, oft in very truth
 Impossible still seems possible. Then speak, say on! *8965*
Chorus.   Speak and tell us, tell us quickly: how we may escape the awful,
 Odious nooses that so threaten as the very vilest necklace,
 Drawing round our throats. Now in advance we feel it, we poor victims,
 Feel the choking, stifling, unless thou, O Rhea, lofty mother
 Of all gods, hast pity on us. *8970*
Phorkyas.   Have ye the patience silently to hear my whole,
 Long-drawn-out discourse? It involves tales manifold.
Chorus.   Patience enough! The while we listen we still live.
Phorkyas.   If one remains at home and noble treasure guards
 And knows how to cement the lofty dwelling's walls *8975*
 And to secure the roof against the pressing rain,
 It will go well with him all his long days of life;
 But he who over his threshold's sacred limits steps
 With light and fleeting foot in buoyant wantonness,
 Will find indeed on his return the ancient place *8980*
 But all things changed about, if they're not quite destroyed.
Helena.   Whereto the like of such familiar sayings here?
 Thou wouldst narrate, so stir not up what gives offence!
Phorkyas.   It is historical, by no means a reproach.
 A corsair, Menelaus steered from bay to bay; *8985*
 The shores and islands all he skirted as a foe,
 Returning with the spoils that in his house abound.
 Besieging Ilion, he then passed ten long years;
 How many on the voyage home I do not know.
 But how stand matters here with the exalted house *8990*
 Of Tyndareus? How stand they roundabout the realm?
Helena.   So thoroughly incarnate in thee is abuse
 That not a lip of thine can stir without rebuke?
Phorkyas.   Full many years forsaken stood the valleyed hills
 Which northward back of Sparta rise into the sky, *8995*
 Taygetus in the rear whence as a merry brook
 Eurotas tumbles down and then along our vale
 By reed-beds broadly flowing nourishes your swans.
 Remote and still in mountain-vale a valiant race
 Has settled, pressing hither from Cimmerian night, *9000*
 And piled a towering stronghold insurmountable.
 From there they pester land and people as they please.

Helena.   Could they accomplish this? It seems impossible.
Phorkyas.   They had the time, perhaps 'twas nearly twenty years.
Helena.   Is one the lord? and are they many robbers? leagued?   9005
Phorkyas.   They are not robbers and yet one of them is lord.
 I blame him not and though he persecuted me.
 Well could he all have taken but contented him
 With few things which he called not tribute but free gifts.
Helena.   How does he look?
Phorkyas.   Not ill! I like his looks full well.   9010
 He is a man who's cheery, bold, of well-built form,
 A man of sense such as are few among the Greeks.
 Men brand these people as barbarians, yet methinks
 Not one so cruel, not so like a cannibal
 As many a hero proved himself at Ilion.   9015
 His greatness I respect, I'd trust myself to him.
 His castle too! With your own eyes ye should see that!
 It is quite different from the clumsy masonry
 Which your forefathers loosely piled up heedlessly,
 Cyclopean like the Cyclops, hurling undressed stone,   9020
 One on the other. There, contrariwise, ah, there!
 The work is level, plumb, according to a rule.
 Gaze at it from outside! It strives aloft toward heaven,
 All rigid, all well-joined, and mirror-smooth like steel!
 To climb there—why, the very thought slides down!   9025
 And inside are great courts and roomy spaces girt
 By structures roundabout of every kind and use.
 There ye see arches, archlets, pillars, pillarets,
 Balconies, galleries for gazing out and in,
 And scutcheons.
Chorus.   What are scutcheons?
Phorkyas.   Ajax used to bear   9030
 A coiling serpent on his shield, as ye have seen.
 The Seven against Thebes, each one upon his shield,
 A pictured emblem bore, rich in significance.
 One saw there moon and stars in heaven's nocturnal field,
 A goddess, hero, ladder, swords, and torches too,   9035
 And all that fiercely threats good towns with violence.
 Such emblems are borne also by our hero-band,
 Aglow with colour, heritage from primal sires.
 There ye see lions, eagles, also claw and beak,
 Then horns of buffaloes, wings, roses, peacocks' tails,   9040
 Bars also, gold and black and silver, blue and red.
 The like of these hangs there in halls, row after row,
 In long, unending halls, wide as the world is wide.
 There ye can dance!
Chorus.   Oh, say, are dancers also there?
Phorkyas.   The best! a blooming troop of boys with golden   9045
 locks,

Fragrant with youth, so fragrant only Paris was
When he approached too near the Queen.
Helena.   Thou fallest quite
Outside thy role! Come, tell me now the final word!
Phorkyas.   Speak thou that word, say plainly and in earnest: "Yes!"
Then with that castle I'll encompass thee at once.   9050
Chorus.   Oh, speak that little word and save thyself with us!
Helena.   What? Must I fear King Menelaus will transgress
In ways so horrible and do me so much wrong?
Phorkyas.   Hast thou forgot how thy Deïphobus he maimed,
Brother of war-slain Paris? In unheard-of ways   9055
He maimed him who for thee, when a widow, stubborn fought
And happily won as mistress. Nose and ears he lopped
And mangled him still worse: a horror to behold.
Helena.   That did he unto him; for my sake did he that.
Phorkyas.   And he will do the same to thee because of him.   9060
Beauty cannot be shared; who has possessed it quite,
Destroys it rather, cursing all part ownership.
    Trumpets at a distance; the CHORUS *shudders.*
Just as shrill trumpets' blare lays hold with rending might
On ears and bowels, jealousy doth clinch its claws
Within the bosom of a man forgetting not   9065
What once he has owned and now has lost and owns no more.
Chorus.
Hear'st thou not the horn resounding? Dost not see the weapons
flash?
Phorkyas.   Be thou welcome, lord and monarch, gladly give I
reckoning.
Chorus.   Ah, but we?
Phorkyas.   Ye know it well, before your eyes ye'll see her
death.
Mark, your own will be within there. No, there is no help for you.   9070
    Pause.
Helena.   I have thought out what first I dare to venture on.
Thou art a hostile dæmon, this I feel full well
And fear that into evil thou wilt turn the good.
But first to yonder castle I will follow thee.
The rest I know; but what thereby in her deep breast   9075
The Queen mysteriously may hide, be that for each
A secret inaccessible. On, Ancient, lead!

Chorus.

           Oh, how glad do we go hence,
               Hast'ning our footsteps,
           Death in our rear,   9080
           And before us again
           A towering stronghold's
           Inaccessible ramparts.

Grant they may shelter as well
As once did Ilion's walls,   9085
Which fell down at last
Through contemptible craft alone!
Mists spread out, veil the background and now the foreground at
  pleasure.

          How is this? How?
Sisters, gaze around!
Was not serene sunlight here?   9090
Drifts of cloud are swaying aloft
From Eurotas' sacred stream;
Vanished has the beautiful
Reed-engarlanded shore from our sight,
And the swans gliding on   9095
Freely, gracefully, proudly,
Swimming glad together,
Ah, I see them no more!
          Still, though, yes, still
Crying I hear them,   9100
Crying afar their hoarse cry!
Death presaging, so mortals say;
Ah, that only to us too,
Instead of promised salvation's weal,
Doom at last it proclaim not to us,   9105
Doom to us swan-like maids,
Fair, white-throated ones, and ah!
To her, our swan-begotten!
Woe to us, woe! woe!
          All is covered and hid   9110
Roundabout in the mist.
We can see each other no more!
What befalls? Do we move?
Float we only,
Footing uncertainly on the ground?   9115
See'st thou naught? Wings not haply e'en
Hermes ahead? Gleams not his golden wand
Waving, commanding us backward again
To the unenjoyable, grey-glimmering,
With impalpable phantoms teeming,   9120
Over-crowded, ever empty Hades?

Yes, 'tis growing darker swiftly; lifts the mist but leaves no
  sunlight,
Darkly-greyish, brown as walls are. Walls encounter our free
  vision.
Standing stark against our seeing. Is it a court? Is it a dungeon?
Horrible in any case! Sisters, alas, we are imprisoned,   9125
Prisoned as we ever were.

THE INNER COURT OF THE CASTLE

Surrounded by rich, fantastic buildings of the Middle Ages.

Leader of the CHORUS.   Impetuous and foolish, perfect woman-type!
  Dependent on the moment, sport of every breeze
  Of good and evil fortune, neither this nor that
  Can ye with calmness bear. One always contradicts   9130
  The other fiercely, and crosswise the others her;
  In joy and pain alone ye howl and laugh alike.
  Now hush! and waiting hearken what the mistress may,
  High-spirited, resolve both for herself and us.
Helena.   Where art thou, Pythoness? Whatever be thy name,   9135
  Come from the vaulted chambers of this gloomy keep.
  If haply thou art gone to the wondrous hero-lord,
  Announcing me, preparing fit reception thus,
  Then take my thanks and lead me speedily to him;
  I wish an end of wandering. Rest alone I wish.   9140
Leader of the CHORUS.
  In vain, O Queen, thou lookst around on every side;
  That sorry form has vanished, has remained perhaps
  There in the mist from out whose bosom hitherward
  We came, I know not how, but swift and treading not.
  Perhaps she too in doubt strays in this labyrinth   9145
  Of many castles strangely mingled into one,
  Seeking the lord that he may princely welcome thee.
  But see up there a crowd of servants stirring now
  In corridors, past windows, and in wide doorways,
  Hast'ning in ready service, swiftly, to and fro: 9150
  A portent of distinguished welcome for a guest.
Chorus.
            My heart is exalted! See, oh, see there
            How so modestly downward with lingering step
            The fairest of youths becoming move
            In appointed procession. At whose command   9155
            Can appear, so well-taught and so fitly arrayed,
            Of youthful squires this glorious troop?
            What most do I admire? The delicate gait,
            Perhaps the curling hair round the dazzling white brow,
            Perhaps the pair of cheeks like the red of the peach   9160
            And clad like the peach with soft, fleecy down?
            I gladly would bite them but shudder in fear,
            For in similar case was the mouth all filled up—
            Oh, horrible tale!—with ashes.
                        And now the fairest   9165
                        Are coming along;
                        What is it they bear?
                        Steps for a throne,

Carpet and seat,
Hangings and tent—   *9170*
Similar gear;
Now it rolls over,
Wreathing cloud-like festoons
Round the head of our Queen,
Who now, invited,   *9175*
Has climbed to the glorious couch.
Forward advance,
Step upon step, stand
Gravely aligned.
Worthy, oh, worthy, threefold worthy   *9180*
Of her may such a welcome be blessed!

All that the CHORUS *describes occurs by degrees.*

FAUST.

After the boys and squires have descended in a long procession,
FAUST *appears above on the staircase in the knightly court cos-*
tume of the Middle Ages; he descends slowly and with dignity.

Leader of the CHORUS [*observing him attentively*].
If to this man the gods have not, as oft they do,
Lent only for a brief time admirable form,
His amiable presence, his exalted mien,
All transitory, then will he ever succeed   *9185*
In what he undertakes, be it in fights with men
Or in the little war with fairest women waged.
Indeed to many others he may be preferred,
Others whom high-esteemed I've seen with mine own eyes.
With slowly solemn step restrained by reverence   *9190*
I see the prince approaching. Turn and see, O Queen!

Faust [*approaching with a fettered man at his side*].
In lieu of solemn greeting, as were fitting,
In lieu of reverent welcome, I bring thee
This servant fettered fast in manacles,
Whose slight of duty made me slight mine own.   *9195*
Before this noble lady kneel thou down,
To make confession and avow thy guilt.
Exalted mistress, here thou seest the man
Of vision rare who on the lofty tower
Was placed to gaze around, there to survey   *9200*
Keenly the firmament and earth's expanse,
If here and there perchance aught may appear,
Descending by the hill-encircled vale
To our firm castle, be it billowing herds,
Perhaps a marching host; those we protect,   *9205*
Meet these in fight. Today, what negligence!
Thou comest, he reports it not, we fail
To greet most duly and most honourably

So great a guest. His life he wantonly
Has forfeited, should lie now in the blood   9210
Of well-deservèd death; but thou alone
Mayst punish or mayst pardon, as thou wilt.
Helena.   High is the honour that thou grantest me,
As judge, as ruler, and although it were
To test me merely, as I may suspect,   9215
Still, now the judge's foremost duty I
Will do, to give the accused a hearing. Speak!
Lynceus [*the warder of the tower*].
               Let me kneel and gaze upon her,
               Let me live or let me perish,
               Since my all I only cherish   9220
               For this god-sent lady's honour.
               Waiting for the bliss of morning,
               Spying eastward its first glows,
               Lo! the sun, without a warning,
               Wondrous in the south arose.   9225
               Thither did it draw my glances
               Off from gorge and mountain-cone,
               Off from earth's and heaven's expanses,
               Her to see, the Only One.
               Piercing sight to me is given   9230
               As to lynx on highest tree,
               Yet I had to struggle, even
               As from dream's obscurity.
               Could I the delusion banish?
               Ramparts? tower? or bolted gate?   9235
               Vapours rise and vapours vanish,
               Such a goddess comes in state!
               Eye and bosom I turned to her,
               Drinking in her gentle light;
               Beauty, blinding all that view her,   9240
               Blinded my poor senses quite.
               I forgot the warder's duty
               And the horn I swore to wind.
               Threaten to destroy me! Beauty
               Doth all anger ever bind.   9245

Helena.   The ill that I occasioned I dare not
To punish. Woe is me! That fate austere
Pursues me, everywhere the breasts of men
So to infatuate that they themselves
Spare not nor aught else worthy. Ravishing,   9250
Seducing, fighting, harrying hither, thither,
Demigods, heroes, gods, aye, demons also,
To and fro they led me ever wandering.
My first estate confused the world, my second

The more, my third and fourth bring woe on woe.   *9255*
Remove this good man, let him now go free;
Let no disgrace befall the god-befooled!
Faust.   Astonished, I behold alike, O Queen,
The unerring archer and the stricken one;
I see the bow which hath the arrow sped   *9260*
That wounded him. Arrows on arrows fly,
Me do they smite. Criss-cross through keep and court
I feel their feathered whirring everywhere.
What am I now? The faithfulest thou mak'st
At once rebellious to me, insecure   *9265*
My walls. And so my army, I fear now,
Obeys the conquering, unconquered Queen.
What else remains save that I give to thee
Myself and all that I have fancied mine?
Freely and truly let me at thy feet   *9270*
Acknowledge thee as Queen who by her coming
Acquired at once possession and a throne.
Lynceus [with a chest and men who carry chests after him].
                O Queen, thou see'st me back again!
                The rich man begs one glance's gain;
                Poor as a beggar feeleth he   *9275*
                And princely rich when he sees thee.
                    What was I erst? and what now too?
                What is to wish for? what to do?
                What use is sharpest flash of eyes!
                Back from thy throne it bounding flies.   *9280*
                    Out of the East we hither pressed
                And all was over with the West;
                A people far and wide were massed,
                The foremost knew not of the last.
                    The first man fell, the second stood,   *9285*
                The third man's lance was prompt and good;
                Each one was backed a hundredfold,
                Thousands, unmarked, lay slain and cold.
                    We crowded on, stormed on apace,
                Masters were we from place to place;   *9290*
                Where for the day I held control
                Tomorrow another robbed and stole.
                    We looked—and hurried was the look;
                The fairest woman one man took,
                And one the steer both firm and strong,   *9295*
                And every horse must come along,
                    But I delighted to espy
                The things most rare to human eye,
                And what another man possessed,
                For me was dried-up grass at best.   *9300*
                    Upon the trail of treasures bright,

I followed only my keen sight;
At every pocket I peeped in,
Transparent was each box and bin.
   And heaps of gold I made my own,   *9305*
And many a lordly precious stone.
Now on thy breast the emerald green
Alone is worthy to be seen.
   Now swaying 'twixt thy lip and ear
Let ocean's oval pearl appear;   *9310*
Rubies would all their radiance lose
Beside thy glowing cheek's bright hues.
   The treasure greatest and most rare
Before thy presence I lay here;
And to thy feet is brought today   *9315*
The fruit of many a bloody fray.
   As many chests as here I bore,
Of iron chests I have yet more;
Admit me to thy train, I will
Thy vaults with every treasure fill.   *9320*
   For scarce dost thou the throne ascend,
Ere now they bow, ere now they bend,
Intelligence and wealth and power,
Before thy peerless form and flower.
   Firmly I held all this as mine,   *9325*
But now it's free and it is thine;
'Twas precious, sterling, vast, I thought,
But now I see that it was naught.
   Vanished is what I once possessed.
A mown and withered grass at best;   *9330*
Oh, with one happy glance but deign
To give it all its worth again!

Faust.   Quickly remove the burden boldly won,
Indeed not censured but without reward.
Already all is hers that in its depths   *9335*
The castle hides; to offer her aught special
Is useless. Go, pile treasure upon treasure
In order fit. Set up the stately show
Of splendour yet unseen! And let the vaults
Glitter like new-born firmaments, prepare   *9340*
New paradises filled with lifeless life.
Hastening before her steps let flowered rug
On rug unroll; thus may her every tread
Meet kindly footing, may her gaze alight
On splendour blinding all but the divine.   *9345*
Lynceus.
        Easy are the lord's commands,
        Child's-play to the servant's hands:

Beauty in such fair excess
Rules all wealth, rules blood no less.
All the army now is tame,   9350
All the swords are blunt and lame.
By this glorious form, behold!
Even the sun seems faint and cold.
By this wealth of loveliness
All is empty nothingness.   9355

    Exit.

Helena [*to* FAUST].   I wish to speak to thee; up to my side
  Hither I bid thee come! The empty place
  Calls to its lord and thus makes mine secure.

Faust.   First kneeling, let my true devotion gain
  Thy favour, lofty lady; let me kiss   9360
  The gracious hand that lifts me to thy side.
  Confirm me as co-regent of thy realm
  Whose bounds are limitless; win for thyself
  Adorer, servant, guardian, all in one.

Helena.   Manifold marvels do I see and hear.   9365
  Amazement strikes me, I would fain ask much,
  But first I'd ask to know why that man's speech
  Sounded so new and strange, strange and yet friendly.
  It seems that one tone makes way for another,
  And hath a word grown friendly to the ear,   9370
  Another woos caressingly the first.

Faust.   If thou art pleased with this our people's speech,
  Oh, surely then its song will ravish thee,
  Fill ears and mind alike with deep content.
  But best it were to practise it straightway,   9375
  Alternate speech allures it, calls it forth.

Helena.   Then tell me how to learn such lovely speech.

Faust.   It's easy, quite, if from the heart it come.
  And when the breast with longing overflow,
  One looks around and asks—

Helena.   Who shares the glow.   9380

Faust.   The soul looks not ahead in hours like this,
  Nor back; the present only—

Helena.   Is our bliss.

Faust.   It is a pledge, great gain, possession grand;
  What confirmation has it?

Helena.   This, my hand.

Chorus.

Who would think to blame our princess   9385
If she grants the castle's lord
Friendly show of favour?
For confess, we all of us are
Captives, aye, as oft already
Since the infamous overthrow   9390

Of Ilion and the agonizing
Labyrinthian woeful journey.
   Women, used to men's affection,
Are not choosers, yet they are
Well-informed and knowing,   *9395*
And to golden-haired shepherds
Or else to fauns with black bristles,
As occasion may bring about,
Over their fair rounded members
Fully grant they an equal right.   *9400*
   Near and nearer they're sitting now,
Leaning one on the other,
Shoulder to shoulder, knee to knee,
Hand in hand, cradle they them
Over the throne's   *9405*
Richly cushioned magnificence.
Now no scruples has majesty
In its revealing
All its intimate pleasures
Thus before all the eyes of the people.   *9410*

Helena.   I feel so far away and yet so near
  And all too glad I say: Here am I! Here!
Faust.   I scarcely breathe, words tremble, check their pace;
  It is a dream, vanished are time and place.
Helena.   I feel I'm lived-out sheer, and yet so new,   *9415*
  Blent with thee here, to thee, the unknown, true.
Faust.   Probe not the dower of this rare destiny;
  Though life's but an hour, our duty's still to *be.*
Phorkyas [*entering hastily*].

Spell love's primer through, enjoying
Lovesick brewing, cooing, toying;   *9420*
Brew and coo on, idle, cloying,
Yet for that 'tis not the day.
Feel ye not a dull storm growing?
Hearken to the trumpet's blowing!
Ruin is not far away.   *9425*
Menelaus hither urges
All his host in mighty surges.
Arm ye for a bitter fray!
By the victor's host entangled,
As Deïphobus was mangled,   *9430*
For this gallantry thou'lt pay.
When this trash hangs on a halter,
Straight she'll die upon the altar,
To the sharpened axe a prey.

Faust.   Bold interruption! Odious it presses in;   *9435*

In danger itself I can't stand senseless violence.
Ill-message uglifies the fairest messenger;
Only bad messages bringst, ugliest, thou with joy.
But this time thou shalt not succeed. With empty breath
Go, shatter thou the air. There is no danger here,   *9440*
And even danger itself would seem an idle threat.

   Signals, explosions from the towers, trumpets and cornets. Mar-
     tial music, a powerful armed force marches past.
Faust.

            No, heroes heart-united ever
            Forthwith assembled thou shalt see;
            He only merits women's favour
            Who can protect them valiantly.   *9445*

To the leaders of the army who detach themselves from their col-
umns and step forward.

            With bated, silent fury's power,
            Sure pledge of victory to come,
            Ye, of the North the budding flower,
            Ye, of the East the mighty bloom,
               In steel encased, light round them breaking,   *9450*
            Hosts that crushed realm on realm at will,
            They come, the very earth is shaking,
            They stride along, it thunders still.
               We came to Pylos, there we landed,
            The agèd Nestor is no more,   *9455*
            And all the kinglets thither banded
            Our free hosts routed on the shore.
               Back from these walls with voice of thunder
            Drive Menelaus to the sea;
            There let him rove, waylay, and plunder;   *9460*
            It was his wish and destiny.
               I hail you dukes as forth ye sally,
            Such the command of Sparta's Queen;
            Now at her feet lay hill and valley,
            And yours be all the realm ye win.   *9465*
               Thine, German! be to stand defending
            At wall and rampart Corinth's bay.
            Achæa's hundred vales unending
            I bid thee, Goth, to hold and sway.
               Toward Elis, march, ye Frankish legions,   *9470*
            Messenia be the Saxons' gain,
            Ye Normans, clear the ocean's regions
            And great make Argolis again.
               Then each, within his walls abiding,
            Will be prepared the foe to meet;   *9475*
            Sparta, over you all presiding,
            Shall be the Queen's ancestral seat.
               She'll see you one and all retrieving

The land whose weal no want can blight,
Ye at her feet, assured, receiving   9480
Authority and law and light.

*FAUST descends, the princes form a circle around him in order to
hear better his commands and instructions.*

Chorus.

Who the fairest one coveteth,
Be before all things able
And let him weapons prudently seek.
Flattering he may win indeed   9485
What all the earth holds highest;
But in peace possesseth he not.
Crafty rogues will entice her from him,
Robbers boldly will snatch her from him;
This to prevent let him be on his guard.   9490
  Therefore do I praise our prince,
Prize him higher than others,
That he, so wise and brave, drew allies
And the mighty, obeying, stand
Waiting his every signal.   9495
Faithfully they fulfil his hest,
Each for himself, for his own gain
And the ruler's enguerdoning thanks,
Both winning thus the supreme meed of fame.
  For who will now ravish her   9500
From the mighty possessor?
His is she, to him granted be she,
Granted twofold by us whom he
Gathered to her, safe within sheltering walls,
Guarded without by a mighty host.   9505

Faust.

Gifts have I granted, great and glorious,
To each of these a goodly land,
Let them march on, through war victorious,
Here in the midst we take our stand.
  And they in rivalry protect thee,   9510
Half-island, lapped by dancing main,
While slender, fair, green hills connect thee
With the last link of Europe's mountain-chain.
  This land, the land of lands, forever
May it be blessed to every race,   9515
Won for my Queen's enduring favour.
It early gazed upon her face,
  When from the shell she burst and gleaming
Rose mid Eurotas' reedy sighs,
On mother, brother, sister beaming   9520
With light that overcame the eyes.
  This land presents its choicest flower

To thee, it turns to thee alone;
From all the world which owns thy power,
Oh, choose thy fatherland, thine own!   9525
   And even if the jagged peak uprearing
Doth on its back the sun's cold arrow bear,
We see a green tinge on the rock appearing;
The wild goat nibbling crops his scanty fare.
   Springs leap and plunging brooks unite in revel;   9530
Already gorges, slopes, and meads are green.
Upon a hundred hillsides' broken level
The moving, fleecy herds spread out are seen.
   With measured step, divided, steady,
Horned beasts draw near the dizzy ledge's fall,   9535
But shelter for them all is ever ready
In hundred caves arched in the rocky wall.
   Pan shields them there, enlivening nymphs are
      dwelling
In bosky chasms' moist, refreshened lee,
And, yearningly toward higher regions swelling,   9540
Aloft crowds branch-abounding tree on tree.
   Primeval woods! The mighty oak is standing
With branch on branch crooked wilfully and bowed;
The gentle maple, with sweet juice expanding,
Shoots cleanly upward, playing with its load.   9545
   And in that silent realm of shadows
Warm mother's milk for child and lambkin wells;
Fruit is not far, the ripe food of the meadows,
And honey from the hollowed tree distils.
   Here comfort is the birthright of a nation,   9550
Both cheek and lips express serenity,
Each is immortal in his age and station,
Healthy they live and happily.
   And thus the lovely child develops, gaining
The father's strength as bright day follows day.   9555
We marvel, in our minds a doubt remaining
If they are gods, if men are they.
   Thus was Apollo shepherd-like in feature,[1]
Only the fairest was as fair as he;
For where in a pure orbit ruleth Nature,   9560
All worlds unite and blend in harmony.

Taking his seat beside HELENA.
   Thus hath success both thee and me attended,
Now let the past be past, behind us flung;
Oh, feel thyself from highest god descended,
Thou of the primal world whence thou art sprung!   9565
   Thee shall no fortress keep in hiding!

[1]See Euripides, *Alcestis,* 1. ff.

Still in eternal youth, stands, as it stood,
A wide domain for us, for blissful biding,
Arcadia in Sparta's neighbourhood!
    Enticed to dwelling in this blessed harbour,   9570
Hast fled into the brightest destiny!
Now let our thrones become an arbour,
Arcadian be our bliss and free!

THE SCENE CHANGES ALTOGETHER

Closed arbours lean against a series of rocky caverns. A shady grove
extends to the surrounding cliff-walls. FAUST *and* HELENA *are*
not visible. The CHORUS *lies sleeping, scattered here and there.*

Phorkyas.   How long these maidens may have slept I cannot tell.
If they allowed themselves to dream that which mine eyes   9575
Saw bright and clear, that likewise is unknown to me,
And so I'll wake them. This young crowd should be amazed,
Ye long-beards too, who sit and wait down there below
To see at length how wonders credible turn out.
Awake! arise! and quickly shake your curly hair,   9580
Sleep from your eyes! And blink not so, but list to me!
Chorus.
Speak and tell us, tell whatever marvellous events have happened;
Most of all we like to hear of what surpasses our believing,
For we're bored, and greatly bored, from looking only on these
    rocks.
Phorkyas.
With your eyes rubbed open scarcely, children, are ye bored so soon? 9585
Hearken then! Here in these caverns, in these grottoes, in these
    arbours,
Shield and shelter have been given, as are given to pairs idyllic,
To our lord and to our lady.
Chorus.   How? Within there?
Phorkyas.   Separated
From the world, they summoned me, me only, to their quiet service.
Highly honoured I stood near them, yet, as doth beseem the trusted, 9590
Looking around for something else. So I turned me hither, thither,
Seeking roots and barks and mosses, skilled in all things efficacious,
And so they remained alone.
Chorus.
Truly thou dost speak as if within there were vast world-wide
    spaces,
Forest, lakes and brooks and meadow; what a fairy tale dost spin! 9595
Phorkyas.
To be sure, ye inexperienced! Those are depths no one hath
    fathomed:

Hall on hall and court on court which musingly I followed through.
But there echoes all at once a laughter through the spacious caverns;
I look thither, lo! a boy who from the woman's lap is leaping
To the man, and from the father to the mother; the caressing,   9600
Dandling, pranks of foolish fondness, cries of fun, and shouts of
    pleasure
Deafen me alternately.
Naked, without wings, a genius, faun-like but with nothing bestial,
On the firm ground he is leaping, yet the ground, in turn reacting,
Speeds him up to airy heights, and in the second or the third leap   9605
Doth he touch the lofty arch.
Anxious calls the mother: "Leap! and leap again, and at thy
    pleasure,
But beware of flying: flight unfettered is denied to thee."
And thus warns the faithful father: "In the earth lies power elastic
That impels thee upward, only with your toe-tips touch the surface   9610
And at once thou wilt be strengthened like Antæus, son of earth."
And so on these rocky masses he goes skipping from one cornice
To the other and around, as leaps a ball when it is struck.
   All at once, though, in the crevice of a rugged gorge he's vanished,
And he now seems lost to us. The mother wails, the father comforts, 9615
Anxiously I shrug my shoulders. But again now what a vision!
Are there treasures lying hid there? Garments striped with
    broidered blossoms
He has donned becomingly.
   From his arms are tassels waving, round his bosom flutter
    ribbons,
In his hands the golden lyre; completely like a little Phoebus,   9620
He steps boldly to the brink, then to the precipice. We marvel
And the parents in their rapture clasp each other, heart to heart,
For around his head what splendour! It is hard to say what glitters,
Is it gold-work or the flame of some transcendent spirit-power?
And he moves and gestures, even now though but a boy, proclaiming 9625
Him the future master of all beauty, through whose every member
Melodies eternal stir; and thus ye too will hearken to him,
And will see him thus, with wonder ye have never felt before.
Chorus.

        Call'st thou a wonder this,
        Thou Crete-begotten?   9630
        Hast to poetical speech
        Pregnant with thought not listened?
        Never yet hast heard Ionia's,
        Never hast listened to Hellas'
        Vast store of tales ancestral   9635
        Celebrating gods and heroes?
          All that may happen now
        While we are living
        Reëchoes gloomily

Grandeur of days ancestral;   9640
Nor can thy narration equal
That which a lovely fiction,
More credible than truth is,
Sang of him, the son of Maia.
   Him a delicate babe but strong,   9645
Nurseling, scarce more than born yet,
Straight has the nurses' chattering flock,
Full of unreasoning fancy,
Wrapped in the purest swaddling-fleece,
Bound fast in fine, costly wrappings,   9650
But now the strong, though dainty rogue
Draws forth his delicate limbs,
Firm, elastic, and supple,
Craftily thence, the purple shell,
Which so grievously bound him,   9655
Leaving quietly in its place,
Like the perfected butterfly
Which from the cramping chrysalis
Deftly slips with unfolding wings,
Through the sunlit, radiant ether   9660
Boldly, wantonly fluttering.
  So too did he, the agilest,
That to thieves and to tricksters
And all seekers of gain he'd be
Ever a favouring genius.   9665
This straightway he makes manifest
Through most clever devices.
Swift the trident of ocean's lord
Steals he, and slyly from Ares' self
Steals the sword from the scabbard,   9670
Arrow and bow from Phoebus too,
Also the tongs from Hephaestus,
Even from Zeus the father's bolt
Would have had, but was frightened by fire.
Eros too he overcomes   9675
In a leg-tripping wrestling match,
And when Cypris caresses him, steals
From her bosom the girdle.

A charming, purely melodious music of stringed instruments re-
sounds from the cave. All become attentive and soon seem to be
deeply stirred. Henceforth to the pause indicated, there is a
full musical accompaniment.

Phorkyas.

    Hear the loveliest chords resounding,
    Quick, be free from myths long gone,   9680
    And your gods, of old abounding,

Let them go! Their day is done.
   None will understand your singing,
We demand a higher mart;
From the heart it must come springing,   9685
If it hopes to touch the heart.

She retires toward the rocks.

Chorus.

   If these witching tones, dire creature,
Find a welcome in thine ears,
We feel healed, of a new nature,
Softened to the joy of tears.   9690
   Let the sun's bright splendour perish
If a dawn within us rise,
If in our own hearts we cherish
What the whole wide world denies.

HELENA, FAUST, EUPHORION *in the costume described for* **him.**

Euphorion.

   Hear ye children carols singing,   9695
Ye at once in sport take part;
When ye see my rhythmic springing,
As a parent's leaps your heart.

Helena.

   Love, in human wise to bless us,
Makes Two One in sympathy,   9700
But us godlike joy possesses
When Love forms a precious Three.

Faust.

   All is found, our love's requited,
I am thine, and mine art thou;
And so stand we here united,   9705
Were it always thus as now!

Chorus.

   Many years of purest pleasure
In the mild light of the boy
Crown this pair in plenteous measure.
How their union stirs my joy!

Euphorion.   9710

   Let me be skipping,
Let me be springing!
In all the breezes
Through ether winging
Is now my passion;   9715
It hath me won.

Faust.

   But gently! gently!
Don't be rash! Check thee
That plunge and death may

Not overtake thee,   *9720*
That we may not perish
Through our dear son.

Euphorion.

I will no longer
Stand earthly stresses;
Let go my hands,   *9725*
Let go my tresses,
Let go my garments,
They are all mine.

Helena.

Oh, think—believe us—
To whom thou belongest!   *9730*
How it would grieve us,
And how thou wrongest
The fair fortune won,
Mine, his, and thine!

Chorus.

The bond, I fear me,   *9735*
Soon is undone!

Helena and Faust.

Curb, thou tempestuous!
For us who love thee,
Over-impetuous
Forces that move thee!   *9740*
In rural leisure
Grace thou the plain.

Euphorion.

But for your pleasure
I will refrain.

Winding among the CHORUS *and drawing them forth to dance.*

Round this gay company   *9745*
Hover I light;
Now is the melody,
Now is the movement right?

Helena.

Yes, that is neatly done!
Lead all the beauties on,   *9750*
Artfully dance!

Faust.

Oh, that an end might be!
Ne'er can this roguery
My joy enhance.

EUPHORION *and the* CHORUS, *dancing and singing, move about in*
   interlocking dance.

Chorus.

When thy twin arms so fair   *9755*
Charming thou raisest,

Radiant thy curly hair
Shaking displacest,
When thou with foot so light
Skimmest the earth in flight,   9760
Hither and off again,
Dancing a linkèd chain,
Thou hast thy goal attained,
Thou lovely child;
All of our hearts beguiled,   9765
All hast thou gained.

Pause.
Euphorion.

O all ye lithesome
Roes never staying,
Quickly and blithesome,
On, to new playing!   9770
I am the hunter,
Ye are the game.

Chorus.

Wilt thou us capture,
Be not unruly
For we, in rapture,   9775
Only would truly
Closely embrace thee,
Thy beauty claim!

Euphorion.

Through groves and rubble,
Over stock and stubble!   9780
Lightly attainable,
That I detest;
Hardly obtainable
Pleases me best.

Helena and Faust.

Oh what madness! Oh what daring!   9785
There's no hope of moderation.
Hark! It sounds like trumpets' blaring
Over vale and woods resounding;
What a tumult! What a brawl!

Chorus [*entering singly and quickly*].

He ran past us, left us lagging,   9790
Scorned and mocked us, onward bounding;
See how hither he is dragging
Now the wildest one of all.

Euphorion [*bearing a young maiden*].

Here I drag the sturdy maiden
Hither to enforced enjoyment;   9795

For my rapture, for my zest,
I press her resisting breast,
Kiss her lips reluctant still,
Showing thus my strength and will.

Maiden.

Loose me! In this form and cover   *9800*
Spirit-strength and courage stay,
And our will, like thine moreover,
Is not lightly swept away.
In a strait dost think me truly?
For thine arm great strength dost claim!   *9805*
Hold me fast, fool, and I'll duly
Scorch thee well, a merry game.

She turns to flame and flashes up in the air.
To the buoyant breezes follow,
To the caverns' dreary hollow,
Come the vanished prize to claim.   *9810*

Euphorion [*shaking off the last flames*].
Rocks all around me here,
Thickets and woods among,
Why should they bound me here?
Still am I fresh and young.
Wild winds are dashing there,   *9815*
Billows are crashing there,
Both far away I hear,
Would I were near!

He leaps higher and higher up the rocks.

Helena, Faust, and the Chorus.
Like a chamois wouldst aspire?
Dreadful fall we fear for thee.

Euphorion.   *9820*
Higher must I climb and higher,
Ever farther must I see.
Now I know where I stand,
Midst of great Pelops' land,
Midst of an isle are we,   *9825*
Kin to the earth and sea!

Chorus.
Wilt not mid wood and hill
Linger contented?
Soon we shall seek at will
Grapes in rows planted,   *9830*
Grapes on the hillsides fanned,
Figs and gold apples rare.

Ah, stay in this fair land,
Stay thou so fair!

Euphorion.

Dream ye of days of peace?   *9835*
Dream on whom dreams may please!
"War!" is the signal cry,
Echoed by "Victory!"

Chorus.

Who in peace ever
Wishes war back again,   *9840*
Himself doth sever
From hope's rich gain.

Euphorion.

They whom this land hath led
Out of dread into dread,
Free, of undaunted mood,   *9845*
Not sparing of their blood:
To their unbreakable,
Consecrate chain,
Fighters unshakeable,
May it bring gain!   *9850*

Chorus.

Look aloft! How high he's mounting!
Yet to us not small he seems,
As if armed, on triumph counting,
As of bronze and steel he gleams.

Euphorion.

Not on walls or moats enduring,   *9855*
On his own strength each must rest;
Fortress firm and all-securing
Is a man's own iron breast.
Would ye live unconquered freemen,
Arm, and off to combat wild!   *9860*
Amazons will be your women,
And a hero every child.

Chorus.

Hallowèd Poesy,
Soar aloft heavenly,
Shine on, thou fairest star,   *9865*
Farther and still more far,
Yet dost thou reach us still,
Yet do we hear and thrill,
Joyous we are.

Euphorion.

No, not a child am I appearing,   *9870*
A youth in armour I come on,
Who, joined with strong men, free and daring,
Great deeds in spirit now has done.

Away!

No stay,   9875

On to the path where fame is won.

Helena and Faust.

Scarcely thou to life art given,

Scarcely knowing day's glad beam,

Yearning dizzily art driven

To the field where sorrows teem.   9880

Are then we

Naught to thee?

Is the lovely bond a dream?

Euphorion.

Hear ye the thundering on the ocean?

How thunder back the vale and wood?   9885

In dust and foam, in fierce commotion,

Host charges host in weltering blood,

And for all

"Death!" 's the call,

That of course is understood.   9890

Helena, Faust, and the Chorus.

How we shudder! How we quiver!

Does death summon thee to fall?

Euphorion.

From afar look on? No, never!

Worry, need—I'll share it all.

The Above.

Danger his rashness brings,   9895

Fatally bold!

Euphorion.

Still must I!—See the wings

That now unfold!

Thither! I must! I must!

Grudge not the flight!   9900

He casts himself into the air, his garments bear him up for a moment, his head is irradiated, a trail of light follows him.

Chorus.

Icarus! Icarus!

Piteous plight!

A beautiful youth falls at his parents' feet. We think we recognize a familiar form[1] in the dead body; but the corporeal vanishes at once, the aureole rises like a comet toward heaven. The robe, mantle, and lyre remain lying on the ground.

Helena and Faust.

Quick on joy followeth

Dire pain and moan.

[1]That of Byron, whom **Goethe identified** with Euphorion "as a representative of the most recent era in poetry."

Euphorion's Voice [*from the depths*].

> Leave me in realms of death,   *9905*
> Mother, not all alone!

Pause.

Chorus [*a Dirge*].

> Not alone!—where'er thou bidest,
> For we think that well we know thee;
> Ah! and if from life thou hidest,
> Never will a heart forgo thee.   *9910*
> For thee scarcely know we sadness,
> Enviously we sing thy fate,
> For thou hadst in pain and gladness
> Songs and courage high and great.
>
> Born with earthly bliss thy dower,   *9915*
> Great thy strength, proud thy descent,
> Soon lost to thyself, the flower
> Of thy youth was from thee rent.
> Keen thy sight, the world discerning,
> Feeling for each heart-throb known,   *9920*
> For fair women's passion yearning,
> And a song thy very own.
>
> But thy tamelessness engaged thee
> In a net without a flaw,
> And in headlong strife enraged thee   *9925*
> Against custom, against law;
> But at last an aim transcendent
> Gave thy noble courage weight,
> Thou wouldst win a fame resplendent—
> But success was not thy fate.   *9930*
>
> Who succeeds?—A dismal query,
> Shunned by Fate who gives no heed,
> When, on days ill-starred and dreary,
> Silently the people bleed.
> But new songs afresh create them,   *9935*
> Deeply bowed lament no more:
> Earth again will generate them
> As it ever did of yore.

Complete pause. The music ceases.

Helena [*to* FAUST].   Alas, an ancient truth is verified in me:

> That bliss and beauty never lastingly unite.   *9940*
> The bond of life is rent no less than that of love;
> Bewailing both, I say with sorrow: Fare thee well!
> And cast myself once more, once only, in thine arms.
> Receive, Persephone, receive the boy and me.

She embraces FAUST, *she herself vanishes, robe and veil remain in*
    his arms.

Phorkyas [*to* FAUST].   Hold fast what now alone is left to thee!   *9945*
  Let not the garment go. Already demons
  Are twitching at its skirts and they would like
  To snatch it to the lower world. Hold fast!
  It is no more the goddess whom thou lost,
  But godlike is it. Make use of the high   *9950*
  And priceless boon, and rising soar aloft.
  Swift over all things common will it bear thee
  Away through ether while thou canst endure.
  We'll meet again, far, far away from here.
    HELENA's *garments dissolve into clouds, surround* FAUST, *lift him*
    in the air, and move away with him.
Phorkyas [*picks up* EUPHORION's *robe, mantle, and lyre from the*
    ground, steps forward to the proscenium, lifts up the memen-
    toes, and speaks].

                A lucky find, although belated!   *9955*
                The flame, in truth, is dissipated,
                Yet for the world I've no distress.
                Here is enough to start the poet
                And swell his tribe with jealousness;
                And talent? Though I can't bestow it,   *9960*
                I can at least bestow the dress.

    She sits down in the proscenium at the foot of a column.
Panthalis.   Now hasten, maidens! From the sorcery we're free,
  From the mad tyranny of the Thessalian hag,
  Freed from the wildering, jangling tones that dazed us all,
  The ear confounding and still worse the inner sense.   *9965*
  Hence, down to Hades! where our Queen has hastened on,
  With solemn steps descending. Let her footsteps be
  Directly followed by the steps of faithful maids.
  Her shall we find beside the throne of the Inscrutable.[1]

Chorus.

                Everywhere indeed do queens ever like to be,   *9970*
                And in Hades too do they stand supreme;
                Proudly with their peers are they allied,
                With Persephone most intimate.
                We, however, in the background
                Of deep, asphodelian meadows,   *9975*
                With far-reaching poplars
                And unfruitful willows joined,
                What diversion shall we have there?
                Bat-like to squeak and twitter
                In whispers undelighting, spectral.   *9980*

[1]Persephone.

Panthalis.   Who hath not won a name nor wills a noble deed,
 Belongs but to the elements, so fare thy way!
 Hotly I wish to join my Queen. Not merit alone,
 Faithfulness too preserves our personality.
  Exit.
All

     Back to the light of day are we now restored, *9985*
     Truly persons no more.
     We feel it, we know it too,
     But to Hades we go back never;
     For ever-living Nature lays
     Claim to us spirits, *9990*
     We to her lay claim that is valid.

A Part of the CHORUS.
 In these thousand branches' quivering whisper, in their murmuring
  swaying,
 Toying gently, we'll entice up from the roots the vital currents
 To the twigs; and now with leafage, now with blooms in great
  profusion
 We'll adorn the fluttering tresses freely for an airy growth. *9995*
 Falls the fruit, at once will gather life-enjoying herds and people,
 Quickly coming, briskly crowding, for the picking, for the tasting;
 They will all bow down around us as before primeval gods.
Another Part.
 In the smooth, far-gleaming mirror by these rocky walls we'll nestle,
 Moving in the gentle wavelets to and fro, caressingly. *10000*
 To each sound we'll hearken, list to songs of birds and reedy fluting.
 Be it Pan's own fearful voice, a ready answer is at hand.
 Doth it murmur, we too murmur; thunders it, we roll our thunders
 Overwhelming, doubly crashing, threefold, tenfold echoing back.
A Third Part.
 Sisters, we more nimble, we will hasten with the brooklets onward, *10005*
 For those yonder distant, richly-mantled mountain ranges charm
  us.
 Ever downward, ever deeper, while meandering we'll water
 Now the meadow, now the pasture, then the garden round the
  house,
 It is marked by slender cypress tree-tops soaring into ether
 Over landscape, winding shore-line, and the mirror of the stream. *10010*
A Fourth Part.
 Roam ye others where it please you; we'll engirdle, we will ripple,
 Round the thickly planted hillside where the trellised vines grow
  green;
 There the grower of the vine in anguish ponders hour- and day-long
 How uncertain is the promise of devoted industry.
 Now with hoe and now with shovel, now with hilling, pruning,
  tying, *10015*

Unto all the gods he prayeth, to the sun-god best of all.
Pampered Bacchus frets himself but little for his faithful servant,
Rests in bowers, lolls in caverns, prattling with the youngest faun.
What he ever needed for his half-intoxicated dreaming,
He has always near at hand in wineskins, pitchers, divers vessels,   *10020*
Right and left in cool recesses for eternal ages stored.
But if all the gods together, Helios the most important,
Fanning, moistening, warming, glowing, filled with grape-vine's
    horn of plenty,
Where the quiet vintner laboured, there new life will soon be
    stirring,
With a rustling in each trellis and a rush from stock to stock.   *10025*
Baskets creak and buckets clatter, tubs groan on the bearer's back;
To the great vat all are going, to the treaders' vigorous dance;
And thus is the sacred plenty of the pure-born, juicy berries
Rudely trodden, foaming, spurting, crushed to an unsightly mass.
Now the ear is pierced by brazen clash of cymbals and of timbrels,   *10030*
For the veil of mystery hath Dionysus cast aside;
He comes forth with goat-foot satyrs, whirling goat-foot satyresses;
And amid them brays, untamed and shrill, Silenus' long-eared
    beast.
Naught is spared! For cloven hoofs are trampling down all decent
    custom;
For the senses whirling stagger, horribly the ear is stunned.   *10035*
For the cup the drunken fumble, over-full are heads and bellies.
Careful still is this and that one, but he heightens thus the tumult,
For to garner this year's juices, they drain swiftly the old skin.

    The curtain falls, PHORKYAS *in the proscenium rises to a gigantic
    height, descends from the cothurni, casts aside mask and veil,
    and appears as* MEPHISTOPHELES *in order, as far as may be nec-
    essary, to comment on the piece by way of epilogue.*[1]

[1]This epilogue was never written.

ACT IV

A HIGH MOUNTAIN RANGE

*Bold jagged rocky peaks. A cloud approaches, pauses as it touches
a peak, and sinks down on a projecting ledge. It divides.*

Faust [*steps forth*].   Looking to deepest solitudes beneath my feet
I walk in thoughtfulness along this summit's verge,   *10040*
Relinquishing my chariot of clouds that bore
Me gently over land and sea through smiling days.
Slowly, not scattering, it drifts away from me.
Off to the east the mass strains, rolling on and on;
The eye strains after it, admiring and amazed.   *10045*
It breaks while moving, billow-like and changefully,
Yet seems re-shaping.—Yes, my eyes deceive me not!
On sun-illumined pillows gloriously reclines—
Of giant size, in truth—a godlike woman's form.
I see it! Like to Juno, Leda, Helena,   *10050*
It floats in lovely majesty before my sight.
Alas! It's shifting! Formless, broad, and towering,
It resteth in the east like distant ice-clad peaks,
And, dazzling, mirrors swift days' great significance.
    Yet round me floats a light and tender misty wreath,   *10055*
Around my breast and brow, cheering, caressing, cool.
Now it mounts high and higher, lightly, lingering.
It draws together.—Doth a rapturing form deceive
Mine eyes, youth's first, long-unenjoyed and highest bliss?
The earliest, deepest treasures of my heart break forth;   *10060*
The dawn of love, so light of wing, it typifies,
The swiftly-felt, the first scarce comprehended glance,
Outshining every other treasure, if held fast.
Like beauty of the soul the lovely form becomes
More fair, dissolving not, but through the ether soars   *10065*
And draws the best of all my being on and on.

> *A seven-league boot comes thumping forward. Another soon
> follows.* MEPHISTOPHELES *steps out of them. The boots stride
> on hastily.*

Mephistopheles.   That I call striding briskly ended!
But say, what kind of whim is this?
Why midst such horrors here descended,
By ghastly yawning precipice?   *10070*
I know them well but not in this high station,
For such things really were Hell's own foundation.
Faust.   Of foolish tales you've always had a store
And now begin to deal them out once more.

245

Mephistopheles [*seriously*].

 When God the Lord—I know well the occasion—   *10075*
 Banned us from air into the deeps profound,
 Where, glowing from earth's centre all around,
 Eternal fire waxed hottest past all bound,
 We found us midst too great illumination
 In a most crowded, irksome situation.   *10080*
 The devils, every one, began a coughing,
 Above, below, at every vent-hole puffing;
 Hell was with sulphur-fumes so much inflated
 And such a gas therefrom was generated,
 That very soon the earth's flat crust—no wonder!—   *10085*
 Thick as it was, was forced to burst asunder.
 So now we have a different situation;
 What's now a peak was once a deep foundation.
 On this men base the doctrines that they boast,
 Turning the lowest into uppermost.   *10090*
 Thus from that slavish hot cave did we fare
 To an excessive lording in free air,[1]
 An open secret but one well concealed
 And to the common crowd but late revealed. *(Ephes.* **6.** 12)[2]

Faust. To me a mountain-mass stays nobly dumb,   *10095*
 I ask not wherefore nor from whence it come.
 When Nature in herself her own self founded,
 The globe of earth she formed and neatly rounded,
 In summits and in gorges took delight,
 Ranged rock on rock and mountain height on height;   *10100*
 The hills in easy slopes she downward moulded,
 Till gently into valleys they unfolded.
 There all is verdant growth and for her gladness
 She has no need of such convulsive madness.

Mephistopheles. That's what you say! To you it seems quite clear *10105*
 But he knows better who beheld it near.
. I was at hand when still below was surging
 The deep abyss, when streamed a fiery tide,
 When Moloch's hammer rock on rock was forging
 And scattering mountain-ruins far and wide.[3]   *10110*
 Earth still abounds in ponderous strange masses.
 Such power in hurling who can well explain?
 As wise men know, their reason it surpasses.
 The rock lies evermore where it has lain.
 We've racked our brains, to our disgrace, **in vain.**   *10115*
 Only the faithful common people know
 And let none shake them in their story:
 (Their wisdom ripened long ago)

[1]See Ephesians, 2. 2.
[2]This reference was inserted, not by Goethe, but by his secretary, Riemer.
[3]Cf. Leviticus, 18. 21; *Paradise Lost,* i. 392ff.

It is a miracle, and Satan gets the glory.
My pilgrim on his crutch of faith limps on   *10120*
To Devil's Bridge, to Devil's Stone.
Faust.   There is indeed remarkable attraction
In seeing a devil's view of Nature's action.
Mephistopheles.   Be Nature what she will! What do I care?
Honour's at stake! Satan himself was there!   *10125*
We are real people, great things we attain.
Violence, tumult, nonsense! See, the sign is plain!—
But—to say something now that's wholly clear—
Has nothing pleased you in our upper sphere?
You have surveyed a boundless territory,   *10130*
The kingdoms of the world and all their glory; *(Matt. 4)*[1]
Still—with that discontented air—
Did you not lust for something anywhere?
Faust.   I did! A great work lured me on.
Divine it!
Mephistopheles.   That can soon be done.   *10135*
I'd seek some city, at its heart
A horrid city victuals-mart,
Tortuous alleys, pointed gables,
Beets, kale, and onions on the tables;
Meat-stalls where blue flies take life easy,   *10140*
Feasting on roasts well-done and greasy;
There you will always surely find
Stench and activity combined.
Then ample squares, broad streets between,
Where one can stalk with lordly mien,   *10145*
And lastly, where no town-gates bar,
The suburbs boundless, stretching far.
There I'd enjoy the coaches' rolling,
The noisy hither and thither bowling,
Eternal running hither and thither   *10150*
Of scattered ants that swarm together.
And whether driving, whether riding,
The centre of them all abiding,
Honoured by thousands would be I.
Faust.   With that I cannot be contented!   *10155*
One likes to see the people multiply
And in their way live comfortably,
Even develop, learn thereby—
And yet, in fine, rebels are thus augmented.
Mephistopheles.   Then, swelling with self-conscious pride I'd raise *10160*
A pleasure-castle in a pleasant place.
Hill, level, meadow, field, and forest glade
Into a splendid garden I'd have made,
Before green walls of verdure, velvet meadows,
[1]See note to line 10094.

And measured paths and art-directed shadows, *10165*
Cascading falls among the rocks designed,
And fountain-sprays of every kind,
One rising proud and stately in the middle,
While at the sides a thousand spraylets spurt and piddle.
And then I'd build, for loveliest women meet, *10170*
Sung villas, each an intimate retreat.
I'd pass there endless time in joyous mood,
Blessed by the dearest social solitude.
"Women," I say, for here, as everywhere,
I think in plurals of the ladies fair. *10175*
Faust. Sardanapalus![1] Vile and new, I swear!
Mephistopheles. Who could divine toward what you would
    aspire?
It must have been sublimely bold, in truth,
Toward the moon you'd soar and ever nigher;
Did you mad quest allure you *there* forsooth? *10180*
Faust. By no means! For this earthly sphere
Affords a place for great deeds ever.
Astounding things shall happen here,
I feel the strength for bold endeavour.
Mephistopheles. So you'd earn glory? One can see *10185*
You've been in heroines' company.
Faust. Lordship, possession, are my aim and thought!
The deed is everything, the glory naught.
Mephistopheles. Yet poets will come forward all the same
To blazon to the later world your fame, *10190*
Through folly more fools to inflame.
Faust. Of all this naught is known to you.
How should you know what men will woo?
Your bitter, sharp, and hostile mood,
How does it know what men count good? *10195*
Mephistopheles. So be it with you then as best it pleases!
Confide to me the range of your caprices.
Faust. Mine eye was drawn out toward the open ocean
That swelled aloft, self-towering and vaulting,
And then drew back its billows in commotion, *10200*
The broad expanse of level shore assaulting.
And that irked me, as always insolence
Irks the free soul who prizes every right,
Whose blood, stirred up to passionate vehemence,
Is fired with feelings of a harsh despite. *10205*
I thought it chance and gazed more sharply at the main.
The billows paused and then rolled back again,
Withdrawing from the goal so proudly won.
The hour returns, again the game's begun.

---

[1]A type of luxury-loving despot, revived in people's memories by Byron's tragedy,
Sardanapalus.

Mephistopheles [*to the spectators*].
 There's nothing new in that for me to know;   *10210*
 I knew it a hundred thousand years ago.
Faust [*continuing passionately*].
 It steals along, in countless channels flowing,
 Fruitless itself and fruitlessness bestowing;
 It swells and grows and rolls and spreads its reign
 Over the loathsome, desolate domain.   *10215*
 Strong with a mighty will there wave on wave rolls on,
 Reigns for a while, retires, and naught is done.
 Even to despair it could harass me, truly,
 The aimless force of elements unruly!
 Here dares my soul above itself to soar;   *10220*
 Here would I fight, of this be conqueror.
 And it is possible! For though the tide
 May rise, it fawns along each hillock's side.
 It may bestir itself and bluster oh! so loudly,
 A little height will meet and daunt it proudly,   *10225*
 A little depth will draw it on amain.
 So plan on plan flashed swiftly through my brain:
 "Win for thyself great joy, a costly store:
 Push back the lordly ocean from the shore;
 Limit the bounds of that vast, watery deep   *10230*
 And force it, far away, within itself to keep."
 Thus step by step I knew I could explain it.
 This is my wish, now dare to help me gain it!
  Drums and martial music at the rear of the spectators, at a dis-
   tance, on the right hand.
Mephistopheles. How easy! Do you hear the drums afar?
Faust. What, war again? The wise man likes not war. *10235*
Mephistopheles. Be it war or peace! From every circumstance
 The wise man tries to draw himself some profit.
 One watches, notes each favouring chance.
 Now is the moment, Faustus, make use of it!
Faust. Spare me such riddle-mongering, my friend! *10240*
 Be brief, explain, what is it you intend?
Mephistopheles. As I came here, it was not hid from me,
 Our Emperor suffers great anxiety;
 You know him well. The while that we amused him
 And with illusive show of wealth abused him,   *10245*
 He thought the whole world could be had for pay.
 For when a youth, the throne fell to his sway
 And wrongly he concluded at his leisure
 Two things one could quite well combine—
 Which would be most desirable and fine—   *10250*
 To rule and also take one's pleasure.
Faust. A great mistake. Whoever would command,
 Must in commanding feel his greatest blessing.

A lofty purpose must his breast expand,
But what he wills must be beyond all guessing.   *10255*
What he to his most faithful whispereth:
It's done! Amazed, all subjects hold their breath.
Thus always will he have the most exalted place,
The worthiest, he! Enjoyment doth debase.

Mephistopheles.   Not such is he! Enjoy? how didn't he?   *10260*
Meanwhile the realm was rent by anarchy,
Where great and small warred criss-cross with each other
And brother drove from home or slaughtered brother,
Castle with castle, town with town in feud,
Guild against noble, all in fiercest mood.   *10265*
Chapters and flocks against their bishops rose.
If men but saw each other, they were foes.
In churches murder, homicide; outside each gate
Each merchant, traveller, waits the self-same fate.
Boldness in all grew to no mean extent.   *10270*
To live meant self-defence!—Well, now, that went.

Faust.   It went, it staggered, fell, and up it jumped,
Fell over itself, and in a heap it plumped.

Mephistopheles.   And such conditions no one dared to blame;
Some standing each could, each would, claim.   *10275*
As peer of any has the least man passed,
But for the best, things grew too mad at last.
The capable arose then in their might
And said: "Who gives us peace is lord by right;
The Emperor cannot, will not—let us choose   *10280*
A new one, one who will infuse
New life into the realm he safeguards duly,
Where peace and justice govern truly
The world he strengthens and renews."

Faust.   That sound like priestcraft.

Mephistopheles.   Priests they were, be sure.   *10285*
Their own well-nourished paunch they made secure.
More than all others were they implicated.
The riot grew, riot was consecrated.
Our Emperor, to whom we gave delight,
Is drawing near, perhaps for his last fight.   *10290*

Faust.   I pity him, so kind and frank was he.

Mephistopheles.   While there is life, there's hope. Come, let
us see.
Let's liberate him from this narrow vale!
A single rescue doth a thousand times avail.
Who knows how yet the dice may fall?   *10295*
Grant him good luck, vassals he'll have withal.

> *They climb over the middle range of mountains and survey the*
> *disposition of the host in the valley. Drums and martial music*
> *resound from below.*

Mephistopheles.   They've taken their position well, I see;
  We'll join them and complete the victory.
Faust.   What is there to expect, I'd like to know?
  Fraud! Dazzling magic! Hollow show!   *10300*
Mephistopheles.   Nay, stratagem to win the fight!
  Just fix your gaze upon a lofty height
  And only think of your high aim.
  If we preserve the Emperor's throne and land,
  Then you can kneel and justly claim   *10305*
  In feudal right a boundless strand.
Faust.   Much have you ere now carried through;
  Come then and win a battle too.
Mephistopheles.   No, you will win it; For, in brief,
  You'll be the General-in-Chief.   *10310*
Faust.   A really lofty post for me, commanding
  In places of which I've no understanding!
Mephistopheles.   You let the General Staff provide
  And the Field Marshal's safe whate'er betide.
  Lack of war-counsel I have long since traced,   *10315*
  Hence a war-council I have straightway based
  On primal mountains' primal human might;
  Blest he who can its elements unite.
Faust.   What do I see there bearing arms?
  Have you stirred mountain-folk with your alarms?   *10320*
Mephistopheles.   No! I have called, like Peter Quince,
  Of all the lot of quintessence.
    The THREE MIGHTY MEN *appear (II Sam. 23, 8).*
Mephistopheles.   You see my fellows coming there!
  Of different ages are they, surely,
  In different garb and outfit they appear;   *10325*
  With them, I know, you'll not fare poorly.
    To the spectators.
  Now every child delights to see
  A knight's bright collar and his armour;
  And allegoric though the rascals be,
  Each is but all the more a charmer.   *10330*
Fight-hard [*young, lightly armed, in motley dress*].
  If anyone should look me in the eyes,
  Straight at his jaw my fist shall fare,
  And if a coward from me flies,
  I'll catch him by his streaming hair.
Get-quick [*manly, well armed, richly clad*].
  Such empty brawls are farces dreary,   *10335*
  We lose what such occasion brings;
  Only in taking be not weary,
  Look afterward to other things.
Hold-fast [*along in years, strongly armed, without attire*].
  Not much is thus accumulated;

Great riches are soon dissipated,   *10340*
Adown life's stream they rush as swift as thought.
To take is good, better to keep when taken;
Let the old greybeard rule unshaken
And none shall plunder you of aught.
    They descend together.

ON THE HEADLAND

EMPEROR. GENERALISSIMO. BODYGUARDS
Drums and martial music from below.
The EMPEROR'S *tent is being pitched.*

Generalissimo.   The project still seems well deliberated,   *10345*
    That back in this convenient vale
    Our army all be drawn and concentrated;
    I trust this disposition will avail.
Emperor.   How things will go now we must soon be seeing;
    But I dislike this giving way, this semi-fleeing.   *10350*
Generalissimo.   Look here, my prince, at our right flank's
        position.
    In war such ground's a longed-for acquisition:
    Not steep the hills, yet not for easy faring,
    To us propitious, to the foe ensnaring.
    Half hidden on the billowy field are we;   *10355*
    They will not venture here with cavalry.
Emperor.   I can but praise, and hope the best;
    Now arm and heart can meet the test.
Generalissimo.   There where the level ground stretches away,
    You see the phalanx eager for the fray.   *10360*
    Through morning's fragrant mist in sunshine rare
    The lances glint and sparkle in the air.
    How dark the mighty square is surging to and fro!
    For great achievements all the thousands glow.
    The mass's power you thus can comprehend;   *10365*
    The enemy's power I trust them now to rend.
Emperor.   For the first time I have so fair a view.
    An army such as this can count as two.
Generalissimo.   Of our left flank I've nothing to report.
    Stout heroes guard that beetling rocky fort.   *10370*
    The stony cliffs, lit by the weapons' sheen,
    Protect the vital pass to the ravine.
    Here I foresee, what little they expect.
    Our foes will in the bloody brawl be wrecked.
Emperor.   Yonder they come, false kinsmen, one and other,   *10375*
    Even as they styled me Uncle, Cousin, Brother,
    Who've more and more presumed, all ties have sundered,
    The sceptre of its might, the throne's respect have plundered,

Then, in their feuds, the realm have devastated
And now rebel against me, federated.   *10380*
The rabble wavers in uncertain spirit,
Then streams along wherever the stream may bear it.
Generalissimo.   A trusty scout, for tidings sent in quest,
  Hastes down the rocks. May he have been well blessed!
First Scout.

                Fortune fair on us has waited.   *10385*
                Through our bold and crafty skill
                Here and there we penetrated;
                But the news we bring is ill.
                Many are pure homage swearing,
                They and many a soldier true;   *10390*
                But they plead, for not appearing,
                Inner ferment, danger too.

Emperor.   Through selfishness one learns self-preservation,
  Not honour, thanks, affection, obligation.
  Do you not think, when your accounts fall due,   *10395*
  Your neighbour's burning house will burn up you?
Generalissimo.   The second comes, but slowly down he clambers;
  The weary man trembles in all his members.
Second Scout.

                Wild confusion we detected
                First of all, were highly cheered;   *10400*
                Then at once and unexpected,
                A new emperor appeared.
                And in fore-determined manner
                Through the plain the rabble sweep;
                His perfidious unfurled banner   *10405*
                They all follow—they are sheep.

Emperor.   A rival emperor I esteem a gain,
  Now know myself an emperor not in vain.
  As soldier only did I armour don,
  Now for a higher aim is it put on.   *10410*
  At every feast, though brilliant it might be
  And naught seemed lacking, danger lacked to *me*.
  When ring-sports you advised—whatever your intent—
  My heart beat high, I breathed the tournament.
  And had you not from war dissuaded me,   *10415*
  Renowned for bright heroic deeds I'd be.
  What self-reliance did I feel, what fortitude!
  When mirrored in that realm of fire I stood!
  The element leapt toward me, infuriate,
  'Twas only semblance, yet a semblance great.   *10420*
  I dreamed confusedly of victory and fame,
  Now I'll retrieve my fault and expiate my shame.

*The heralds are despatched to challenge the rival emperor to
single combat.*

FAUST *in armour, with half-closed visor. The* THREE MIGHTY MEN
armed and clothed as above.

Faust.   We come and hope that we are welcome here;
　　Foresight avails even when no need is near.
　　You know the mountain-people think and pore,　　　　　*10425*
　　Well-studied in all rocks' and nature's lore.
　　The spirits, long since vanished from the plain,
　　Of rocky heights are more than ever fain.
　　Silent they work through devious crevasses
　　In rich metallic fumes of noble gases.　　　　　　　*10430*
　　On sundering, testing, blending, they are bent,
　　Their only impulse, something to invent.
　　With the light touch of spiritual power
　　They build transparent figures, hour by hour;
　　The crystal then in its eternal silence glasses　　　*10435*
　　What in the upper world above them passes.
Emperor.   I've heard it and believe that it may be;
　　Yet, gallant man, say: what is that to me?
Faust.   The Norcian necromant, of Sabine race,
　　Your faithful, worthy servant, sends me in his place.　*10440*
　　What fate once threatened him, so monstrous, dire!
　　The fagots crackled, leapt the tongues of fire;
　　Dry billets, lattice-like, were round about him fixed,
　　With pitch and bars of sulphur intermixed.
　　Rescue through devil, man, or god was vain.　　　　*10445*
　　Your Majesty it was who burst the fiery chain!
　　It was in Rome. Still of most grateful mood,
　　He pays heed to your path with deep solicitude.
　　He has forgotten self from that dread moment on;
　　He questions stars and depths for you alone.　　　　*10450*
　　He charged us, as our task the most immediate,
　　To stand by you. The mountain's powers are great;
　　Here Nature works omnipotently free.
　　The priests' dull wits chide it as sorcery.
Emperor.   On festal days when guest on guest we're greeting,　*10455*
　　Who come for joy and hope for joyous meeting,
　　We like to see them shoving, pushing, one and all,
　　So many men as make the rooms seem small.
　　But still most highly welcome must the good man be
　　If to our aid he comes with energy　　　　　　　*10460*
　　Some morning hour when many dangers wait,
　　And doubtful hang the balances of Fate.
　　But here at this hour's critical demand
　　Take not the willing sword in your strong hand;
　　Honour the hour when many thousands stride　　　*10465*
　　To fight against me or upon my side.

Self is the man! Who asks a throne and crown
Must in himself be worthy such renown.
The spectre who against us has arisen,
Himself as Emperor, Lord of our lands, doth christen,   *10470*
Our army's Duke, our nobles' feudal Lord, he must
With mine own hand into the realm of death be thrust!
Faust.   Though it be done to end the noble undertaking,
You do not well, your head thus to be staking.
Is not your helm with plume and crest bedecked?   *10475*
The head which fires our zeal it doth protect.
Without the head what could the limbs avail?
For if it's drowsy, all droop down and fail;
If it is hurt, at once all have a wound,
Arise afresh, if quickly it grows sound.   *10480*
To give its laws effect, swift is the arm,
It lifts the shield to guard the skull from harm.
Instantly doth the sword its duty know,
Parries with vigour and returns the blow.
The active foot shares in the other's weal   *10485*
As on the slain man's neck it plants its heel.
Emperor.   Such is my wrath, him thus I fain would treat,
Make his proud head a footstool for my feet.
Heralds [come back].

       Little honour, little glory
       Met us yonder at our coming;   *10490*
       At our noble, valiant story
       Laughed they as a vapid mumming:
       "Vanished is your Emperor yonder,
       But an echo through the vale;
       If on him we are to ponder,   *10495*
       'There was once'—so runs the tale."

Faust.   As your best men have wished, it doth betide;
Both staunch and true they're standing at your side.
There comes the foe, your troops impatient wait.
Order attack, the hour is fortunate.   **10500**
Emperor.   Here I surrender the supreme command.
    To the GENERALISSIMO.
So be your duty, Prince, in your own hand.
Generalissimo.   Then let our right wing march on to the field!
The enemy's left wing, that just now is ascending,
Ere they complete their final step, shall yield   *10505*
Before the tested constancy of our defending.
Faust.   I beg you then to let this hero gay
Be added to your ranks without delay,
Be fully in your ranks incorporated;
His sturdy strength will much avail, so mated.   *10510*
    He points to the right.

Fight-hard [*steps forward*]. Who shows his face to me turns not
    away
  Till both his cheek- and jawbones get a mangling,
  Who turns his back, limp on his nape straightway
  Are neck and head and scalp right grimly dangling.
  And if your men then strike and lunge   *10515*
  With sword and mace as I go raging round,
  Man after man, the foe will plunge
  And in their own hot blood be drowned.
    Exit.

Generalissimo.   Let now our centre phalanx follow slow,
  With caution but in full force meet the foe.   *10520*
  See, on the right, now fiercely overtaken,
  Their schemes our force has desperately shaken,

Faust [*pointing to the man in the middle*].
  Then let this hero too your hest obey.
  He's quick and in a rush sweeps all away.

Get-quick [*steps forth*].   The imperial host's heroic spirit   *10525*
  Will rise with hope for booty near it;
  The goal, set up for all, shall be
  The rival emperor's rich marquee.
  Upon his seat he will not swagger long,
  I'll take my place and lead the phalanx strong.   *10530*

Speed-booty [*sutler-woman, fawning on him*].
  Although his wife I may not be,
  My dearest lover still is he.
  For us a harvest rare is ripe.
  Women are fierce to grab and gripe,
  In robbing ruthless and uncowed.   *10535*
  Forward in conquest!—All is allowed.
    Exeunt both.

Generalissimo.   Against our left, as was to be expected,
  Their right flank has been vigorously directed.
  The narrow, rocky pass they seek to gain;
  To thwart the furious onset ours will strain.   *10540*

Faust [*beckons to the left*].   I beg you, Sire, also to note this one:
  When strength adds to its strength, no harm is done.

Hold-fast [*steps forward*].   For your left wing dismiss all care!
  For where I am, safe is possession there;
  Thus age asserts itself, we're told;   *10545*
  No lightning shatters what I hold.
    Exit.

Mephistopheles [*coming down from above*].
  Look at the background, see how surges
  Out of the jagged, rocky gorges
  A host of armed men—how they pour,
  Crowding the narrow pathways ever more—   *10550*
  With helmet, armour, sword, and spear

To build a rampart at our rear,
Waiting the signal to strike home.
   Aside to the knowing ones.
You must not ask from whence they come.
Industriously I've quite cleared out   *10555*
The halls of armour roundabout.
There were they all, on foot or mounted,
As if lords of the earth they still were counted;
Knight, emperor, king, they were of yore,
Now empty snail-shells, nothing more;   *10560*
Full many a ghost is thus adorned for strife,
Bringing the Middle Ages back to life.
Whatever devilkin is thus bedecked,
They'll now create a rare effect.
   Aloud.
Hark how in anger now they chatter,   *10565*
With clank of tin each other batter!
And torn old flags on standards flutter free,
That waited stirring breezes restlessly.
Reflect, an ancient folk stands ready there
And in this modern conflict fain would share.   *10570*
   Fearful resounding of trumpets from above, a perceptible waver-
      ing in the enemy's army.
Faust.   Already the horizon darkles,
   Yet meaningful anon there sparkles
   A crimson-red, portentous light;
   And now the weapons glitter bloody,
   The air, the woods, and cliffs are ruddy;   *10575*
   The whole sky mingles in the fight.
Mephistopheles.   The right flank stoutly holds its station;
   But towering midst them, self-reliant,
   I see Jack Fight-hard, nimble giant,
   Busy and swift in his own fashion.   *10580*
Emperor.   At first I saw one arm engaging,
   But now I see a dozen raging;
   No law of Nature's working here.
Faust.   Have you not heard of mists that over
   Sicilian sea-coasts sweep and hover?   *10585*
   There, in the daylight, swaying, clear,
   Uplifted into mid-air spaces
   And mirrored in especial hazes,
   One sees a vision strange appear:
   There cities hover backward, onward,   *10590*
   There gardens waver up- and downward,
   As form on form breaks through the air.
Emperor.   Yet how suspicious! For I see the tall
   Spear-heads flash lightning, one and all;
   Behold our phalanx' shining lances!   *10595*

On each a nimble flamelet dances.
Too spectral seems to me this sight.
Faust.   Oh, pardon, Sire, those are the traces
Of spiritual natures, vanished races,
Pollux' and Castor's reflex, the great pair   *10600*
By whom all sailors used to swear;
They gather here their final might.
Emperor.   But say: to whom are we indebted
That Nature hath us so abetted
As here her rarest powers to unite?   *10605*
Mephistopheles.   To whom except that lofty Master
Who bears your fate within his breast?
Your foe's strong menace of disaster
Has stirred his soul to deep unrest.
You would he thank and save and cherish   *10610*
Though he himself should thereby perish.
Emperor.   They joyed to lead me round, with pomp invested;
I felt my power and wished to test it;
Fitting it seemed—though I was scarce aware—
To give to that white beard the cooling air.   *10615*
I spoiled a pastime that the clergy savour
And truly thus did not acquire their favour.
Now shall I, when so many years have passed,
Reap the returns of that glad deed at last?
Faust.   Rich is the interest of a generous deed.   *10620*
Look upwards! For he soon will send us,
If I err not, a sign portentous.
It will reveal itself at once, give heed!
Emperor.   An eagle soaring high in heaven I see,
A griffin wild pursues him threateningly.   *10625*
Faust.   Give heed: auspicious seems the sign.
The griffin is of fabled line;
Can he forget his foe is regal?
How dare he fight a genuine eagle?
Emperor.   And now in circles far extending   *10630*
They wheel around, and in a flash
They straight upon each other dash,
Each other's throat and bosom rending.
Faust.   Mark how the sorry griffin, torn
And ruffled sore, finds naught but injuries   *10635*
And with his drooping lion's tail, forlorn,
Plunging in tree-tops, vanishes.
Emperor.   Even as the sign, be the event!
I accept it all with wonderment.
Mephistopheles [*toward the right*].   Under crushing blows repeated *10640*
Has the foe perforce retreated;
Fighting in uncertain fashion,
They crowd toward their right wing's station,

Leave their left wing undirected,
In confusion, unprotected.   *10645*
Now our phalanx, firmly tight'ning,
Moves to right and like the lightning
At the foe's weak spot it flashes.—
Now, like waves the tempest dashes
Spuming, equal powers are raging,   *10650*
Twofold conflict wildly waging;
Never was aught planned more glorious,
In this battle we're victorious!

Emperor [*on the left to* FAUST].   Look! In jeopardy is our position,
If I'm right in my suspicion.   *10655*
Not a stone do I see flying.
Mounted are the rocks low-lying,
But the upper stand deserted.
Now!—To one huge mass converted,
Press the enemy on and on,   *10660*
Now perhaps the pass have won.
Toil unholy thus ends fruitless!
And your arts have all proved bootless.
    Pause.

Mephistopheles.   Here come my pair of ravens winging,
What may the message be they're bringing?   *10665*
I fear we're in an evil plight.

Emperor.   What are these doleful birds portending?
Hither their sable sails they're bending
From the hot combat on the height.

Mephistopheles [*to the ravens*].   Perch near my ears. Lost is he never *10670*
To whom you grant your guardian favour,
For your advice is sound and right.

Faust [*to the* EMPEROR].   You've surely heard of pigeons flying
Back to their food and nestlings, hieing
From farthest lands to their own coast.   *10675*
We find a difference here obtaining:
Pigeon-post serves while peace is reigning,
But war demands the raven-post.

Mephistopheles.   A fate's reported that distresses.
See yonder how the enemy presses   *10680*
Around our heroes' rocky wall.
The nearest heights have been surmounted
And if the pass be theirs accounted,
We'll find it hard to stand at all.

Emperor.   So then deception was played on me!   *10685*
Into these meshes you have drawn me;
I shudder in this tangling net.

Mephistopheles.   Courage! All has not failed as yet.
Have patience, craft, for the last knot.
The usual end is fierce and hot.   *10690*

My trusty messengers I have at hand;
  Command that I may give command.
Generalissimo [*who has arrived meanwhile*].
  These men with whom you are confederated
  Have all the time made me feel irritated.
  No stable luck doth magic earn.   *10695*
  As for this conflict, I can't mend it;
  'Twas they began it, let them end it.
  My staff of office I return.
Emperor.   Keep it until a better hour
  Which luck perchance has in its grip.   *10700*
  Before this ugly chap I cower,
  Him and his raven-fellowship.
      To MEPHISTOPHELES.
  I cannot grant the staff to you;
  You do not seem the proper man.
  Command! and seek to make us free anew,   *10705*
  Then happen all that happen can.
      Exit into the tent with the GENERALISSIMO.
Mephistopheles.   The blunted staff—may he have safety of it!
  Us others it could little profit,
  There was a kind of cross thereon.
Faust.   What's to be done?
Mephistopheles.   It is already done!—   *10710*
  Now haste, black kin, in service fleeting
  To the great mountain-lake! The undines greeting,
  Beg them their torrents' semblance to prepare.
  Through women's arts, beyond our seeing,
  They can part semblance from real being,   *10715*
  And that it is real being, each will swear.
      Pause.
Faust.   Those water-maidens, look! them must our ravens
  Have quite enveigled from their havens,
  For yonder is a trickling you can see.
  From many a barren, dry place in the mountain   *10720*
  Arises now a full, swift-flowing fountain.
  It's over with our enemy's victory.
Mephistopheles.   To such strange greeting they're not used.
  The boldest climbers are confused.
Faust.   With might now brook to brook is downward rushing;   *10725*
  From many a gorge redoubled they come gushing.
  One cascades in an arch adown the trail,
  Soon spreading outward on a rocky level,
  Foaming and rushing to and fro in revel,
  Leaping down step by step into the vale.   *10730*
  What boots heroic, brave resistance?
  The mighty flood sweeps them past all assistance.
  Before so fierce a surge I too must quail.

Mephistopheles. Naught do I see of water and illusion;
Men's eyes alone are subject to confusion. 10735
In this odd case I take a great delight.
The crowds rush on, are fain to leap and bound.
The fools! they think that they'll be drowned,
And, as if swimming, drolly thrash around,
Panting and snorting on the solid ground. 10740
Confusion now is at its height.
    The ravens have returned.
I'll praise you to the lofty Master[1] duly.
Now if you'll prove that you are masters truly,
Hasten ye to the glowing smithy
Where tireless dwarf-folk on their stithy 10745
Strike sparks from metal and from stone.
Ask, while at length you prate and flatter,
For fires that beam and flash and scatter,
Such as to their deep minds are known.
It's true, sheet lightning in the distance dancing 10750
And fall of stars from height of heaven glancing
May happen any summer night;
Sheet lightning, though, amid entangled bushes
And stars that hiss among the quenching rushes:
Not often seen is such a sight. 10755
Don't worry much, but be, with understanding,
At first entreating, then commanding.
    Exeunt the ravens. All takes place as prescribed.
Mephistopheles. Before the foe there falls a thick, dark curtain!
Their step and tread become uncertain!
Everywhere flitting scintillations, 10760
Sudden and blinding illuminations.
That's fine, methinks, and has succeeded.
But now a sound of terror's needed.
Faust. The hollow armour from the vaulted chambers
Revives in open air in all its members; 10765
There it's been rattling, clattering all around,
A wondrous-strange, discordant sound.
Mephistopheles. Quite right! They're now past all restraining.
Hark to the sound of blows those knights are raining
As in the dear old times of yore. 10770
Brassards and cuisses, charging, rearing,
As Guelph and Ghibelline appearing,
Renew the everlasting strife once more.
Their enmity still unabated,
Firm in the hate their fathers hated, 10775
Both far and wide resounds the wild uproar.
Hate between parties is the devil's
Best helper still in all his revels,
    [1]Lucifer.

Till the last horror ends it all;
Abhorrent sounds of panic panic,   *10780*
From time to time sharp, shrill, satanic,
Through all the valley rise and fall.
  Warlike tumult in the orchestra, finally passing over into lively
    martial airs.

THE RIVAL EMPEROR'S TENT

THRONE, RICH SURROUNDINGS

GET-QUICK. SPEED-BOOTY.

Speed-booty.
                 So we're the first ones here, I see!
Get-quick.
                 No raven flies as fast as we.
Speed-booty.
                 Oh, what a store lies here heaped up!   *10785*
                 Where shall I start? Where shall I stop?
Get-quick.
                 How full indeed the whole place stands;
                 I don't know where to lay my hands.
Speed-booty.
                 This rug is just the thing I need;
                 My couch is oft too hard indeed.   *10790*
Get-quick.
                 Here hangs a club with many a spike;
                 I long have wished to have its like.
Speed-booty.
                 The scarlet mantle, golden-hemmed,
                 Of such a one I've often dreamt.

Get-quick [*taking the weapon*].
                 With this the job is quickly done;   *10795*
                 One strikes his man dead and goes on.
                 You've piled so much now on your back
                 But nothing worth while's in your sack.
                 That rubbish, leave it where it lay,
                 Take one of these small chests away!   *10800*
                 The army's destined pay they hold,
                 In this one's belly naught but gold.
Speed-booty.
                 This thing's a killing weight, I swear it;
                 I cannot lift it, cannot bear it.
Get-quick.
                 Quick! Duck down! Stoop! and I will pack   *10805*
                 The booty on your sturdy back.

Speed-booty.

> Oh, woe! Oh, woe! I'm done for! Whew!
> That load will break my back in two.

The chest falls and springs open.

Get-quick.

> There lies in heaps the ruddy gold;
> Quick, rake it up, fall to, lay hold!   *10810*

Speed-booty [*crouches down*].

> Quick to the work, fill up my lap!
> 'Twill be enough for any hap.

Get-quick.

> And so enough! Make haste and go!

She stands up.

> Your apron has a hole! Oh, woe!
> Go where you will or stand, I see   *10815*
> You sowing treasures all too free.

Bodyguards of our EMPEROR.

> This spot is sacred! What are you up to?
> Rifling the Emperor's treasure? Shame on you!

Get-quick.

> We risked our limbs for little pay
> And fetch our portion of the prey.   *10820*
> In enemies' tents it's custom so,
> And we, we're soldiers too, you know.

Bodyguards.

> In our profession that won't do.
> A carrion-thief and soldier too!
> Who nears our Emperor must be   *10825*
> A soldier used to honesty.

Get-quick.

> Yes, honesty—we know that same
> And "Contribution" is its name.
> All of you lie under one same cover:
> The password of your trade's "Fork over!"   *10830*

To SPEED-BOOTY.

> Away and drag off what you've got,
> Since welcome guests here we are not.

Exeunt.

First Bodyguard.

> Say, why did you not straightway slap
> His cheek? the dirty, saucy chap!

Second.

> I don't know, strength had gone from me,   *10835*
> So spectre-like they seemed to be.

Third.

> Things all went bad before my sight;
> They flickered, I could not see right.

Fourth.

How to express it I know not;
The whole day long it was so hot,   *10840*
Fearsome, oppressive, close as well.
While one man stood, another fell.
We groped and struck both high and low;
A foeman fell at every blow.
Before us swayed a kind of mist,   *10845*
And something hummed and roared and hissed.
Thus it went on—here are we now!
It happened but we don't know how.

The EMPEROR *enters accompanied by four* PRINCES. *The* BODY-
GUARDS *retire.*

Emperor. Now be it as it may! The battle's won! And shattered,
Over the level plain the fleeing foes are scattered.   *10850*
Here stands the empty throne; with tapestry hung round,
The traitor's store of treasure blocks up all the ground.
With our own bodyguards in honour due protecting,
The people's envoys we're imperially expecting;
Glad messages are coming in from every side,   *10855*
In happy loyalty the realm is pacified.
Though in our fight, in truth, we've been by magic aided,
For our own selves alone we fought—so be it stated.
To combatants, we know, chance often works some good:
From heaven falls a stone, upon the foe rains blood,   *10860*
From caves may echo strains, great wonders radiating,
Lifting our hearts on high, the foeman's palpitating.
Doomed to eternal scorn, the vanquished bit the sod;
The victor, while he boasts, exalts the favouring God.
Without command, this thanks all men unite in bringing: *10865*
"We praise Thee, God our Lord," a million throats are singing.
It rarely happed before, but now in highest praise
On my own grateful breast I turn my pious gaze.
A young and merry prince may give his days to pleasure,
But he will learn in time the moment's fitting measure.   *10870*
Wherefore I choose for counsel wholly to consort
With you four worthy men in realm and house and court.

To the FIRST PRINCE.[1]

You, Prince, achieved the host's well-ordered disposition,

---

[1]The Emperor proceeds to invest four generals with the ceremonial offices which the Golden Bull (established by Charles IV in 1356) assigned to the four lay electors of the Holy Roman Empire. According to the Bull the Duke of Saxony was appointed Arch-Marshal, the Margrave of Brandenburg Arch-Chamberlain, the Count Palatine of the Rhine Arch-Steward, and the King of Bohemia Arch-Cupbearer. The other three electors of the Empire were the Archbishops of Mainz, Trier, and Cologne, but Goethe combines the three in one and has him appear now in the one and now in the other of his dual capacity as Archbishop (10951 and later) and Arch-Chancellor (10961). Both the content and the form of the scene parody the stiff formality and the love of pomp at the court of the Holy Roman Empire as well as those at "our" Emperor's court.

Then, when the crisis came, moved it with bold precision.
Be active now in peace, just as the times suggest;   *10875*
Arch-Marshal you I dub and with the sword invest.
Arch-Marshal. Your army, tasked till now to keep the civil
    order,
When it has made your throne secure along the border,
Then at your festive throngs we'll ask it as our care
In wide ancestral halls the banquet to prepare.   *10880*
The bright sword I will bear before you, hold beside you,
Your Majesty Supreme, ever to guard and guide you.
Emperor [*to the* SECOND]. Who as a gallant man doth show a
    pleasing grace,
Shall be Arch-Chamberlain, no easy task and place.
The master you shall be of those of household station,   *10885*
Whose quarrels make their service oft a sore vexation.
You as a model to be honoured I install
To show how one can please the lord and court and all.
Arch-Chamberlain.
To further what his lord intends brings one to favour:
To help the best men on, to harm even bad ones never,   *10890*
Be frank and free from guile, reserved without deceit!
If you, Sire, read my heart, then is my joy complete.
But may my fancy now on to the banquet hasten?
When you go to the board, I'll hand the golden basin;
I'll hold your rings for you that so on gala days   *10895*
Your hands may be refreshed as I am by your gaze.
Emperor. To think about a feast, too grave I'm feeling, truly;
Yet be it! Festal moods promote glad actions duly.
    To the THIRD.
I choose you as Arch-Steward. Henceforth you shall guard
The game-preserves, the manor-farm, and poultry-yard.   *10900*
Give me a choice of favourite foods at every season
As each month brings them forth, prepared with care and reason.
Arch-Steward. Strict fasting be my highest duty, dearest wish,
Until I've placed before you some delighting dish.
The kitchen servants all shall be with me united;   *10905*
What's far will be brought near, the season expedited.
True, far-fetched early things with which the board is graced,
Do not attract you. Plain and hearty fare you'd taste.
Emperor [*to the* FOURTH]. Since here to feasts the talk is ever-
    more diverted.
As cupbearer to me, young hero, be converted.   *10910*
Arch-Cupbearer, take care that every cave of mine
Be stored most plentifully with the best of wine.
Be temperate yourself, let not a gay occasion
Lead you to yield yourself to happy chance's suasion.
Arch-Cupbearer.
The young themselves, my prince, when trust in them is shown,   *10915*

Before one is aware, stand forth as men full-grown.
So I at that high feast shall duly take my station
And to your sideboard's pomp add noblest decoration,
Rare, gorgeous vessels, gold and silver, all set up.
Beforehand, though, I'll choose for you the loveliest cup: *10920*
Of clear Venetian glass wherein delight lies waiting,
Enhancing wine's good taste but never inebriating.
On such a wondrous prize men oft too much depend,
But you, most noble Sire, your temperance doth defend.

Emperor.   What I've designed for you in this most solemn hour,   *10925*
You've heard with confidence because I speak with power.
The Emperor's word is great and makes each gift secure,
Yet needs his noble script to make the matter sure;
It needs his signature. And in due form to make it,
Here comes the fitting man this fitting hour to take it.   *10930*

    The ARCHBISHOP-ARCH-CHANCELLOR *enters.*

Emperor.   If in the keystone doth a vaulted arch confide,
Then is it built securely against time and tide.
You see the princes four! We have but just now noted
How next the state of house and court might be promoted.
Now what the realm contains, in all its breadth enclosed,   *10935*
Shall be with weight and power upon you five imposed.
In lands you shall outshine all other men and orders,
So of your property I'll now extend the borders
Out of the lands once left to that disloyal band.
To you who're true I grant full many a lovely land,   *10940*
With this the lofty right to widen these possessions,
As chance occurs, by barter, purchases, successions,
To practise undisturbed—be this secured to you—
Whatever sovereign rights, as landlords, are your due.
As judges it's for you to make the last decisions,   *10945*
And these shall suffer no appeals and no revisions.
Then imposts, interest, tributes, rents, safe-conduct, toll,
Dues from the mines, salt-works, and mints, yours is the whole,
For that my gratitude be fully demonstrated,
Nearest to Majesty you have I elevated.   *10950*

Archbishop.   In deepest gratitude to you we all unite,
You make us strong and firm and strengthen your own might.

Emperor.   Yet honour to you five I'll give in fuller measure.
I still live for my realm, to live is still my pleasure;
Ancestral chains, however, draw men's gaze from hours   *10955*
Of swift endeavour to the doom that always lowers.
In time I too shall part from all whom I hold dear;
Then you must choose the man who shall succeed me here.
Crown him and on the holy altar lift him high;
May then peace end what now began so stormily.   *10960*

Arch-Chancellor.   With pride at heart, yet humbly, as each mien
   convinces,

Here stand, before you bowed, the first of earthly princes.
As long as loyal blood through our full veins doth thrill,
We are the body which obeys your lightest will.

Emperor.   So, to conclude: what we've ordained and manifested,   *10965*
For all the years to come be it written and attested.
As lords, in truth, you've your possessions wholly free,
But on condition that they never parcelled be.
What you receive from us, however you expand it,
Shall to the eldest son be undivided handed.   *10970*

Arch-Chancellor.   At once I'll put on parchment in most joyous
   mood
This statute weighty for the realm's and for our good;
Engrossment, seal—thus shall the chancery invest it,
Your sacred signature, the lord's, will then attest it.

Emperor.   Thus I dismiss you so that each of you now may   *10975*
With tranquil mind reflect upon the glorious day.
   The secular PRINCES *withdraw.*

The Archbishop [*remains and speaks with feeling*].
The Chancellor went away, the Bishop stays before you;
A warning spirit bids him straightway to implore you.
With deep concern for you his father's-heart doth quake.

Emperor.   In this glad hour what makes you apprehensive? Speak! *10980*

Archbishop.   With what a bitter pang I find that in this hour
Your consecrated head's in league with Satan's power.
True—as it seems—you're on the throne, secured by right,
But woe! in the Lord God's, in Father Pope's despite.
Which when the Pontiff learns, swift judgment he'll deliver,   *10985*
His holy bolt will crush your sinful realm forever.
He has not yet forgot—the day that you were crowned,
A solemn time—you had the sorcerer unbound.
And from your crown, where Christian honour hung suspended,
The ray of pardon first on that damned head descended.   *10990*
But smite your breast, and straightway from your wicked gain
Give back a moderate mite unto the holy fane;
That broad and hilly space where your tent stood erected,
Where by an evil spirits'-league you were protected,
Where to the Prince of Lies you lent attentive ear,   *10995*
Devote the land to holy use in pious fear,
With hill and forest dense, as far as they're extending,
With heights all clad in green, rich luscious pasture lending,
Clear lakes alive with fish, uncounted brooks that flow
Swiftly and serpent-like and plunging as they go,   *11000*
Then the broad vale itself with mead and lea and hollow.
Thus is remorse expressed, and pardon soon will follow.

Emperor.   My horror of this grievous fault is so profound
The borders of the land yourself shall measure round.

Archbishop.   First, where one so has sinned, the spot, so desecrated, *11005*
Be to the Most High's service straightway dedicated.

My spirit sees the massive walls mount swiftly higher;
The morning sun's first rays already light the choir;
The growing edifice a cross's form is taking;
The nave grows long and high, believers' joy awaking;   *11010*
Through solemn portals they stream in with ardent zeal,
While over hill and dale resounds the bell's first peal.
It sounds from lofty towers aspiring up to Heaven.
Now comes the penitent to whom new life is given.
The consecration day—oh, may it soon be sent!—   *11015*
Your presence then will be the highest ornament.
Emperor.   Let this great work be done, a pious proclamation
That God the Lord I praise and seek my expiation.
Enough! I feel my soul already mounting high.
Archbishop.   As Chancellor I'll conclude the last formality.   *11020*
Emperor.   Produce a formal deed to show that I resign it
To Holy Mother Church, and I will gladly sign it.
Archbishop [*has taken his leave but turns back as he is about to
    go out*].
Then to the work as it proceeds you'll not refuse
All tribute, interest, tithes—the land's whole revenues—
Forever. 'Twill need much for worthy sustentation   *11025*
And heavy are the costs of wise administration.
That we may build it fast on such a desert spot,
Some gold from all your booty surely you'll allot.
Besides, one has to have—I needs must seem insistent—
Wood, lime, and slate, and other things from places distant.   *11030*
The people will haul these, thus from the pulpit taught;
The Church doth bless a man who serving her has wrought.
    Exit.
Emperor.   Great is the sin and heavy that I've loaded on me;
These tiresome sorcerers—sore damage have they done me.
Archbishop [*returning again, with a very low obeisance*].
Pardon, O Sire, you gave that most notorious man   *11035*
The empire's coast; but he'll be smitten by the ban
Unless due penance to the Holy Church you tender
And there tithe, interest, gifts, and revenues surrender.
Emperor [*vexed*].   The land is not yet there; far out at sea it lies.
Archbishop.   A man who's right and patient sees his day arise.   *11040*
May your word in its strength forever be our stay!
Emperor [*alone*].   I might as well cede my whole realm this very day.

ACT V

OPEN COUNTRY

Wanderer.   Yes, the lindens stand there gloomy,
  Stand there yet in sturdy age,
  Now again appearing to me   *11045*
  After my long pilgrimage!
  It's the old place, and still standing
  Is the hut that sheltered me
  When the storm-tossed billow, stranding,
  Hurled me duneward from the sea!   *11050*
  And my hosts? I fain would greet them,
  Helpful folk, a valiant pair,
  But today I'll scarcely meet them;
  Agèd in those days they were.
  Pious they, in God believing!   *11055*
  Shall I knock or raise my voice?
  Hail! if you, a guest receiving,
  Still in kindly deeds rejoice.
Baucis [*a little woman, very old*].
  Stranger dear! Hush, hush! You're breaking
  My good husband's peaceful rest.   *11060*
  Sleeping long gives the brief waking
  Of an old man active zest.
Wanderer.   Tell me, mother, is it you really,
  Here to take the thanks of one
  Whose young life you saved so freely,   *11065*
  You and your good spouse alone?
  Are you Baucis who devoutly
  My half-dying lips restored?
      The husband enters.
  You Philemon who so stoutly
  Wrested from the wave my hoard?   *11070*
  'Twas your hurried flames ascending,
  'Twas your silver-chiming bell,
  Brought to me a happy ending
  Of adventure dread and fell.
  Let me step forth that I may there   *11075*
  Gaze upon the boundless sea;
  Let me kneel and let me pray there,
  Sore my heart oppresses me.
      He strides forward on the dune.
Philemon [*to* BAUCIS].   Hasten, pray, and set the table
  Where the garden blooms serene.   *11080*
  Let him run, be dazed, unable
  To believe what he'll have seen.

Standing beside the WANDERER.
Where fierce billows did maltreat you,
Where waves, wildly foaming, rolled,
There a garden now doth greet you, 11085
Fair as Paradise of old.
Older grown, I was not able
To give help as once of yore;
As my limbs grew more unstable,
Far the waves drew from the shore. 11090
Wise lords' menials, bold and daring,
Dug the trenches, dammed the sea,
Ocean's ancient rights not sparing,
Lords, instead of it, to be.
See green meadows far extending, 11095
Garden, woodland, field, and town.—
Come, enjoy the meal attending,
For the sun will soon go down.—
Sails are gliding far out yonder,
Nightly to safe ports they fare. 11100
To their nests the sea-birds wander,
For the harbour now is there.
Far away, you scarce can see it,
Lies the blue sea and its strand;
Right and left, though far may be it, 11105
Spreads a thickly-peopled land.
    The three at table in the little garden.
Baucis.   Silent still? and is there going
   To your starved lips not a bit?
Philemon.   Fain the wonder he'd be knowing;
   Fond of talking, tell him it. 11110
Baucis.   'Twas a wonder if there's any!
   Even today it troubles me;
   For the whole thing was uncanny,
   It was not as things should be.
Philemon.   Can the Emperor be called sinning 11115
   Who bestowed on him the strand?
   Did a herald-trumpet's dinning
   Not proclaim it through the land?
   From our dunes a little distance
   First they set foot as we've seen: 11120
   Tents and huts!—Soon to existence
   Springs a palace midst the green.
Baucis.   Vainly slaves by day were storming,
   Pick and shovel, stroke on stroke;
   Where by night the flames were swarming, 11125
   Stood a dike when we awoke.
   Wails of human victims bleeding
   Nightly to our ears were borne;

Torches toward the ocean leading,
A canal was there at morn.   *11130*
Godless is the man; our labour,
Grove, and cottage covets he,
Such an overlording neighbour,
Master of us will he be.

Philemon.   Be it so, he's offered to us   *11135*
Fair estate in his new land!

Baucis.   Little good will marsh-land do us;
On your own height keep your stand!

Philemon.   To the chapel let's awaying,
There the sun's last rays behold,   *11140*
Ring the bell and kneeling, praying,
Trust us to the God of old.

PALACE

Spacious, ornamental garden; broad, straight canal.
FAUST, in extreme old age, walking about, reflecting.

Lynceus [the warder, through a speaking-trumpet].
The sun is setting, ships are nearing
The safe home-port with song and cheer.
A mighty barge is just appearing   *11145*
On the canal; 'twill soon be here.
Their motley flags the breeze caressing,
The rigid masts stand up to view;
In you the seaman finds his blessing,
And Fortune at your prime greets you.   *11150*
   The little bell rings on the dune.

Faust [starting up].   Accursèd bell! Base clangour sending,
It wounds like spiteful shot from slings;
Before mine eyes my realm's unending,
Yet at my back vexation stings.
The envious bell is aye recalling: *11155*
From blemish is my realm not free!
The lindens, brown hut, church half-falling,
Not one of these belongs to me.
And if I'd seek rest, there repairing
I'll shudder as with alien fear,   *11160*
A thorn to feet and eyes, unsparing!
Oh, would that I were far from here!

Warder [as above].   How blithely doth the gay bark glide
Before the breeze of eventide!
How tower, as it swiftly sails,   *11165*
The chests and boxes, sacks and bales!

   A splendid bark, richly and variously laden with products of
   foreign countries.

MEPHISTOPHELES. THE THREE MIGHTY COMRADES.

Chorus.

> Here do we land,
> Come from on board.
> Hail to our patron,
> Hail, our Lord!   *11170*

They disembark; the goods are brought ashore.

Mephistopheles.   We've proved ourselves as it behooves,
> Pleased if our patron but approves.
> With but two ships we sailed away,
> With twenty we're in port today,
> The great things we have done—how great,   *11175*
> That can be seen well from our freight.
> The free sea sets the spirit free.
> Who'll stop to think when he's at sea!
> What helps is suddenness of grip.
> You catch a fish, you catch a ship,   *11180*
> And when you're once the lord of three,
> You hook the fourth one easily;
> Then is the fifth in sorry plight,
> You have the Power and so the Right.
> You ask not *How* but *What* it be.   *11185*
> I know not how the sea is charted
> If war and trade and piracy
> Are not triune and can't be parted.

The Three Mighty Comrades.

> He doesn't greet!
> He doesn't thank!   *11190*
> As if we brought
> Our lord what stank.
> See what a
> Wry face he has got,
> The royal wealth   *11195*
> Doth please him not.

Mephistopheles.

> Do not await here
> Further pay;
> You took indeed
> Your share away.   *11200*

The Comrades.

> That took we but
> As pastime fair;
> We all demand
> An equal share.

Mephistopheles.

> First range in order,   *11205*
> Hall on hall,

The costly objects,
One and all.
When this rich sight
He comes to see   *11210*
And reckons all
More narrowly,
A niggard he'll
Not be at least;
He'll give the fleet   *11215*
Feast after feast.

Tomorrow come the gay birds here;
For them I shall provide good cheer.
    The cargo is taken away.
Mephistopheles [*to* FAUST].
With gloomy gaze, with brow austere,
Of your supreme good luck you hear.   *11220*
High wisdom has been crowned. 'Tis done,
The shore and ocean are at one.
Now from the shore, for their swift trips,
The willing ocean takes the ships.
So say what's true: from this high place   *11225*
Your arm doth all the world embrace.
Here it began: here once there stood
The first rude shanty made of wood.
A little ditch was dug away
Where busy oars now toss their spray.   *11230*
Your will, your people's industry,
Have won the prize of earth and sea.
From here—
Faust.   Oh, that accursèd *here!*
That is the burden hard to bear.
Wise one, to you I must declare it.   *11235*
It gives my heart sting after sting;
It is impossible to bear it,
And yet I'm shamed to say the thing.
The old folks there should make concession,
I'd have the lindens for my throne;   *11240*
The few trees there, not my possession,
Spoil me the world I call my own.
There I would fain, for world-wide gazing
From branch to branch a scaffold raising,
Open to view the course I've run,   *11245*
That I might see all I have done,
View at one glance, before me brought,
The masterpiece of human thought,
Which made a fact shrewd wisdom's plan
And won broad dwelling-place for man.   *11250*
    Thus suffer we the sorest rack,

Midst riches feeling what we lack.
The chime, the scent of linden-bloom,
Close round me as with church and tomb.
The power of my all-conquered will   *11255*
Breaks down before that sandy hill.
How shall I ever free my spirit?
The bell rings and I rage to hear it!

Mephistopheles.   Of course! Some paramount distress
Must gall your life to bitterness.   *11260*
Who doubts it? To each noble ear
That jangle seems a hostile fleer.
And that accursed bim-bam-booming,
The cheerful evening sky be-glooming,
Mingles in each event that passes,   *11265*
From the first bath to burial-masses,
As if all mortal life should seem,
Twixt *bim* and *bam,* a vanished dream.

Faust.   Their opposition, stubbornness,
Spoil the most glorious success,   *11270*
Till in deep, angry pain one must
At last grow tired of being just.

Mephistopheles.   Why are you troubling? temporizing?
Aren't you long used to colonizing?

Faust.   Then go and shift them to one side!   *11275*
You know the farm—it's small but fair—
I've chosen for the agèd pair.

Mephistopheles.   We'll bear them off and on new ground
They'll stand before one looks around.
For violence that's past and done   *11280*
A pretty dwelling will atone.
    He whistles shrilly. THE THREE *enter.*

Mephistopheles.   Come! Do the lord's command—'tis meet!—
Tomorrow he will feast the fleet.

The Three.   The old lord gave us naught but slights;
A feast that's fleet is ours by rights.   *11285*
    Exeunt.

Mephistopheles [*to the spectators*].   Here haps a hap of long ago;
With Naboth's vineyard it happed so. (*I Kings 21*)

DEEP NIGHT

Lynceus [*the warder singing on the watch-tower of the castle*].
                    Keen vision my dower,
                    Placed here for my sight,
                    And sworn to the tower,   *11290*
                    In the world I delight.
                    I gaze at the far,
                    I look at the near,

The moon and the star,
The wood and the deer.   *11295*
In all things around me
Is grace without end,
And as they astound me,
Myself I commend.
Thou fortunate vision,   *11300*
Thou mayest have seen
Whatever there may be,
Yet fair hath it been.

Pause.

But not only to delight me
Am I stationed here on high;   *11305*
What a gruesome sight, to fright me,
Threatens from the dark world nigh!
Flashing sparkles I see gushing
Through the lindens' twofold night;
Ever stronger rages, rushing,   *11310*
Fanned by draughts, a glowing light.
Ah! inside the cabin's flaming,
Though moss-grown and damp it stand;
Speedy succour is it claiming
And no rescue is at hand.   *11315*
Ah, those good old folk whom duty
Once made careful of the fire,
Now of smoke become the booty!
What a misadventure dire!
Flames are flaring, now they wave them   *11320*
Through the black, moss-covered shell;
Could the good folk only save them
From that furious burning hell!
Brilliant tongues of flame are flashing,
Through the leaves and branches lashing; *11325*
Withered boughs that flare up, burning,
Swiftly glow, plunge from the tree.
Must ye eyes—such things discerning—
Must I, so far-sighted be?
Down the little chapel crashes,   *11330*
Burdened under branches' fall.
Winding upward, pointed flashes
Seize upon the tree-tops tall.
To their roots the trunks, ignited,
Hollow, purple-red, glow on.   *11335*

Long pause. Song.

Gone what once the eye delighted,
With the centuries is gone.

Faust [on the balcony, facing the dunes].

What song hear I of lamentation?

Too late, the word or tone to heed.
My warder wails, and deep vexation   *11340*
Stirs me for this impulsive deed.
Yet though the lindens, grown so thickly,
Now half-charred trunks, defile the place,
An outlook-point is builded quickly,
Where I can gaze through endless space.   *11345*
Thence too I'll see the new-made dwelling
Which for that agèd pair I'll raise,
Who, of my kind forbearance telling,
Will there enjoy their latter days.

Mephistopheles and The Three [*below*].
Here we're coming at full trot,   *11350*
But pardon us! well went it not.
We rapped on it, we chapped on it,
And still not opened was a slit;
We rattled on, we pounded more,
Till down there lay the rotten door.   *11355*
We called, a loud and threatening call,
But found no hearing there at all.
As in such case has oft occurred,
They would not, so they had not heard.
We tarried not long thereabout;   *11360*
Swift, as you bade, we cleared them out.
The couple suffered scarce a jot;
From fright they fell dead on the spot.
A stranger, hid there, made a show
Of fight but he was soon laid low.   *11365*
But in the brief and furious fray,
From embers that around us lay,
The straw caught fire. It's blazing free,
A funeral pyre for all the three.

Faust.   To my commands then deaf were ye?   *11370*
Exchange I meant, not robbery.
This unconsidered, savage blow,
I curse it! Share the curse and go!

Chorus.   The old saw says—it echoes still—
To violence submit thy will!   *11375*
If bold and steadfast, stake thy pelf,
Thy house and home and—thine own self.
      Exeunt.

Faust [*on the balcony*].
The stars conceal their light and glow,
The fire is sinking, flickering low;
A cool wind fans it with its wings.   *11380*
Vapour and smoke it hither brings.
Rash the command, too quick obeyed!—
What hovers hither like a shade?

MIDNIGHT

FOUR GREY WOMEN *enter.*

First.   My name, it is Want.
Second.   And my name is Guilt.
Third.   My name, it is Worry.
Fourth.   And mine is Distress.   *11385*
Three Together.   The door is locked fast, we cannot get in:
  A rich man dwells there, we may not go in.
Want.   Here I turn to shadow.
Guilt.   Here I cease to be.
Distress.   The pampered ones turn their faces from me.
Worry.   Ye sisters, ye cannot, may not go within   *11390*
  But even at the keyhole will Worry slip in.
    WORRY *vanishes.*
Want.   Grey sisters, away! Ye must vanish from here!
Guilt.   I'll bind me beside thee and keep me quite near.
Distress.   Distress keepeth pace with you, still as a breath.
The Three.   Fast gather the clouds, they blot out each star!   *11395*
  Behind there! behind! From afar, from afar,
  There cometh our brother, there cometh he . . . Death.
    Exeunt.
Faust [*in the palace*].   Four saw I come and only three go hence;
  Of what they said I could not grasp the sense.
  "Distress" one seemed to say—'twas like a breath—   *11400*
  A gloomy word then followed—"Death."
  Hollow the sound, with spectral message fraught.
  My way to freedom I have not yet fought.
  Could I all magic from my pathway banish,
  Could quite unlearn its spells and bid it vanish   *11405*
  Nature, could I face thee, in thy great plan,
  Then were it worth the pain to be a man.
    Such was I once ere I the gloom explored
  And cursed me and the world with impious word.
  The air so teems with many a ghostly shape,   *11410*
  No way appears whereby one may escape.
  If one day, bright with reason, on us beams,
  The night entangles us in webs of dreams.
  From young green fields we homeward turn, elate;
  A bird croaks, and his croaking tells—ill-fate.   *11415*
  Thus superstitions all our hours entwine,
  With happening, with warning, or with sign.
  And thus abashed, we find ourselves alone.
  The portal creaks, and no one enters—none!
    Agitated.
  Is someone here?
Worry.   The question claims an "Aye!"   *11420*

Faust.   And thou, who art thou then?
Worry.   Enough!—'Tis I.
Faust.   Away! Begone!
Worry.   I am where I should be.
Faust [*first furious, then appeased, to himself*].
   Take care and say no word of sorcery.
Worry.

             Though the ear hear not my droning,
             Yet the heart doth feel it, moaning.   *11425*
             In a variable guise
             Cruel force I exercise.
             On the pathway, on the billow,
             Ever-agonizing fellow,
             Always found though never sought,   *11430*
             Flattered, cursed, in word and thought.
  Is Worry still to thee unknown?
Faust.   Through the world I have but flown.
  Whatever I craved, I seized it by the hair,
  Whatever sufficed not, I let fare.   *11435*
  Whatever escaped, I let it go.
  I've but desired and but achieved, each hour,
  And then again have wished, and so with power
  Stormed through my life; at first with power and greatness;
  But now life moves with cautious, wise sedateness.   *11440*
  Well do I know the sphere of earth and men.
  The view beyond is barred to mortal ken;
  A fool! who thither turns his blinking eyes
  And dreams he'll find his like above the skies.
  Let him stand fast and look around on earth;   *11445*
  Not mute is this world to a man of worth.
  Why need he range through all eternity?
  Here he can seize all that he knows to be.
  Thus let him wander down his earthly day;
  When spirits spook, let him pursue his way;   *11450*
  Let him find pain and bliss as on he stride,
  He! every moment still unsatisfied.
Worry.

             Whom I once possess will ever
             Find the world not worth endeavour;
             Endless gloom around him being,   *11455*
             Rise nor set of sun he's seeing.
             Be each outer sense excelling,
             Still is darkness in him dwelling;
             He cannot through any measures
             Make him lord of any treasures.   *11460*
             All luck turns into caprices;
             Him midst plenty hunger seizes.
             Be it joy or be it sorrow,

He postpones it till the morrow,
Waiting for the future ever   *11465*
And therefore achieving never.

Faust. Be still! Not so wilt thou get hold of me!
    I do not care to hear such drivel.
    Begone! That wretched litany
    Could even befool the wisest man to evil.   *11470*
Worry.

Go or come? How shall he guide him?
All decision is denied him;
Though with but a smooth road coping,
He takes half-steps, wavering, groping,
Wandering as if bemisted,   *11475*
Everything he sees as twisted;
Burdening himself and others,
Breathing deeply, still he smothers,
Though not smothered, lifeless faring,
Not resigned and not despairing.   *11480*
Rolling on without remission,
Painful quitting, loath submission,
Freedom now, now subjugation,
Semi-sleep, poor recreation,
Bind him fast within his cell   *11485*
And prepare the wretch for Hell!

Faust. Ill-omened spectres, ye! Thus mangle ye still
    The human race on thousands of occasions;
    Indifferent days themselves entangle ye still
    In a vile web of mingled tribulations.   *11490*
    It's hard, I know, from spirits to get free;
    The strenuous spirit-tie we cannot sever.
    Still, Worry, though it great and stealthy be,
    Thy power I shall not acknowledge ever.
Worry.

Then learn it now. My parting curse thou'lt find   *11495*
Swift and forever thee attending.
Throughout their lives are mortals blind;
So, Faustus, be thou too at thy life's ending!
    She breathes on him and goes.

Faust [*blinded*]. Night presses round me, deep and deeper
        still.
    And yet within me beams a radiant light;   *11500*
    What I have planned, I hasten to fulfil;
    Only the master's word has weight and might.
    Up from your couches, vassals, every man!
    Bring happily to sight my daring plan.

Seize shovel, spade! With all your tools lay on!   *11505*
The work staked out must with all speed be done.
Strict order and swift diligence
Result in fairest recompense.
To consummate the greatest enterprises
One spirit for a thousand hands suffices.   *11510*

GREAT OUTER COURT OF THE PALACE

Torches

Mephistopheles [as overseer, leading the way].
This way, this way! Come on, come on,
Lemurs,[1] ye shambling creatures,
Of tendons, sinews, and of bones
Ye patched-up semi-natures.
Lemurs [in chorus].
We come at once, are at your hand,   *11515*
And it's our half-impression
The call concerns a spacious land
Where we shall have possession.
The pointed stakes, here are they all,
Long chains with which to measure;   *11520*
But we've forgotten why the call
Came to disturb our leisure.

Mephistopheles.   An artist's zeal would here be wrong;
You need no measure but your brothers'.
Let him who's longest lay his length along,   *11525*
And you, lift up the turf round here, you others.
As for our fathers it was done,
Dig out a square, a longish one!
Out of the palace to the narrow home,
So stupidly at last the end doth come.   *11530*
Lemurs [digging with mocking gestures].
When I was young and lived and loved,
Methought it very sweet,
When joy rang out and all was gay,
Then merrily went my feet.
But now Old Age with his stealthy steps   *11535*
Hath clawed me with his crutch;
Over a grave's door stumbled I,
Why yawned the door so much?

Faust [coming out of the palace, gropes his way by the door-posts].
The click of spades—ah, how it heartens me!
It is my crowd that toils the while,   *11540*
[1]Wicked dead.

Earth with itself to reconcile,
To set fixed limits to the sea
And gird it with a rigid zone.
Mephistopheles [*aside*].   And yet you work for us alone
  While you for dikes and pens are caring,   *11545*
  Since now for Neptune you're preparing—
  That Devil of the Sea—a great repast.
  In every way you're lost and lorn;
  To aid us every element is sworn,
  And ruin is the end at last.   *11550*
Faust.   Overseer!
Mephistopheles.   Here!
Faust.   Be it done as it may,
  Bring crowd on crowd of workmen here!
  Spur them with rigour and good cheer,
  Entice, coerce, give ample pay!
  I wish each day fresh news of what's been done,   *11555*
  How the groove lengthens that we have begun.
Mephistopheles [*half aloud*].   The talk was—when the news they
      gave—
  Not of a groove but of a grave.
Faust.   A marsh extends along the mountain-chain
  That poisons what so far I've been achieving;   *11560*
  Were I that noisome pool to drain,
  'Twould be the highest, last achieving.
  Thus space to many millions I will give
  Where, though not safe, yet free and active they may live.
  Green fertile fields where straightway from their birth   *11565*
  Both men and beast live happy on the newest earth,
  Settled forthwith along the mighty hill
  Raised by a daring, busy people's will.
  Within, a land like Paradise; outside,
  Up to the brink may rage the mighty tide,   *11570*
  And where it gnaws and would burst through or sap,
  A common impulse hastes to close the gap.
  Yes, to this thought I hold unswerving,
  To wisdom's final fruit, profoundly true:
  Of freedom and of life he only is deserving   *11575*
  Who every day must conquer them anew.
  Thus here, by danger girt, the active day
  Of childhood, manhood, age will pass away.
  Aye! such a throng I fain would see,
  Stand on free soil among a people free.   *11580*
  Then might I say, that moment seeing:
  "Ah, linger on, thou art so fair!"
  The traces of my earthly being
  Can perish not in æons—they are there!
  That lofty moment I now feel in this: *11585*

I now enjoy the highest moment's bliss.

    FAUST *sinks back, the* LEMURS *take him up and lay him on the*
      ground.

Mephistopheles.   Him could no pleasure sate, suffice no bliss,

   So wooed he ever changeful phantoms' favour.

   The last vile, empty moment—this!—

   The poor wretch wished to hold it fast forever.   *11590*

   Him who against me stoutly held his stand,

   Time conquers—here the old man lies in sand.

   The clock stands still—

Chorus.   Stands still! No sound is heard.

   The clock's hand falls.

Mephistopheles.   It falls, 'tis finished.

Chorus.   'Tis past.

Mephistopheles.   "Past"—'tis a stupid word.   *11595*

   Past—why?

   Past and pure Naught, sheer Uniformity!

   Of what avail's perpetual creation

   If later swept off to annihilation?

   "So it is past!" You see what that must mean?   *11600*

   It is the same as had it never been,

   And yet whirls on as if it weren't destroyed.

   I should prefer the Everlasting Void.

BURIAL

Lemur Solo.

          Who hath so badly built the house

          With shovel and with spade?   *11605*

Lemurs Chorus.

          For thee, dull guest, in hempen vest,

          It all too well was made.[1]

Lemur Solo.

          Who hath so badly decked the hall?

          Not chairs, not table, any!

Lemurs Chorus.

          'Twas loaned for a short interval;   *11610*

          The creditors are so many.

Mephistopheles.   The body lies, and ere the spirit flee,

   I'll quickly show the blood-writ scroll;

   But they've so many means—alas for me!—

   To cheat the Devil out of many a soul.   *11615*

   If one pursues the old way, one's resisted,

   And to the new we do not feel commended;

   I could of old have done it unattended,

   But now I have to be assisted.

     In all things, wretched is our plight!   *11620*

[1]For lines 11604-7, cf. the third stanza of the Grave-diggers' Song in *Hamlet.*

Transmitted custom, ancient right—
Naught's to be trusted now as in the past.
The soul once with its last breath left its house;
I watched my prey, and like the swiftest mouse,
Snap! in my firm-shut claws I held it fast.   *11625*
Now it delays, won't quit the dismal place,
The wretched corpse's house so nauseating;
The elements, each other hating,
Will finally expel it in disgrace.
And though for days I fret till I am weary,   *11630*
When? how? and *where?* that is the tiresome query.
In power swift and strong Old Death's played out;
Even the *whether* long has been in doubt.
With lust I've often watched the rigid members—
'Twas but a sham; they moved: life stirred the embers.   *11635*
   Gestures of conjuration like those of a fantastic fugleman.
Lords of the straight, lords of the crookèd horn,
Come quick! in double time! and show your fettle,
You of old diabolic cut and metal,
And with you let the maw of Hell be borne.
True, many maws hath Hell, in short,   *11640*
To use as due to rank and dignity;
But henceforth in this final sport
Not so particular shall we be.
   The horrible maw of Hell opens up on the left.
Tusks yawn; and from the vaulted gorge profound
The furious, fiery torrents flow,   *11645*
And at the rear, in seething vapours wound,
I see the flaming city in eternal glow.
Up to the very teeth the crimson billow dashes,
The damned, in hope of help, swim into view;
But now the huge hyena bites and gnashes,   *11650*
And their hot course the agonized renew.
Much more is left to spy in corners there,
In narrowest space horrors supreme!
You do well, sinners to affright and scare,
But they'll think it a lie and sham and dream.   *11655*
   To the fat devils with short, straight horns.
You fat-paunched rogues with cheeks like hell-fire burning,
You glow so fattened by Hell's sulphur and its steam;
What necks, so thick-set, short, and never turning!
Watch here below for phosphorescent gleam:
That's the wee soul, Psyche with fluttering wing;   *11660*
Don't pluck the wings, 'twere else a nasty worm.
I'll stamp my seal upon the beastly thing,[1]
Then off with it in whirling-fiery-storm.
   These lower regions, watch them duly,

[1]Cf. Revelation, 16. 2; 19. 20.

You bladders—that's the duty you've to show;   *11665*
If it was pleased to live there, truly,
That we do not so accurately know.
It feels at home in navels, there's no doubt;
So heed my words, for there it may pop out.
    To the lean devils with long, crookèd horns.
You clowns, huge fuglemen, bashaws,   *11670*
Clutch at the air—no respite take or give;
Stretch out your arms, show your sharp claws,
That you may catch the fluttering fugitive.
In its old home bad surely is its plight;
Genius is quick to soar, so too will be this sprite.   *11675*
    Glory, from above, on the right.

A Heavenly Host.

                    Heavenly kindred,
                    Envoys unhind'red,
                    Follow in flight:
                    Sinners forgiving,
                    Making dust living!   *11680*
                    Bring while ye're swaying,
                    Lingering, staying,
                    To all things living
                    A trace of delight.

Mephistopheles.   Discords I hear, a most disgusting humming   *11685*
  That with unwelcome light comes from above;
  It is that boyish-girlish bungling strumming
  That sanctimonious tastes are prone to love.
  You know how we in deep depravèd hours
  Planned the destruction of the human race;   *11690*
  The shamefullest we planned with all our powers
  In their devotion finds a perfect place.
    The canting tribe, they come in foppish fettle!
  Many they've snatched away before our eyes;
  With our own weapons are they giving battle;   *11695*
  They're devils too, though in disguise.
  If you lose here, in endless shame you'll sink;
  On to the grave and hold fast by the brink!

Chorus of Angels [*strewing roses*].

                    Roses, ye glowing ones,
                    Balsam-bestowing ones,   *11700*
                    Fluttering and soaring,
                    Sweet life restoring,
                    Branchlets revealing,
                    Fresh buds unsealing,
                    Blooming be seen!   *11705*

> Springtime, awake him
> In purple and green;
> Paradise take him,
> The sleeper serene.

Mephistopheles [*to the* SATANS].
  Why duck and jerk? Is that Hell's wonted rule?   *11710*
  Do stand your ground and let them scatter.
  Back to his place, each gawky fool!
  They think perhaps that with such flowery matter
  They'll snow hot devils in and make them cool.
  Your breath will melt and shrivel it.—Now puff,   *11715*
  You puffers!—Hold! It is enough, enough!
  Your foul breath bleaches all the fluttering stuff.—
  Be not so violent! Shut your jaws and noses!
  You've blown indeed too strongly at the roses.
  Oh, that the proper measure you would ever learn!   *11720*
  They shrivel—yes, they scorch, they char, they burn!
  With poisonous bright flames they're floating hither.
  Stand fast against them and press close together!
  Your strength dies out, your courage is all spent!
  A strange, voluptuous glow the devils scent.   *11725*
Chorus of Angels.

> Blossoms ethereal,
> Flamelets empyreal,
> Love now are bearing they,
> Bliss are preparing they,
> All hearts they sway.   *11730*
> Words of true charity
> In ether's clarity,
> Bring hosts in verity
> Infinite day.

Mephistopheles. Oh, curses, shame on such an idiot band!   *11735*
  Upon their heads the Satans stand.
  Head over heels fat ones are curving,
  Plunging in Hell ass-uppermost.
  So be your bath as hot as you're deserving!
  But I'll remain here at my post.   *11740*
    Fighting the hovering roses.
  Off, will-o'-the-wisp! However bright your flake,
  When caught, you're but a sticky, filthy cake.
  Why flutter thus? Away with you and quick!—
  Like pitch and sulphur they cling to my neck.
Chorus of Angels.

> What ye've no title to,   *11745*
> Ye may not share it;
> What bringeth pain to you,

Ye must forbear it.
If we'll press in with might,
Valiantly must we fight.   *11750*
Only the loving
Does Love lead to light.

Mephistopheles.   My head burns, heart and liver too. I scent
A more than devilish element,
Sharper by far than Hell's own fire!—   *11755*
And hence your wailing, monstrous, dire,
You haplessly enamoured! who, when spurned,
Toward your darlings keep your faces turned.
    I too! What draws my head in that direction?
Am I not sworn to its complete rejection?   *11760*
To see it I was once so bitterly averse!
Has something alien pierced me through and through?
Now these most charming youths I love to view.
What holds me back that I can't curse!—
And if I let myself be fooled and baited,   *11765*
Who henceforth fool-in-chief will be?
The stunning rascals whom I've always hated,
Charming beyond words do they seem to me!—
    Tell me, sweet children, that I may not miss you!
Aren't you too of the race of Lucifer?   *11770*
You are so fair I'd truly like to kiss you;
To say you come just right, I scarcely err.
I feel so much at home, so natural,
As though we'd met a thousand times before;
So stealthy, kitten-like, desirable,   *11775*
At every glance your beauty charms me more.
Oh, do draw near! Grant me one glance, I pray!
Angels.   We're coming now, why do you shrink away?
We're drawing near, remain now if you can.
    The ANGELS *hover around and occupy the whole space.*
Mephistopheles [*crowded into the proscenium*].
You call us damnèd spirits! You,   *11780*
You are yourselves the wizards true,
For you seduce both maid and man.
Oh, what a damnable event!
Is this indeed love's element?
A raging fire fills all my frame,   *11785*
My neck scarce feels the scorching flame.—
You hover to and fro—come down, I say,
Bestir your lovely limbs in a more worldly way;
In truth, it suits you well, that serious style,
But just for once I'd like to see you smile!   *11790*
'Twould be for me eternally entrancing.
I mean like lovers at each other glancing,

A flicker round the mouth, done easily.
You tall boy, you would I possess most gladly;
That priestly mien befits you very badly,   *11795*
Do look at me a little lustfully!
More nude, yet decently, could you appear,
That flowing shirt is over-moralizing—
They turn around—To see them from the rear!
The little rogues are quite too appetizing.   *11800*

Chorus of Angels.

> Flames, love revealing,
> Grow ever clearer;
> To damned through error
> May truth bring healing,
> That they from evil   *11805*
> Find glad retrieval,
> In the All-Unity
> Blessèd to be.

Mephistopheles [*recovering his self-possession*].
What's happ'ning to me!—Like Job I've boil on boil
From head to foot so that I shrink to view me,   *11810*
Yet triumph still when I search through and through me
And place my trust in my own self and kin.
My noble parts are saved despite the broil;
The love-spell works no deeper than the skin.
Now are the damned flames burned out past recall,   *11815*
And as is right, I curse you one and all!

Chorus of Angels.

> Ardours of Heaven!
> Round whom they brood,
> In life is given
> Bliss with the Good.   *11820*
> Laud ye together,
> Rise to your goal;
> Cleansed is the ether,
> Breathe thou, O Soul!

> *They rise aloft, bearing away* FAUST's *immortal part.*

Mephistopheles [*looking around*].
How's this?—Where have they gone, I wonder?   *11825*
You have surprised me, young folk though you be,
And flown away to Heaven with the plunder.
Hence played they round this grave so wantonly!
A treasure great, unique, they've confiscated.
The lofty soul, to me hypothecated,   *11830*
Out of my hands they've smuggled craftily.
    To whom now shall my sad case be presented?
Who'll get for me my well-earned right?

In your old age you have been circumvented,
But you deserved it, wretched is your plight.   *11835*
I have mismanaged in disgraceful fashion;
Great outlay shamefully I've thrown away.
A vulgar lust, an absurd, lovesick passion,
Led the well-seasoned Devil far astray.
Since with this childish, silly folderol   *11840*
I—shrewd and would-be wise—obsessed me,
In very truth the folly is not small
That in conclusion has possessed me.

MOUNTAIN GORGES

FOREST, ROCKS, DESERT

HOLY ANCHORITES *scattered up the mountain-side,*
dwelling among the clefts.

Chorus and Echo.

Forests are swaying here,
Rocks weight them downward sheer,   *11845*
Roots clutching rocks appear,
Trunk close by trunk is near.
Wave dashes after wave,
Shelter hath deepest cave.
Lions, soft-footed, dumb,   *11850*
Friendly around us come,
Honouring the sacred place,
Refuge of love and grace.

Pater Ecstaticus [*hovering up and down*].

Endless ecstatic fire,
Glow of pure love's desire,   *11855*
Pangs of the yearning breast,
Rapture in God to rest.
Arrows, pierce through me here,
Lances, subdue me here,
Bludgeons, come, batter me,   *11860*
Lightnings, come, shatter me,
That my mortality
Flee from reality,
Endless star shine above,
Core of eternal love.   *11865*

Pater Profundus [*Lower Region*].

As chasms at my feet descending
Burden the chasms more profound,
As a thousand radiant streams are wending
To foaming cataracts' awesome bound,

As, by its own strong impulse driven,   11870
The tree mounts upward, straight and **tall,**
So to Almighty Love 'tis given
To fashion all, to cherish all.
    All round me is a savage roaring
As if swayed wood and rocky steep;   11875
Yet plunges, lovely in its pouring,
The wealth of water to the deep,
Summoned below, the vale to brighten,
The bolt that fell with sudden flare,
The atmosphere to cleanse and lighten   11880
Which in its bosom poison bare,
    Heralds of love are they, proclaiming
Creative powers that us enfold.
May they, my inner self inflaming,
Quicken my soul confused and cold,   11885
Its blunted senses galled unceasing,
Bound fast in chains that cramp and smart.
O God! these thoughts of mine appeasing,
Illumine Thou my needy heart!

Pater Seraphicus [*Middle Region*].
    What a morning cloudlet hovers   11890
    Through the pine trees' tossing hair!
    Do I guess what life it covers?
    They are spirits young and fair.
Chorus of Blessèd Boys.
    Tell us, father, whither go we?
    Tell us, kind one, who are we?   11895
    Happy are we all, that know we;
    Sweet, oh, sweet it is to be.
Pater Seraphicus.
    Boys! At midnight born, with only
    Halfway opened sense and brain,
    Straightway lost to parents lonely,   11900
    For the angels sweetest gain.
    If ye feel that in this place is
    One who loves, then hither fare;
    But of earth's rude ways no traces
    Do ye happy spirits bear.   11905
    In mine eyes descend, pray choose them,
    Organs meet for earthly sphere;
    As your own eyes ye can use them,
    Gaze upon this landscape here.

He receives them into himself.
    Those are trees, and cliffs are yonder,   11910
    There a stream that downward leaps,

Rolling with the voice of thunder
Down its short way to the deeps.

Blessèd Boys [*from within*].
    Grand the scene to which we're waking,
    But too full of gloom and woe;   *11915*
    We're from fright and terror quaking,
    Noble, kind one, let us go!

Pater Seraphicus.
    On to higher spheres ascending,
    Unawares grow endlessly,
    As in fashion pure, unending,   *11920*
    God's high presence strengthens thee.
    That is spirits' sustentation,
    In free ether all effecting,
    Endless loving's revelation,
    To beatitude perfecting.   *11925*

Chorus of Blessèd Boys [*circling round the highest peaks*].
    Hand in hand clinging,
    In a glad ring unite,
    Soaring and singing,
    Feeling a pure delight.
    Godlike the yearning,   *11930*
    Confident be;
    For whom we're yearning,
    Him shall ye see.

Angels [*soaring in the higher atmosphere, bearing* FAUST's *immortal part*].
    Lo! rescued is this noble one
    From evil machination;   *11935*
    "Who e'er aspiring, struggles on,
    For him there is salvation."
    And if to him Celestial Love
    Its favouring grace has given,
    The Blessèd Host comes from Above   *11940*
    And welcomes him to Heaven.

The Younger Angels.
    Roses sainted women spended,
    Penitent through mercy glorious,
    Helped to make the fight victorious,
    That the lofty work be ended,   *11945*
    That be won this spirit-treasure.
    Demons shrank in sore displeasure,
    Devils fled the roses' flinging.
    Not with wonted hell-pangs stinging,

Love-pangs brought them to disaster   *11950*
Even the old Satan-Master
By sharp pain was penetrated.
Shout with joy! It's consummated!

The More Perfected Angels.

Still earthly rests remain
Which have oppressed us;   *11955*
They'd not be pure of stain,
Though of asbestos.
When every element
Strong spirit-forces
Have borne away and blent,   *11960*
No angel divorces
The natures two in one,
So close they weave them;
Eternal Love alone
Can ever cleave them.   *11965*

The Younger Angels.

Mist-like round yonder height,
I'm just discovering
Where in approaching flight
Spirit-life's hovering.
The clouds are growing clear,   *11970*
I see a host draw near
Of Blessèd Boys,
Freed from the stress of earth,
Circling, united!
They taste the joys   *11975*
Of spring in their new birth,
Therein delighted.
Let him at once begin
Perfected joy to win,
With these united!   *11980*

The Blessèd Boys.

Glad we're receiving now
Him as a chrysalis,
Thereby achieving now
Pledge of angelic bliss.
Loosen all earthly flakes   *11985*
That cling around him;
Fair and great now he wakes,
Divine life has crowned him.

Doctor Marianus [*in the highest, purest cell*].

Here is the outlook free,
The soul uplifting.   *11990*
Women I yonder see,

Heavenward drifting,
And glorious, midway seen,
Star-crowned, yet tender,
Heaven's own lofty Queen!   *11995*
It is Her splendour.

Enraptured.

Highest mistress of the world,
Let me, of Thy pleasure,
See Thy mystery unfurled
In the vaulted azure.   *12000*
Look with grace on what doth move
Human hearts to greet Thee
And with holy bliss of love
Bears them up to meet Thee.
All invincible we feel   *12005*
When supreme Thou willest,
Swiftly tempered is our zeal
When its glow Thou stillest.
Virgin, pure in fairest sense,
Mother sweet, supernal,   *12010*
Chosen Queen of our defence,
Peer of gods eternal!
Little clouds circle
Around Her splendour:
Penitent women,   *12015*
Of natures tender,
Ether respiring,
At Her knees pleading,
Her mercy needing.
O Thou of immaculate ray,   *12020*
From Thee 'tis not taken
That those lightly led astray
Come with trust unshaken.
Rapt away, to weakness prone,
It is hard to save them.   *12025*
Who by their own strength alone
Rend the lusts that slave them?
Whose foot does not slip awhile
On steep, slippery places?
Whom befool not glance and smile,   *12030*
Flattery's breath and phrases?

The MATER GLORIOSA *soars into view.*
Chorus of Penitent Women.

To heights art soaring
Of realms eternal,
Hear our imploring,
Matchless, Maternal,   *12035*
Of grace supernal!

Magna Peccatrix (St. Luke, 7. 36).

   By the love that ever glowing
   For Thy Son, the Heaven-born,
   Shed warm tears to balsam flowing
   Spite of Pharisaic scorn;   *12040*
   By the box whose ointment precious
   Dropped its perfume rare and sweet;
   By the locks whose gentle meshes
   Dried the Saviour's holy feet—

Mulier Samaritana (St. John, 4).

   By the well to which were driven   *12045*
   Abram's herds in days of yore;
   By the pitcher once 'twas given
   Our dear Saviour to restore;
   By the spring, rich and supernal,
   Whence flow waters far and wide,   *12050*
   Overflowing, bright, eternal,
   Pouring through the worlds their tide—

Maria Aegyptiaca[1] *(Acta Sanctorum).*

   By the sacred place where mortals
   Our dear Master's body laid;
   By the arm which at the portals   *12055*
   Warningly my entrance stayed;
   By the forty years' repentance
   Truly passed in desert-land;
   By the blessèd farewell sentence
   That I wrote upon the sand—   *12060*

All Three.

   Thou who women greatly sinning
   Grantest to come nigh to Thee,
   By sincere repentance winning
   Bliss through all eternity,
   Grant to this good soul Thy blessing,   *12065*
   Who but once herself forgot,
   Who knew not she was transgressing,
   Pardon meet refuse Thou not!

Una Pænitentium [formerly named GRETCHEN, *drawing closer].*

   Bend, oh bend now,
   Matchless, attend Thou,   *12070*
   Thy radiance spend now,
   Look on my bliss in charity.
   My early lover,
   His troubles over,
   Comes back to me.   *12075*

[1]Like Mary Magdalen and the Woman of Samaria, Mary of Egypt had committed the sin of sensuality.

Blessèd Boys [*hovering in a circle*].

> Mighty of limb, he towers
> Already above us;
> Soon for this care of ours
> Richly he'll love us.
> Early were we removed,   *12080*
> Life did not reach us;
> But he has learned and loved
> And he will teach us.

The One Penitent [*formerly named* GRETCHEN].

> Girt by the noble choir of Heaven,
> Himself the new-come scarcely knows,   *12085*
> Scarce feels the fresh life newly given
> Ere like the holy throng he grows;
> See! how each earthly bond he's riven,
> From that old vesture freed at length,
> Now in ethereal garb of Heaven   *12090*
> Appears his pristine, youthful strength,
> Oh, grant that I may now instruct him,
> Since blinds him still the new-born day.

Mater Gloriosa.   Come, rise to higher spheres! Conduct him!

> If he feels thee, he'll go thy way.   *12095*

Doctor Marianus [*prostrate, adoring*].

> Penitents, look up, elate,
> Where ye see salvation;
> Grateful, to you blessèd fate
> Grow through re-creation.
> May each better sense be keen   *12100*
> In Thy service precious;
> O Thou Virgin, Mother, Queen,
> Goddess, be Thou gracious!

Chorus Mysticus.

> All earth comprises
> Is symbol alone;   *12105*
> What there ne'er suffices
> As fact here is known;
> All past the humanly
> Wrought here in love;
> The Eternal-Womanly   *12110*
> Draws us above.

FINIS

PRINTED IN THE U.S.A.

THE GREAT IDEAS, *Volumes 2 and 3*